Lincoln

MODERNITY AND POLITICAL THOUGHT

Series Editors:
Morton Schoolman
State University of New York at Albany
and
Kennan Ferguson
University of Wisconsin–Milwaukee

This unique collection of original studies of the great figures in the history of political and social thought critically examines their contributions to our understanding of modernity, its constitution, and the promise and problems latent within it. These works are written by some of the finest theorists of our time for scholars and students of the social sciences and humanities.

Titles in the Series

The Augustinian Imperative: A Reflection on the Politics of Morality by William E. Connolly
Emerson and Self-Reliance by George Kateb
Edmund Burke: Modernity, Politics, and Aesthetics by Stephen K. White
Jean-Jacques Rousseau: The Politics of the Ordinary by Tracy B. Strong
Michel Foucault and the Politics of Freedom by Thomas L. Dumm
Reading "Adam Smith": Desire, History, and Value by Michael J. Shapiro
Thomas Hobbes: Skepticism, Individuality, and Chastened Politics by Richard E. Flathman
Thoreau's Nature: Ethics, Politics, and the Wild by Jane Bennett
G. W. F. Hegel: Modernity and Politics by Fred R. Dallmayr
The Reluctant Modernism of Hannah Arendt by Seyla Benhabib
William James: Politics in the Pluriverse by Kennan Ferguson
Merleau-Ponty and Modern Politics after Anti-Humanism by Diana Coole
Aquinas and Modernity: The Lost Promise of Natural Law by Shadia Drury
Carl Schmitt and the Intensification of Politics by Kam Shapiro
Impressions of Hume: Cinematic Thinking and the Politics of Discontinuity by Davide Pangia
Publius and Political Imagination by Jason Frank
Lincoln: The Ambiguous Icon by Steven Johnston

Lincoln

The Ambiguous Icon

Steven Johnston

ROWMAN & LITTLEFIELD
Lanham • Boulder • New York • London

Published by Rowman & Littlefield
An imprint of The Rowman & Littlefield Publishing Group, Inc.
4501 Forbes Boulevard, Suite 200, Lanham, Maryland 20706
www.rowman.com

Unit A, Whitacre Mews, 26-34 Stannary Street, London SE11 4AB

Copyright © 2018 by The Rowman & Littlefield Publishing Group, Inc.

All rights reserved. No part of this book may be reproduced in any form or by any electronic or mechanical means, including information storage and retrieval systems, without written permission from the publisher, except by a reviewer who may quote passages in a review.

British Library Cataloguing in Publication Information Available

Library of Congress Cataloging-in-Publication Data

Names: Johnston, Steven, author.
Title: Abraham Lincoln : the ambiguous icon / Steven Johnston.
Description: Lanham : Rowman & Littlefield, 2018. | Series: Modernity and political thought | Includes bibliographical references and index.
Identifiers: LCCN 2018010307 (print) | LCCN 2018011362 (ebook) | ISBN 9781442261310 (Electronic) | ISBN 9781442261303 (cloth : alk. paper) | ISBN 9781442261310 (electronic : alk. paper)
Subjects: LCSH: Lincoln, Abraham, 1809–1865—Philosophy. | Lincoln, Abraham, 1809–1865—Political and social views. | Presidents—United States—Biography.
Classification: LCC E457.2 (ebook) | LCC E457.2 .J64 2018 (print) | DDC 973.7092—dc23
LC record available at https://lccn.loc.gov/2018010307

Contents

Series Editor's Introduction — vii

Acknowledgments — xv

Preface — xvii

Introduction: Lincoln's Ambiguity — 1

1. Lincoln's Decisionism and the Politics of Elimination — 15
2. Democratic Ironies of Lincoln's Cinematic Exceptionalism — 53
3. A "Humble Offering": The (First) Lincoln Memorial — 83
4. Lincoln's Persistent Racial Ambivalence: Colonization — 109
5. What to the Indian Is the Gettysburg Address? — 149
6. American Exceptionalism or American Narcissism? The Second Inaugural — 179

Conclusion: Lincoln's Tragic Revenge — 205

Index — 211

About the Author — 215

History is not the past. It is the present. We carry our history with us. We are our history. If we pretend otherwise, we literally become criminals.

—James Baldwin

Series Editor's Introduction

Steven Johnston's book is the nineteenth volume in Modernity and Political Thought (MPT), the Rowman & Littlefield series in contemporary political theory. It follows the publication of recent MPT volumes on John Rawls by J. Donald Moon, Publius by Jason Frank, David Hume by Davide Panagia, Carl Schmitt by Kam Shapiro, and Gilles Deleuze by Nicholas Tampio.[1] Planned volumes beyond these include works on Paul by Char Roone Miller, Friedrich Nietzsche by David Owen, and Edward Said by Jeanne Morefield. MPT has long served as a series that both reintroduces and refigures important and canonical political theorists and philosophers in relation to the politics of our modern world and includes works by distinguished political thinkers of today. Previous volumes have focused on Augustine (William Connolly), Hobbes (Richard Flathman), Burke (Stephen White), Emerson (George Kateb), Rousseau (Tracy Strong), Thoreau (Jane Bennett), Adam Smith (Michael Shapiro), Foucault (Thomas Dumm), Hegel (Fred Dallmayr), Arendt (Seyla Benhabib), William James (Kennan Ferguson), Merleau-Ponty (Diana Coole), and Aquinas (Shadia Drury).[2]

Each study has proposed critical interpretations and arguments about key figures in the history of political theory, figuring their importance in the structure of modernity. Contributors to Modernity and Political Thought critically examine ways in which major political theorists shape our understanding of modernity—not only its origins and constitution but also its overt and latent problems, promises, and dangers. In addition to the works themselves, the series illustrates how the history of political thought can be brought to bear on modernity's political present to acquire deeper insight into its possible political futures. As a whole, MPT offers an unparalleled presentation of the discussions and debates that define much of political theory today.

Steven Johnston's analysis of American politics has made him an important democratic theorist of our time. In *Lincoln: The Ambiguous Icon*, Johnston takes on one of the arguably most significant and controversial figures in U.S. history. In his many books in political theory, Johnston has engaged the various dynamics of the democratic polity: nationalism, memorialization, violence, patriotism, and, above all, tragedy. For Johnston, the genre of tragedy best explains the particular crux in which modern thought finds itself. Constantly looking for a clear path forward, it finds instead diverging, opposed, and contradictory ethical and moral choices. Out of this thicket of competing claims, no singular and absolute political solution can or should be found.

Tragedy forms the groundwork of politics, Johnston has long held, though many in the contemporary world (especially in the United States) instead assume a progressive teleology of resolution and improvement, or, conversely, a consistent and lamentable decline. Though it is grounded in Greek theater, tragedy proves to be the most modern of genres. Politics is always a clash, most often between sides that see themselves as driven by truth, morality, and historical destiny. As such, it will always contain an agonistic element as its very fundament, and those ideological apparatuses and national myths that attempt to deny these intrinsic antagonisms of politics will be ineluctably drawn into numerous cruelties and violences in their attempt to insist on unity. The gift of tragedy, at least formally, is its ability to dramatize the irrevocability and irreconcilability of critical situations. Its protagonists, caught between fate and law, or between competing moralities, or between order and family, cannot escape; while they may never realize the consequences of the decisions they make, trying to resolve the irresolvable, the audience can. Tragedy shows that there may be no perfect solution, no easy way out. It therefore realizes contradiction and demands attention to the practices and consequences of refusing to believe in the tragic condition of humanity.

This tragic sensibility can be found in the famous work of many political thinkers, though contemporary readers—working to discover lessons for today—often ignore or discount it. For Johnston, Jean-Jacques Rousseau serves as one emblematic philosopher of tragedy. Its appearance in Rousseau's thought is marked not by his self-awareness, but rather by the clash between his intellectual analytic of politics and his faith in the relative infallibility of the best-laid plan. Above all else, this thinker of the modern condition trusted in the ability to look ahead with conviction, to set up a system that would work in solving any political problem facing it. But such dreams can have no end but tragic ones.

The failure of Rousseau's ideal underpins the analysis of Johnston's first book, *Encountering Tragedy: Rousseau and the Project of Democratic Order* (1999). Rousseau, Johnston shows, well understood the particulars of politics, but elided these insights when attempting to formulate grandiose political goals. Famously, *On the Social Contract* calls for a totalization of the state as community, the subsumption of individual and group differences into the "general will." But looking at Rousseau's writings on specific political issues shows that he in fact well understood the impossibility of such concord. In writings such as his *Letter to d'Alembert*, *Political Economy*, *Considerations on the Government of Poland*, and *Constitutional Project for Corsica*, Rousseau focuses on government, rather than on ideal legal and political goals. These texts, especially taken together, show the impossibility of concord and resolution, instead highlighting how politics is the ability to continue to negotiate through discord and irresolution. Governmentality is particular, responsive, and concerned with the granular details of people in these works—precisely the opposite of the usual reading of *On the Social Contract* and the *Second Discourse*.

Johnston's attention to the relationships between national mythos and governmentalism are further explained as he turns his attention to the democratic project of the United States. In *The Truth about Patriotism* (2007), Johnston examines the affective experience of loving a country. The contradiction of patriotism, he argues (following Rousseau), is that its love encourages the overcoming of liberal individualism, in service of the greater good, while also demanding eternal sacrifice as well as constant jealousy and antagonism. In a representational political system, this leads to war, empire, militarism, and ultimately an antidemocratic mien. Ultimately, he holds, this love "seems perpetually poised to bring about the ruin of the republic that it is supposed to guarantee."[3]

Rather than the usual suspects of American Political Thought, such as Publius's *The Federalist Papers* or Tocqueville's *Democracy in America*, the texts of *The Truth about Patriotism* are the everyday locales where U.S. patriotism is today experienced. Movies, novels, memorials, and song make up our social world of patriotism, and in them Johnston finds not only the most contradictory and self-defeating idioms of American exceptionalism, but also potentially redemptive moments. Look at the practices of memorialization, for example, which make up the central chapters. Statues and other national architectural commemorations, Johnston argues, are locations where death is used to promote a national unity and interest. And he traces the debates over the Vietnam Veterans Memorial(s) and the World War II memorials to explain just how the death and putative sacrifice of young people sent abroad to kill are reconciled and reformulated with that national unity and interest. While he admits that some designs prove far more satisfactory and evocative than others (Maya Lin's black and reflective wall of death certainly works better than the neoclassical World War II coliseum), every attempt to memorialize war proves to be an attempt to channel the force of death into serving the nation.

"Death specifies patriotism's linchpin—moral, political, and affective."[4] By highlighting this operation, Johnston specifically aims at those who see in patriotism a redemptive possibility, political figures and philosophers as diverse as Richard Rorty, George W. Bush, John Schaar, Socrates, and Steven Spielberg. The machinery of the patriotic nation runs on death, generating a sort of love inseparable from the destruction of life. In contrast, Johnston offers an alternative relationship to the nation, one that he finds in the music and lyrics of Bruce Springsteen. Springsteen offers meditations on the ironies of belonging, collectivity, and identification, while foregrounding the price demanded by these systems. He understands the mythos of American identity but has no interest in promulgating an unthinking reliance upon it. Instead, he attends to the particularities of people's lives: workers, soldiers, young men (and sometimes women) who end up marginalized and sometimes killed by the loyalties demanded of them. Springsteen loves life, not death.

In *American Dionysia: Violence, Tragedy, and Democratic Politics* (2015), Johnston presses these issues by examining how democratic energies emerge not only from the consolidation of death but from its furtherance. The tragic nature of democratic practices ineliminably consolidates violence and government. Too often, this seems to be merely an issue of temporality: in the past, democracy may have been violent, as no founding is innocent, but "we" have now moved beyond that. In truth, Johnston argues, democracies rely on the continuing perpetuation of war, sacrifice, and bloodshed, yet human death proves insufficient for this project. Johnston recognizes that violence in all its forms includes a wide range of actors, including such nonhuman beings as dogs and horses. Again, he notes the role of memorials in the making of national narratives: the early years of this century have seen the emergence of a number of war memorials to animals. While nonhuman actors have long been part of military efforts, from homing pigeons to attack dogs, recent years have seen the overt sanctification and memorialization of particular nonhumans. These animals have sacrificed themselves for the nation—though, of course, they had no choice in the matter.

Why do nonhuman animals work so well in this narrative? Because the central ethos of democracy, Johnston argues, is that of loss: these animals must be loved, trained, and then lost. Their deaths must hurt (unlike the deaths of, say, millions of other animals in the meat-processing industry). For their sacrificial qualities to work, we must mourn their loss—but we must mourn it in the process of aiding the building or protection of the country. The democratic practices of a nation demand "life's conformity to its political-military projects and dictates."⁵ Why, for example, are there no monuments to car-accident victims or people killed by smoking? Because their deaths were in vain—*to the patriot they count for nothing.*

Johnston does not think that violence can be eliminated from democratic practice. The idea that governments can operate without death and destruction not only proves idealistic and naïve, but also encourages practices of ignoring and unseeing the kinds of violence that must occur. This sort of blind, pollyannaish obscurantism, commonly known as "patriotism," demands a farcical assumption that evil is a result only of our enemies and that all we do is good. Far better, he argues, to keep all visible—the "candor and respect" needed "for hard truths regarding life and world, which democracy requires given its (often) unbearable combination of commitments made and failures produced."⁶

Hence Abraham Lincoln, the most tragic of political figures—a creative legalist unable to keep the United States' constitutional order; the commander-in-chief of a powerful army powerless to stop the Civil War; a man dedicated to reconstructing the United States and assassinated before the process could begin. Lincoln was, in many ways, a failure, as his election proximately caused the fracture of the nation and his death left his major project barely begun.

Yet we are often left with someone far different: a tophatted, bearded sage, a figure of deracinated leadership unconnected to the particularities of mid-nineteenth century America. This Lincoln—the Lincoln of the log-cabin upbringing, the penny, and the stern, paternal visage—is the figure most often memorialized in the U.S. imaginary. This remembering, Johnston shows, is meant to overdetermine the project of U.S. power—simplifying his life into iconography allows the current wide range of uses of Lincoln. The resolution of the tragic into the triumphant serves the nation, or at least the rationalization of various national projects.

This new work excavates the particulars of our memorializations of Lincoln to show the complexities of the real Lincoln alongside the very different complexities of our contemporary uses of him. In doing so, Johnston rightly criticizes the simplifications that go into making Lincoln a flat character meant to promote the idea of America, whether as the marbleized statuary of the Lincoln Memorial or the filmic re-creations of a John Ford or Steven Spielberg. In doing so, however, Johnston also rededicates our attention to a complex, contradictory, and eminently engaging man. Lincoln, both as president and as man, maps closely upon the American experience, but not in the usual panegyric ways. Instead, our memories of Lincoln bend and shape him into a wide variety of contradictory forms, each for its own projection of an American—and an America—never truly existent.

* * *

We are grateful to Jon Sisk, vice president and senior executive editor for American government, American history, public policy, and political theory at Rowman & Littlefield, for the thoughtfulness and professionalism that make it possible for authors and editors alike to produce their best work. His support of a series dedicated to examining authors through the lens of modern thought has led to a compilation of volumes that, as a whole, refigure the relationship between critical thinkers and the contemporary world. Editors and publisher together strive to provide an indispensable set of volumes that, taken in their totality, provide a guide to the complexities and nuances of history's most important political philosophers. Under his stewardship, Rowman & Littlefield's Modernity and Political Thought continues to define the critical importance of the study of classical, medieval, modern, and contemporary political theory today.

Kennan Ferguson, University of Wisconsin at Milwaukee
Morton Schoolman, State University of New York at Albany

NOTES

1. J. Donald Moon, *John Rawls: Liberalism and the Challenges of Late Modernity* (Lanham, MD: Rowman & Littlefield, 2014); Jason Frank, *Publius and Political Imagination* (Lanham, MD: Rowman & Littlefield, 2013); Davide Panagia, *Impressions of Hume* (Lanham, MD: Rowman & Littlefield, 2013); Kam Shapiro, *Carl Schmitt and the Intensification of Politics* (Lanham, MD: Rowman & Littlefield, 2009); Nicholas Tampio, *Deleuze's Political Vision* (Lanham, MD: Rowman & Littlefield, 2015).

2. William E. Connolly, *The Augustinian Imperative: A Reflection on the Politics of Morality* (Lanham, MD: Rowman & Littlefield, 2002); Richard E. Flathman, *Thomas Hobbes: Skepticism, Individuality, and Chastened Politics* (Lanham, MD: Rowman & Littlefield, 2002); Stephen K. White, *Edmund Burke: Modernity, Politics, and Aesthetics* (Lanham, MD: Rowman & Littlefield, 2002); George Kateb, *Emerson and Self-Reliance* (Lanham, MD: Rowman & Littlefield, 2002); Tracy B. Strong, *Jean-Jacques Rousseau: The Politics of the Ordinary* (Lanham, MD: Rowman & Littlefield, 2002); Jane Bennett, *Thoreau's Nature: Ethics, Politics, and the Wild* (Lanham, MD: Rowman & Littlefield, 2002); Michael J. Shapiro, *Reading "Adam Smith": Desire, History, and Value* (Lanham, MD: Rowman & Littlefield, 2002); Thomas L. Dumm, *Michel Foucault and the Politics of Freedom* (Lanham, MD: Rowman & Littlefield, 2002); Fred Dallmayr, *G.W.F. Hegel: Modernity and Politics* (Lanham, MD: Rowman & Littlefield, 2002); Seyla Benhabib, *The Reluc-*

tant Modernism of Hannah Arendt (Lanham, MD: Rowman & Littlefield, 2003); Kennan Ferguson, *William James: Politics in the Pluriverse* (Lanham, MD: Rowman & Littlefield, 2007); and Diana Coole, *Merleau-Ponty and Modern Politics after Anti-Humanism* (Lanham, MD: Rowman & Littlefield, 2007); Shadia Drury, *Aquinas and Modernity: The Lost Promise of Natural Law* (Lanham, MD: Rowman & Littlefield, 2008).

3. Steven Johnston, *The Truth about Patriotism* (Durham, NC: Duke University Press, 2007), 58.

4. Ibid., 161.

5. Steven Johnston, *American Dionysia: Violence, Tragedy, and American Politics* (New York: Cambridge University Press, 2015), 108.

6. Ibid., 5.

Acknowledgments

Thanks to Char Miller, Bill Connolly, Doug Dow, Brian Danoff, Kennan Ferguson, Peter Haworth, Bill Jensen, Benjamin Kleinerman, Dennis Lambert, Eric Lamar, Sarah Pemberton, Mort Schoolman, Susan Sterett, Simon Stow (especially for booing me at a conference), Andrew Valls, Lee Ward, and especially Jane Bennett for their helpful feedback on and assistance with this project. Thanks also to Michaele Ferguson, Andy Baker, the Department of Political Science of the University of Colorado, and its graduate students and faculty for inviting me to give a talk on an earlier version of chapter 2. It was a great experience. A preliminary version of chapter 1 appeared in *Political Theory* 45, no. 4, August 2017. My thanks to Sage Publications for its inclusion here. Finally, I'm deeply indebted and grateful to Bob Gerlits for the fabulous photographs that appear in the book. Bob also assisted me with *The Truth about Patriotism* in 2007. Finally, I'd like to thank Judy Gallant for her unflagging love, faith, enthusiasm, and support. I couldn't have written this book without her.

Preface

> Unless one conceives of time as ending with 1865, the Lincoln of folklore is of more significance than the Lincoln of actuality.
>
> —David Donald, "The Folklore Lincoln"

America reveres Abraham Lincoln. Citizens and scholars alike rate him the nation's best president, especially for his political vision and leadership in a crisis.[1] He sets the standard by which other presidents are judged. George Washington, Thomas Jefferson, Franklin Delano Roosevelt: all are secondary figures despite their considerable accomplishments and substantial gifts. This means the country is always looking for more from its presidents, thus reflecting and reinforcing the immense pride felt for Lincoln. He saved the Union and delivered a new birth of freedom to a people desperately in need of it. He was also violently taken from the nation prematurely. Who knows what might have been achieved had he lived through a second term? The country practices a kind of perpetual mourning for Lincoln, suffering from an unabated sense of loss and privation. Why can't more presidents be like him?

America worships Lincoln, but it also knows his name signifies controversy. He held beliefs (or they held him) and pursued policies, particularly on race, that were less than noble, and his contentious wartime presidency included a number of constitutionally suspect decisions as commander-in-chief that reverberate to this day. These well-known facets of Lincoln do nothing to lessen his standing. If anything, America worships Lincoln even more because of his shortcomings and those of his four-year rule. Lincoln had the courage of his (often unpopular) commitments; he was prepared to do whatever it took, including great wrong, for the Union cause, thereby proving his patriotism; he weathered the unrelenting criticism and condemnation heaped upon him by political elites and a partisan press. In short, America can live with Lincoln's ambiguity, especially insofar as the ambiguity works to reveal his heroics and recuperate his infamy, and especially insofar as the heroics tend to confirm American (in particular white) exceptionalism.

This is the liminal space in which this book operates. It interrogates the fabrication and adulation of an icon whose democratic credentials are dubious. It suspects that America cannot realize the democratic identity it professes as long as it's in thrall to the political spell cast by this troubling figure, which effectively gives the country permission to routinely ignore, even discard, its basic political principles and commitments. Such permission finds expression in one of American political discourse's most popular—and disturbing—exculpatory mantras, "If Lincoln . . .": If Lincoln suspended habeas corpus; if Lincoln silenced and jailed political opponents; if Lincoln suppressed freedom of the press; if Lincoln was ready to save the Union by preserving slavery; if Lincoln didn't believe in full social and political equality between the races; if Lincoln presided over the largest mass execution in American history; if Lincoln waged total war against the South; if Lincoln was willing to sacrifice hundreds of thousands of lives to win the war. In a time of political crisis, in cases of state malfeasance or misconduct, deploying Lincoln's name as an incantation simultaneously admits and absolves any and all manner of problematic state action. The concern here is not that Lincoln is being (mis)used for political purposes. Rather, beneath the (mis)use lies a collective judgment. America accepts, admires, and even endorses Lincoln's notorious underside. In other words, American political culture has created a Lincoln that allows for and welcomes what should be impermissible.

This book asks American democracy to tarry with Lincoln's iconic ambiguity and dwell on its problematic aspects. It harbors the suspicion that the ambiguity tilts noticeably toward the deleterious and should serve as a warning or cautionary tale. Lincoln's ambiguity, in other words, is radical, not superficial—always raising doubts that his legacy should be the subject (when all is said and done) of unquestioned national veneration. Insofar as America considers Lincoln *the* exemplar of the unfinished project of a more perfect union, it affirms a political model more likely to result in something that necessarily falls terribly short of such an aspiration.

Nonetheless, Lincoln can still be of value. His place in American political life and cultural memory indicates that if the country is to achieve a semblance of the democracy to which Lincoln allegedly gestured, it must find ways to overcome and thus make itself worthy of his constitutive failures, however much they are denied or dismissed—because they are America's failures. In the Second Inaugural Lincoln famously considered the possibility that the Civil War was the price God was imposing on America for its greatest sin. Yet the war could never amount to anything more than a partial down payment. For one thing, a full accounting would have to address all of the country's offenses. America could redeem itself in the postwar world, if at all, only with commitments to ideals that it had not begun to imagine, coming at a price it could not conceive paying. Lincoln encompasses these uncomfortable truths, too. If he worked to overcome himself, America must work to overcome Lincoln.

NOTE

1. See, for example, C-SPAN's 2017 survey of presidential historians: https://www.c-span.org/presidentsurvey2017/?category=8.

Introduction

Lincoln's Ambiguity

He was of the people, by the people, and for the people.

—Carl Sandburg, *Abraham Lincoln: The War Years*

There has undoubtedly been written about him more romantic and sentimental rubbish than any other American figure . . . and there are moments when one is tempted to feel that the cruellest [sic] thing that has happened to Lincoln since he was shot by Booth has been to fall into the hands of Carl Sandburg.

—Edmund Wilson, *Patriotic Gore*

Lincoln's iconic status in American life and politics would seem to need little or no explanation. Not only did he save the Union and free the slaves, he came from nowhere and nothing to win the highest office in the land and achieve world-historical success. Had a novelist invented Lincoln, surely the character would have been ridiculed by readers as unduly fanciful. It is therefore altogether fitting that the nation built a towering memorial to Lincoln on the Mall in Washington, D.C., the country's most sacred symbolic ground visited by many millions of wonderstruck citizens each year. If anything, the temple housing Lincoln's regal statue might not be sufficient to mark the significance of his contribution to and place in American history and memory. It's a good thing, then, that scores of Lincoln statues are scattered throughout the country, even the world, to honor him.[1]

Lincoln's story is more complicated, of course, and Lincoln is a controversial figure regardless of his preeminent status in the nation's collective imagination. No president could preside over a Civil War rooted in racial dogmatism and emerge universally and unequivocally admired or loved.

The subject of the internecine conflict was as contentious as the means used to settle it. Lincoln's (un)timely assassination, however, converted him into a martyr for the cause of human freedom and has effectively diluted, if not erased, criticisms of his conduct of the war and his legacy. Criticisms are not ignored or dismissed exactly, but they are blunted and absorbed in many treatments of Lincoln's (wartime) presidency.

LINCOLN'S AMBIGUITY

In 1956 David Herbert Donald noted in a short essay that Lincoln, following his assassination, became a political property of great value—not so much treasured for its own sake but to be deployed solely for partisan advantage. For decades Republicans enjoyed a monopoly on Lincoln, but their unique possession was ultimately challenged by Democrats and, soon enough, Lincoln's imprimatur was sought for any and every good cause. No matter the issue, Lincoln could be its symbol. He favored the righteous. He opposed the wicked. This rendered Lincoln not just an ally to be recruited but an example to be emulated and thus a source of inspiration.

What made Lincoln the ready-made screen of America's myriad projections? According to Donald, the answer could be found not so much in Lincoln's appropriators, but in Lincoln himself: "Perhaps the secret of Lincoln's continuing vogue is his essential ambiguity. He can be cited on all sides of all questions. 'My policy,' he used to say, 'is to have no policy.'" Donald believes that Lincoln's (supposed) opportunism may be anathema to moralists, but moralists (and others) are able to capitalize on his "absence of dogma" for political advantage, a result to which Lincoln would not (necessarily) have objected.[2] After all, Lincoln did not hesitate to advance strong political positions as occasion permitted (or dictated). More importantly, perhaps, he often articulated them with a flair for elaborate formulations (convolutions) that made it difficult to fix their meaning with confidence. Lincoln championed and defended constitutional government, but he also claimed the Constitution permits exceptions and applications that run counter to the very idea of limited state power. Lincoln affirmed First Amendment guarantees to freedom of speech and press, including the right of citizens to criticize the government, but also insisted on the government's right to abridge these liberties when the public safety required it, especially during wartime. Lincoln advocated emancipation for people enslaved for generations, but also directed a state apparatus that did not hesitate to silence or imprison those who, in his judgment, interfered with freedom's realization in the war. Given these fraught combinations, Lincoln, in the collective political imagination, has come to represent the best, but he also concretizes the worst, in America. Simply put, Lincoln's legacy is ambiguous, a fusion of great performance and concomitant vice. Rather than adjudicate between (indisputably) good and bad Lincolns, however, there is a way to approach him that recognizes both his best and worst; that appreciates the constitutively ambiguous combination; but that also fears that much of the worst has been willfully and dangerously downplayed, rationalized, or forgotten.[3]

ON AMBIGUITY

What, though, is this thing called ambiguity? What is its political import? Simone de Beauvoir makes a distinction between absurdity and ambiguity. Absurdity refers to a lack of meaning. Ambiguity refers to a lack of fixed meaning. According to de Beauvoir, meaning is something that "must be constantly won"—because it is always open, a perpetual subject of contestation.[4] Should a meaning be won (fixed), this does not prove it is right. Fixity results from a contingent play of forces that, realigned, might soon produce another outcome altogether, another winner, another "fixed" meaning. Beauvoir's distinction suggests that no single meaning is likely to capture any particular political action, event, deed, doctrine, text, statement, identity, achievement, legacy, memory, or *figure*. Given the plurality of democratic life and the myriad of perspectives from which it is enacted, the presence of ambiguity seems not only inevitable but welcome.

If ambiguity refers to a lack of fixed meaning in something, this undecidability might spring from the copresence of contrary signs or indications. Political action, for example, often produces both great and terrible results, not due to some failure or shortcoming but because of the limitations inherent in acting in the world. A political creed or doctrine, to cite another example, might privilege or prioritize one principle at the expense of another equally worthwhile value, again not due to some conceptual or normative failure or shortcoming but because not all values are compatible and can be harmonized. Or a political figure's legacy might entail in roughly equal measure accomplishments to be praised and misdeeds to be condemned. This, in turn, can lead to a public memory that is unstable, composed of certain aspects of the legacy deemed worthy of commemoration and other aspects of it that should serve as warnings (though the latter may get buried in the glow of the former).

Ambiguity is a political virtue in democracies insofar as it signals room for rival understandings and perspectives, thus disagreement, contestation, and discord. No political figure, party, position, creed, or interpretation can embody or possess a monopoly on truth or right. Ambiguity suggests that even though one meaning is ascendant today, it might be the subject of legitimate reinterpretation and reappraisal tomorrow. What cannot be revisited or rethought in its name? Ambiguity at its best conveys an attractive modesty. It is a sign that things are complicated, tangled, not easily resolved or settled, if at all. Ambiguity thus makes its own contribution to a democratic way of life—as an expression of its ethos.

Ambiguity is also to be valued for what it might forestall. Resentment is an affect that circulates widely in social and political life, perhaps especially in democracies, where the frustration of legitimate expectations may be greater than in, say, authoritarian regimes. A strong notion of responsibility is a common component of resentment. People want to know who initiated political actions and brought about their consequences, thus who can be held accountable and assigned blame for what goes wrong—and something always goes wrong when it comes to the conduct of politics. If, however, one has an appreciation for ambiguity, one may be able to resist or fend off the allure and attraction of resentment. One might see that the doctrine of responsibility presupposes a kind of sovereign power to control events in life that is nothing more than fantasy. The world does not lend itself to human manipulation and fashioning without remainder. Once this is recognized, the will to hold (someone) accountable, to blame and punish accordingly, may recede. Ambiguity, then, foils the will to moralize, the insistence that we are right, that others are wrong, and that the world can be arranged according to a vision of what it should be. Ambiguity goes hand-in-hand with a spirit of forbearance, even generosity. It subverts temptations to dogmatism and points to the legitimacy of alternative claims.

PERILS OF AMBIGUITY

An appreciation of and for ambiguity—whether recognizing it or cultivating it—contributes to the moral and political well-being of democracy. It contributes to its openness, plurality, and freedom. Affectively, it contributes to its mood and temper, softening and soothing it. Does this render ambiguity an unalloyed good? Not necessarily.

An appreciation for ambiguity might undermine or disable a critical response to problematic figures, records, actions, or outcomes. It might make it possible for the authors of moral and political initiatives to sidestep or evade responsibility for their ramifications. A program, position, or policy may be objectionable, indefensible, unworthy of respect, and even deserving of condemnation and punishment—yet the critical mass required to assign and fix accountability fails to materialize. The cultivation of ambiguity, that is, can lead to a paralyzing undecidability. For example, if a president pursues a constitutionally suspect course of action and cites the uncertainties of a political situation or the indeterminacies in the founding text as an explanation or defense, citizens may be prone to extend the benefit of the doubt, sympathetic to the dilemmatic position in which he (supposedly) finds himself. Such a defense might be offered in good faith and the political issue at hand might be susceptible to alternative judgments. It can also serve as a pretext for presidents to exercise powers they believe should be at their disposal—despite the implications for democracy. In this context, a culture of ambiguity can subvert the meaningful possibility of addressing and redressing serious political transgressions with sufficient gravitas.

This kind of result also suggests that a culture of ambiguity can deter the formation of affective energy and involvement in politics. Mobilization, not to mention militancy, does not seem to follow from an appreciation for the ambiguity of a situation, event, action, deed, symbol, or figure. A politics of ambiguity, then, may interfere with the development and formation of critical judgments that can also serve as a prelude to meaningful action—to organize, to resist, to hold accountable, to politically punish where this is democratically indispensable. It may also provide cover for controversial or problematic actions that might not otherwise have been possible. Thus, it must be kept in mind that ambiguity does not suggest that anything goes, that rival perspectives, claims, or ways of life must always be respected or tolerated no matter their substance. It does mean that a plurality of views jostle and contend for attention, adherence, and ascendancy. Nor does ambiguity mean that those on one side of a struggle to fix the meaning of something must reject the superiority of their assessments or concede that those with competing judgments may be right. It does mean the moral and political landscape will be a crowded, busy, contentious place characterized by noise, roughness, and turbulence. Ambiguity promises a world never at rest, often at odds, always in flux. The point here is neither to laud nor censure a politics of ambiguity, but to pinpoint and be alert to the promise and perils that accompany it.

LINCOLN'S ICONIC AMBIGUITY

How do these reflections relate to Lincoln? What does it mean to claim that he is an ambiguous icon? How does his lofty status flow from his ambiguity? How might a deeper affinity for Lincoln's ambiguity affect his circulation and functioning in the American polity? Lincoln's unorthodox iconic identity can be illuminated, first, by exploring his relationship to the American founding, itself an ambiguous historical event. Lincoln revered the birth of the United States—not only for what it introduced into the world but also for what it made possible for what Hamilton called remote futurity, its true mark of greatness. A gratified America returned the compliment and made Lincoln the founding's long-awaited successor. To his credit Lincoln seemed clear-eyed about the nation's problematic beginning, if not necessarily its consequences, but rather than disparage or disown he embraced it. It's crucial that Lincoln did not share the founders' profound moral failings regarding race. He rejected slavery and did not own other human beings. Lincoln thus represented a break from 1776. And while he suffered from his own serious shortcomings on the very same subject, he nevertheless affirmed those shortcomings as principles. Lincoln thus represented continuity with the past. He proclaimed his own racial biases and would, if possible, have left slavery alone where it already existed to preserve the union. On this and other vital national matters, Lincoln avowed noble principles, but not consistently or insistently (except, perhaps, regarding union). If America venerates the founders despite their (gross) failings, it worships Lincoln, in part, precisely because of his (mere) flaws.

Lincoln, then, can be said to represent a modernization of founding ideals that did not place undue moral and political demands on the country and its self-conception (even if Southern fanatics were blind to it). Lincoln transcends George Washington in American folklore insofar as he offered—and continues to offer—America a comfortable reconciliation with its inescapable past—which is also its inveterate present. The United States was born in and as contradiction. Founding did not represent the pinnacle of achievement, the realization of a set of principles and ideals. Nor did it represent the articulation of and aspiration to a set of values that could eventually find fulfillment. Not exactly, anyway. Rather, founding amounted to a perpetual settlement rooted in America's constitutive rivenness. America, that is, entered the world divided against itself along multiple lines of difference, especially racial difference, committed imperfectly—because partially, selectively, hesitantly, ambivalently, and sometimes not at all—to the ideals it espoused. American exceptionalism, as a result, rooted in contradiction, can be understood as a condition that necessarily entails dissimulation, pretension, and affectation insofar as the country maintains a commitment to ideals it supposedly, but doesn't actually believe in, let alone practice.

More specifically, American exceptionalism presupposes and engenders a story the country tells itself about necessary compromises and accommodations in the face of social, political, and economic realities beyond its control, realities responsibility for which it has forgotten (or has chosen to forget) belongs to it. Regarding American national identity, it seems apt to say that compromise and accommodation were always already folded into the ideals themselves. Compromise is constitutive, not incidental, peripheral, or transient. America was born of contrary, contending dispositions congealed as one. America's founding established the principle that principles can always be compromised because they were always already compromised. This applies not just to the ethnic cleansing of Native peoples and the enslavement of blacks. It also applies to the violence, terror, and revenge deployed against loyalists who remained faithful to Great Britain during America's first civil war. It even applies to rebels exploiting and terrorizing those who supported them, whether through safety committees that policed individual thought and conduct or through repeated acts of plundering that Washington did his best to curtail (even as he practiced it himself). The Revolution, contrary to myth, was not a bloodless revolt that witnessed the finest American conduct in a righteous war for independence. It was an inherently violent struggle of extraordinary brutality and cruelty in which founding ideals were effectively undone in the course of their (alleged) actualization. America's ideals turned out to be thoroughly non-ideal. The so-called compromises enabled the "ideals" to be established in the first place.[5]

Lincoln as the reincarnation of the founding generation enables America, finally, to (more fully) embrace the story of its birth (and subsequent life) as an ambiguous achievement—problematic in many ways but an achievement nonetheless and despite everything. To close the gap between ideal and reality: no country has made such an ambition a more central part of its self-understanding. The gap, so the story goes, is the source of discontent and energy. It engenders efforts to close it. At the same time, however, no country has lived as comfortably in and with a (so-called) gap as the United States. Insofar as it's in the nature of this gap that it can't be altogether closed, the discrepancy effectively gives the country permission, even license, to live in the space in between, especially in moments of crisis, real or imagined, when the gap usually tends to widen. Lincoln is the figure who embodies the gap. He allows us simultaneously to condemn slavery and countenance racism; profess love and respect for constitutional ideals and insist on the necessity of violating them in the name of that love; extol democracy and enhance the power of the state; champion individual freedom and suppress political liberties; reject violence in politics and wage total war as its continuation; affirm sovereign power and national unity and embrace colonial expansion. Lincoln enables America to think the best of itself while routinely doing its worst in the world. This ambiguity renders him a limitless political resource that can be drawn on openly but also reflexively and unthinkingly—for almost anything.

In American politics, then, Lincoln's nonpareil presidency, conducted on behalf of the greater good of the American republic, authorizes whatever needs to be done at any given political moment. American culture has always displayed a soft spot for the outlaw, the loner, the gangster who, rather than merely follow the law makes his own, someone who has the strength to flout convention and, driven by his own moral compass, do things his way, and in the process carve out a unique identity and reputation for himself. When this resolute figure also holds high office and dedicates himself to America and its greatness, so much the better. Lincoln is loved for what he achieved but also what he stands for, which is related to what he achieved but also to how he achieved it. Lincoln usurped congressional power and, with a little prodding, Congress subsequently legitimized it. Lincoln abused executive power and, with a few well-chosen words, the people affirmed it. Lincoln waged a ghastly prolonged war through what many considered outrageous means, but he won it. Lincoln negated the due process rights of citizens, but the Supreme Court rebuked him only after the war was won. Lincoln is loved, then, for things both great and terrible. That is, he accomplished "great" things through drastic, often desperate, even despicable means. For this he is celebrated all the more rather than condemned because, like the founders but new and improved, he was willing to do whatever he thought necessary, including turn to the underside of things—for the nation. This is what great powers do, and Lincoln made America a great power, at once magnificent and appalling, and achieved greatness himself as a result.

Thanks to Lincoln, then, America can confirm its ideals as he reinvents and redeems them, especially through their violation. Once again America doesn't have to concern itself with understanding what it actually means to have and to hold ideals. It didn't do so in the eighteenth century. Otherwise, the founding generation would have adjudged its political creation unworthy of life in the form it took. Given, inter alia, the constitutive exploitation and sacrifice of others, it knowingly devalued its ideals to the point of nullification. Yet America came into being—in self-celebration no less. Lincoln inaugurates a new, intensified celebration.

Herbert Croly can be of assistance here. In "The Paradox of Lincoln," Croly makes a distinct contribution to Lincoln exaltation by embracing him as a contradictory figure. In so doing, however, Croly's account calls itself into question, revealing critical aspects of Lincoln's appealing ambiguity. Croly marvels at one of Lincoln's underappreciated intellectual gifts, namely, the skill of "harboring and reconciling purposes, convictions and emotions so different from one another that to the majority of his fellow-countrymen they would in anybody else have seemed incompatible." Lincoln, a wartime president, signifies something more than unique intellectual legerdemain. He "expressed and acted on these usually incompatible motives and ideas with such rare propriety and amenity that their union in his behavior and spirit passes not only without criticism but *almost* without comment." Croly thus appreciates Lincoln's extraordinary attractiveness to the American people. "His fellow-countrymen, who like to consider him a magnified version of the ordinary American and to disguise flattery of themselves under the form of reverence for him, appear not to suspect how different he is from them."[6] Perhaps, but if one respects the intellectual equality of Lincoln's fellow citizens and assumes they were able to see him clearly, it's worth considering whether Croly appreciates the extent to which Lincoln does mirror them. Interestingly, Croly fudges the question whether many of Lincoln's convictions, ideas, and purposes (only some of which Croly discusses) are actually—not just seemingly or usually—incompatible, and whether this discordance, because it was coupled with a willingness to act unashamedly regardless of any potential inconsistency or the problematic consequences likely to result, is precisely why the American people can both identify with and revere him.

Croly's Lincoln myopia is shared by Fred Kaplan, who also does an admirable job of seeing Lincoln in the round. Yet Kaplan, unlike Croly, may overestimate the acuity—and thus mischaracterize the judgment—of the American people. Kaplan insists: "The mythologized, ahistorical Lincoln is an impossible standard. No one can measure up to it, not even Lincoln. He was a great president, *despite* his limited vision and his conciliatory politics; *despite* his inability to embrace some version of abolitionism; *despite* his fixation on colonization; *despite* his belief, almost to the end of his life, that America should remain a white man's country; *despite* his mistakes as commander in chief, especially his attempt to bribe the South back into Union and his counterproductive efforts to keep the Border States from breaking away; and, most of all, *despite* his willingness to buy union at the cost of perpetuating slavery indefinitely."[7] But the American people don't hold Lincoln to an impossible standard. Since they don't believe in such a thing, this is not the source of their love. Rather, they locate his greatness, in part, in the "flaws" and "failings" Kaplan laments, which can account for the identification Croly deems unwarranted. In key respects Lincoln was "a magnified version" of the people.[8]

Enter David Donald's folkloric Lincoln. In an essay written before "Getting Right with Lincoln," Donald surveys the "growth of Lincoln legends" and finds two in competition "One, essentially literary in character and often of New England or Eastern sponsorship, presented a prettified Lincoln, a combination of George Washington and Christ. . . . This Lincoln has the outlines of a mythological hero; he is a demigod." Insofar as this treatment of Lincoln borders on the impossible or unbelievable, he "was saved from . . . deification by a different stream of tradition, frequently Western in origin and more truly folkloric in quality. The grotesque hero . . . is one of the oldest and most familiar patterns in folk literature." Here Lincoln "was the practical joker, the teller of tall and lusty tales. Stupendously strong, he was also marvelously lazy." This Lincoln is no naif, however: "He was shrewd, a manipulator of men, whose art concealed his artfulness. He was Old Abe, a Westerner, and his long flapping arms were not the wings of an angel."[9] Donald recognizes that these contending conceptions of Lincoln are not mutually exclusive and though he does not pursue in detail the possible implications of their combination, these construals of Lincoln as a *problematic demigod*, however accidentally, set the stage for a darker understanding in which his pernicious features emerge.

LINCOLN'S RADICAL AMBIGUITY

This much is known. Lincoln was a wartime president who implemented policies, pursued courses of action, and made decisions that often entailed a terrible price. Many of them were arguably unnecessary. American memory both admits and denies this kind of truth about Lincoln. Ironically, the admission seems to legitimize the denial. It's time, then, to "restore," even deepen Lincoln's ambiguity. Lincoln was also a wartime president who routinely justified his policies, actions, and decisions to the public. This might seem to embody the transparency critical to a democracy's success. Yet Lincoln's political thought often betrays ambiguity, which is critical to the sordidness it helps shroud. Addressing difficult questions, anticipating possible objections, responding to critics, moving in multiple directions, animated by competing ambitions, his thinking does not always follow a single trajectory. It is mobile, elusive, slippery, in short, on the move. It can do things, terrible things. That's the idea. The source of recurring disagreement and dispute, Lincoln's writings take on second, third, and fourth interpretive lives. They do not accommodate a single fixed reading. They are both symptomatic and generative of ambiguity. That is, they are themselves ambiguous; they lend themselves to ambiguity; they seek to introduce and foster ambiguity; they are the occasion for ambiguity. This is America's Lincoln, whether it knows it or not. The figure is both compelling and dangerous.

For this very reason, I try to re-cover Donald's account of Lincoln's essential ambiguity. The project here is not to deny Donald's assessment, but to suggest that Lincoln's ambiguity functions in a peculiar fashion in American political discourse and memory. While few, if any, would deny Lincoln's ambiguity, the affirmation of it actually tends to work in such a way that it deflects, attenuates, minimizes, and even conceals its darker aspects. Nevertheless, while Lincoln can be credited with extraordinary accomplishments, they came at an exorbitant, perhaps excessive or gratuitous price; while Lincoln was attuned to and determined to ameliorate some of the gross injustices characterizing American life, he was blind to and helped perpetuate, even worsen other glaring injustices also marking it; while Lincoln knew that he was conducting the affairs of state on precarious ground, he betrayed little or no sense that it could be of grave democratic significance to make amends and atone for his missteps. This (unstable) combination of political morality and pure power politics devoid of morality, which America reveres, can also be (re)narrated in order to reconfigure Lincoln's iconic status.

What, then, does the ambiguous Lincoln look like that emerges in these pages? He will not be altogether unfamiliar.

Lincoln rejected slavery and condemned its monstrous injustice. He also denied the social and political equality of blacks. It's one thing to repudiate an institution; it's another to extirpate a conviction and feeling. The civic nationalism Lincoln professed, rooted in the Declaration of Independence, receded before the racial nationalism he lived and breathed.

Lincoln resisted the extension and nationalization of slavery. He also assured the South that he would leave it alone where it already existed. Lincoln, that is, was prepared to live with slavery for another one hundred years, by his own accounting, for (a white supremacist) union.

Lincoln worked in the Border States to secure gradual, compensated emancipation. He also insisted that blacks, both those already freed and those who would eventually be liberated, submit to colonization abroad and rebuked black leaders who refused to cooperate.

Lincoln issued a sweeping emancipation proclamation, changing the character of the Civil War and the United States—forever. He also turned to blacks (solely) as a military resource to win the war. Simultaneously he labored behind the scenes to make colonization a success despite all the evidence that it was already a failure and rejected by an overwhelming majority of blacks. The patriotic service of black Americans would, ideally, be rewarded by deportation however voluntary.

Lincoln's nationalism entailed preserving the territorial integrity of the Union and enlarging its (so-called) empire of liberty on the North American continent. Thus Lincoln's racial nationalism reared its ugly façade here, too, as Native American peoples continued to be the subjects of social experimentation, specifically, of perpetual colonization. Lincoln's vision of union did not include them. Rather, it presupposed not only their exclusion but their elimination. This presumption animates Lincoln's denunciation of the Kansas-Nebraska Act.

Lincoln issued an inspiring promise for a new birth of freedom at Gettysburg. It precluded Indians. After the Dakota Sioux War in late 1862, Lincoln presided over the largest mass execution in American history as the country disposed of (some of) its most hated enemies. The thirty-eight Indians he sentenced to hang did not die in vain. Their destruction contributed to white expansion, prosperity, and purity. As Washington's army cleansed Native lands during the Revolutionary War, Lincoln's army did likewise in the War Between the States.

Lincoln managed and won a war more violent and bloody than either side imagined, despite fierce opposition from within loyal Northern states and their citizens, which made fielding a sufficient army a daunting task. Lincoln also, in utter disregard of the First Amendment, never more important than during wartime, did not hesitate to silence and crush those who opposed, with any potential effectiveness, the war or the draft.

Lincoln was a great champion of the founders and what he took to be their remarkable achievement in constitutional government. He also trampled on that achievement repeatedly and extensively, making a mockery of the notion of limited government as the national state experienced a period of unprecedented growth in its powers and thus its reach.

Lincoln appreciated that slavery was an American crime, not just a Southern transgression. He imagined the Civil War as God's way of delivering justice for this extraordinary evil, the costs of which (might) rightly exceed the profits and pleasures derived from it. In this narration of the Civil War, however, it turns out that, for Lincoln, no souls needed saving more than white ones. Lincoln's God's vengeance made whites the center of his concerns.

Lincoln did not bask in the glory of (his) hard-won military triumph and addressed the defeated—and unrepentant—South with remarkable generosity given its responsibility for the war. While he found the North complicit in slavery, his rejection of malice and embrace of charity would ultimately be paid for by those Americans who had suffered unrelentingly since their ancestors were first shipped from Africa.

Given Lincoln's ambiguous record, he might seem an unlikely candidate for America's foremost icon. Granted, American exceptionalism identifies the nation as the world's greatest democracy, and such a polity requires symbols and figures that embody both its character and accomplishments. Lincoln functions beautifully in this capacity not despite but thanks, in part, to his complicated record. To found or refound a polity by violating its basic norms not only requires unrivaled virtuosity. Ironically, it testifies to its superior standing. Lincoln is thus both hero and antihero, which means his iconic status has always required a careful balance of targeted remembrance and selective forgetting. It's time, then, not only to remember Lincoln as a whole, which many claim to have done,[10] but also to take such remembering seriously rather than rhetorically. It's time, that is, to do justice to the dark side of Lincoln's ambiguity, and reimagine his iconicity. Democracy can only be the better for it.[11]

NOTES

1. https://www.deseretnews.com/top/3178/0/32-Abraham-Lincoln-memorials-in-America-and-around-the-world.html.

2. David Herbert Donald, "Getting Right with Lincoln," in *Lincoln Reconsidered: Essays on the Civil War Era* (New York: Vintage Books, 2001).

3. Arthur Schlesinger Jr. typifies America's willfully myopic attitude toward Lincoln. In *The Imperial Presidency*, Schlesinger both admits and denies discomfiting truths about Lincoln, sometimes in the same sentence. Consider these two claims: (1) "Since Lincoln's reputation as the greatest of democratic statesmen is well earned, he obviously did not become a despot lightly." (2) "Driven to extreme policies by unprecedented emergency, he incorporated within himself the written and unwritten checks on presidential absolutism." In the first formulation, Lincoln easily combines democracy and despotism. In the second, Lincoln both transgresses the Constitution and corrects his own transgressions. Arthur Schlesinger Jr., *The Imperial Presidency* (Boston: Houghton Mifflin Company, 1973), 59, 66.

4. Simone de Beauvoir, *The Ethics of Ambiguity* (New York: Citadel Press, 1991), 129.

5. See, for example, Holger Hoock, *Scars of Independence: America's Violent Birth* (New York: Crown, 2017).

6. Herbert Croly, "The Paradox of Lincoln," *The New Republic*, February 17, 1920, https://newrepublic.com/article/79549/the-paradox-abraham-lincoln, emphasis mine.

7. Fred Kaplan, *Lincoln and the Abolitionists: John Quincy Adams, Slavery, and the Civil War* (New York: Harper, 2017, xiii–xiv, emphases mine).

8. There's no question that any assessment of Lincoln's greatness would diverge, at key moments, along racial lines. To reverse Kaplan's valuation is to address a white Lincoln.

9. David Donald, "The Folklore Lincoln," *Journal of the Illinois State Historical Society* 40, no. 4, December 1947, 381, 386.

10. See, for example, Eric Foner's *The Fiery Trial: Abraham Lincoln and American Slavery* (New York: W.W. Norton, 2011).

11. Philip Gourevitch, "Abraham Lincoln Warned Us about Donald Trump," *The New Yorker*, March 15, 2016, https://www.newyorker.com/culture/cultural-comment/abraham-lincoln-warned-us-about-donald-trump; Sidney Blumenthal, "What Would Lincoln Think of Trump?" *LA Times*, July 13, 2017, http://www.latimes.com/opinion/op-ed/la-oe-blumenthal-lincoln-trump-20170713-story.html. Philip Gourevitch (before the 2016 presidential election) and Sidney Blumenthal (after it) credited Abraham Lincoln with anticipating Donald Trump's troubling rise. Lincoln's ostensible prescience can be found in his Young Men's Lyceum Address of 1838. In it he identifies a pair of domestic threats to the American republic: the spirit of lawlessness manifested in vigilante mobs throughout the nation and the likely prospect of a demagogical figure emerging from it who, bent on acclaim and unable to create anything new on his own, sets about destroying America's institutions. What these two don't

consider is whether and how Lincoln—and his subsequent canonization—contributed to Trump's dangerous ascension in the first place. It's not just that Lincoln, a man of deep prejudices shared by much of the country, practiced his own brand of lawlessness by interpreting the Constitution to suit what he insisted were the needs of a country under attack and arrogating newfound powers to the office he held. It's that Lincoln has become a revered figure in American political and military history precisely for disregarding what many take to be legal luxuries the country can't always afford or moral niceties it can't always meet. Trump, then, also a man of deep prejudices shared by much of the country, has occupied a piece of the political and rhetorical space forged by Lincoln's precedents and corresponding exemplarity to promote his own distinct version of what William E. Connolly calls an aspirational (American) fascism. Lincoln is a forerunner of Trump, and Trump, a recognizably American personality, flourishes in part thanks to Lincoln and his iconic status. See William E. Connolly, *Aspirational Fascism: The Struggle for Multifaceted Democracy under Trumpism* (Minneapolis: University of Minnesota Press, 2017).

Chapter One

Lincoln's Decisionism and the Politics of Elimination

> The exception reveals most clearly the essence of the state's authority.
>
> —Carl Schmitt, *Political Theology*

Abraham Lincoln occupies a hallowed place in American memory. His gargantuan temple on the Mall in Washington, D.C., offers a succinct explanation: he saved the union and made possible a democracy to come—and was assassinated for his troubles. Lincoln, of course, was more than a national martyr. He was also a first-rate political thinker and disputant who enjoyed democratic contestation with adversaries and allies alike. Lincoln not only defended the Union in the Civil War, he deployed the Constitution as a weapon in that war, taking democratically problematic actions in the process. Still, his critics generally seem to admire him—not despite but in part because of perceived deficiencies. Was Lincoln a dictator? Perhaps, but if so, he was a benevolent one.[1]

In what follows, however, I argue that Lincoln's political and theoretical legacies are more complicated than his august reputation suggests and that while his accomplishments are many and undeniable, they came at terrible democratic cost. This combination is not the result of unanticipated or unintended consequences. In the events examined below, the first involving Ohio politician Clement Vallandigham, the second involving the Dakota Sioux Indians, Lincoln exercised a sovereign decisionism that enfeebled the democracy it was ostensibly meant to serve, and did so at the kind of moment that tests a nation's commitment to its core political principles. Lincoln thereby modeled a sovereign violence emulated by successors and solidified and extended an American habit of suppressing contentious political speech. Lincoln, that is, practiced a politics of elimination to deal with forces he claimed jeopardized the Union's efforts to defeat an illegitimate rebellion in the South threatening its existence, thus enacting and establishing an untrammeled sovereign power over those who opposed and resisted the conduct of his administration, reducing them to mere disposability. Reduction and elimination—not engagement—defined much of his rule. Lincoln insisted wartime entailed exceptional circumstances that necessitated resort to singular actions, and even those ordinarily suspicious of state power have been inclined to agree.[2]

LINCOLN'S FOUR-FRONT WAR

Lincoln was a wartime president waging a four-front Civil War: against rebellious Southern states; against Northern Democratic opponents of the war; against deserting soldiers; against Native peoples resisting American expansion. Harold Holzer argues: "The fact remains that [Lincoln] was . . . an unrelenting warrior prepared to commit—even sacrifice—men and treasure in unprecedented numbers to secure the kind of peace worth having. And the most powerful evidence of this focus comes from his writings, words that counter the idealized image."[3] Holzer's characterization is correct but partial. Lincoln was prepared to sacrifice more than men and money as he conducted the Civil War. He was also prepared to sacrifice the Constitution to prosecute the war to a successful conclusion. When Lincoln first suspended the writ of habeas corpus, it was argued that the executive trusted to enforce the laws should not break them. Lincoln was blunt in response: "To state the question more directly, are all the laws, *but one*, to go unexecuted, and the government itself go to pieces, lest that one be violated?"[4] Lincoln's alarmist justification for his decision to suspend the writ is contestable, to say the least. More importantly, Lincoln's readiness to achieve political good though it meant not only risking but actually doing serious harm to other political goods remains an example of inestimable value to the American democratic imagination in troubled times. Below I focus on two of the war's four fronts, each a notable incident of political suppression. The first involves the silencing of Clement Vallandigham, a leading figure in Ohio and Democratic national politics.[5] The second involves the killing of thirty-eight Dakota Sioux Indians, the largest mass execution in American history, a state-orchestrated spectacle following an insurrection by a Native American people seeking its own new birth of freedom. In these events Lincoln is at his creative best and cruel worst as sovereign power reinvents itself through and with him.

Lincoln's wartime conduct can be parsed through Carl Schmitt's distinction between commissarial and sovereign dictatorship.[6] In a time of crisis or emergency, a democracy can appoint a dictator empowered to deal with existential threats—from war to domestic upheaval. The dictator acts according to its discretion alone, authorized to do anything it decides—including suspending the legal system, its procedures and protections—except make (new) law. It is bound by no (other) limit. Insofar as commissarial dictatorship constitutes a form of delegation, it can be assigned with great exactitude, specifying the task to be performed and the time allotted to perform it. It can also be revoked at will. This kind of dictator is expected to take extraordinary measures—but only to return the order to its rightful condition prior to the emergency that made it necessary. Restoration of the status quo is its reason for being. Sovereign dictatorship, on the other hand, is tasked to create a new constitutional order. It is truly bound by no limit, but is supposed to do what the commissarial dictator cannot: make new law. In fact, that is its reason for being.

Where does Lincoln fit in Schmitt's typology? Lincoln effectively declared a state of exception and made himself dictator when he initially decided to suspend the writ of habeas corpus in Maryland in 1861, defying (by ignoring) a federal court that ruled he had no authority to do so. He suspended the writ nationwide the following year. This power is (implicitly) granted to Congress in Article I, Section 9 (clause 2), of the Constitution, a section that restricts congressional power by forbidding its particular exercise or imposing conditions and limitations on it. Lincoln tends to model Schmitt's commissarial dictator.[7] Though not at first appointed through a higher authority, namely, the Constitution, Lincoln did invoke it to ground his wartime measures, which he claimed were designed only to save the Union, that is, restore things to the status quo ante bellum. When Congress later ratified Lincoln's usurpation of its suspension power, it also outlined procedures regarding the detention of political prisoners, including conditions for their release, where federal courts remained open. Still, Congress gave Lincoln few meaningfully specific instructions—or serious limitations—regarding the deployment of his newly sanctioned power. Lincoln took advantage of this aporia to exercise a decisionism that defined itself through the details of its enactment. With habeas corpus suspended, political liberties, including freedoms of speech, press, and association, could be negated at will: Lincoln alone would decide whether to negate them and what forms negation would take.

Why would Lincoln even consider negating political liberties? The Civil War lasted longer than anyone anticipated. Its duration posed a number of serious problems for the North, including manpower. In the aftermath of Fort Sumter, Lincoln's call for volunteers elicited a surge of patriotic enthusiasm. Tens of thousands rushed to enlist for battle. Two years, countless casualties, and too many embarrassing military setbacks later, however, the United States faced serious personnel shortages. This led to the first national conscription law in March 1863, which, in turn, broadened and exacerbated already fierce opposition to the war. Conscription, moreover, did not solve the manpower problem. Those subjected to the draft law could hire a substitute or pay a fee to avoid it. Some ignored it. Only 18 percent of those drafted in the first round of conscription donned a uniform.[8] Desertion also plagued the military. Ostensibly, it was not clear how, or whether, the Union would be able to maintain an effective military force to prosecute the war and defeat secession. Anything that even appeared to subvert or weaken the war effort could be disastrous.[9]

Given Democratic opposition to the war and draft, the administration took steps to suppress both. In March 1863 Lincoln appointed General Ambrose Burnside to run the (so-called) Department of Ohio. Burnside, like Lincoln, did not recognize, let alone appreciate, adversarial politics during wartime. He declared martial law and issued General Order No. 38, which regulated public speech on the war, though Burnside tried to conceal its antidemocratic character by claiming that he was only targeting expressions of "sympathies for the enemy," which, by definition, were fair game. The conceit fooled no one and Vallandigham defied Burnside's edict—partly because it had been issued—and continued speaking publicly against the war. Following a speech in Mount Vernon, Ohio, before close to twenty thousand people in which he denounced the war, excoriated General Order No. 38, and asserted a constitutional right to criticize governmental policies, Vallandigham was arrested, tried in military court, convicted, and sentenced to military prison in Boston for the remainder of the war (execution was considered but rejected).[10] The proceedings took two days. Vallandigham ridiculed the legitimacy of the military prosecution, insisting on his right to a jury trial and to his right of political critique. He also reiterated his commitment to effect change by electoral means alone and his total obedience to law.

In prison Vallandigham continued to press his case against the war. He sought a writ of habeas corpus, but federal judge Humphrey H. Leavitt invoked the dubious principle of judicial incompetence in wartime and refused to get involved. Nevertheless, Burnside's heavy-handedness backfired, generating a reaction both immediate and furious. Newspapers nationwide blasted him (and Lincoln) for his assault on the Constitution. (Burnside also shut down, in defiance of a federal judge, the *Chicago Times*, an opposition newspaper, for its political criticism of, among other things, the Vallandigham arrest.) Fighting to save the Union, the administration was destroying it, undermining its most sacred rights and liberties. Critics noted that the same logic that denied citizens the right to speak publicly against the war could be used to deny them the right to vote as well.[11] Many Republicans also lambasted the administration; Vallandigham was not simply a partisan issue.

AMERICAN IN EXILE

Lincoln tried to diffuse all things Vallandigham by revoking his prison sentence and banishing him behind Confederate lines. This political kidnapping effectively stripped him of his citizenship. Determined not to convert Vallandigham into a martyr, Lincoln tried to erase him from the political map instead, a move that did not (seem to) allow for the possibility of restoration once the war concluded. This decision, in other words, gave every appearance of permanence, unlike a jail sentence in a military prison. With the latter, Vallandigham could be released at the end of the war (or even earlier). Lincoln, of course, had no real intention of doing this. Vallandigham was a gifted orator capable of drawing and energizing enormous crowds. Lincoln claimed exile "less disagreeable" to Vallandigham than prison, but Vallandigham would surely have taken exception to Lincoln's characterization of his exceptional move.[12]

In his brutal treatment of Vallandigham, Lincoln may have been channeling ancient Greek predecessors. The Athenian practice of ostracism targeted protean political figures, but not always or necessarily as punishment for (alleged) wrongdoing. Exile could be a response to a citizen whose undue success threatened democracy itself. The only way to preserve equality and freedom was to maintain and, when necessary, restore democratic balance. One might legitimately prevail in the celebrated Greek contest, but too much success could be dangerous to the democracy it helped constitute. Lincoln seems to have been responding to Vallandigham's political prowess, but he refused to couch his response to Vallandigham in political terms and did not challenge Vallandigham on the field of political battle. In fact, Lincoln's resort to exile suggested, if anything, that he was unable to match Vallandigham on that field. Exile could be considered a tacit admission of agonistic defeat. Democracy was not enhanced as a result of Lincoln's decision nor could it plausibly be claimed that the Union's security improved. Not only did Vallandigham's treatment reveal how precarious individual life had become. It also suggested the self-defeating, self-destructive trajectory of the Union. In the immediate aftermath of Vallandigham's arrest, his fellow Dayton citizens assembled at the city's Republican newspaper, the *Dayton Journal*, and torched its offices. Burnside then declared martial law.[13] These were needless, self-inflicted wounds. As David Bromwich notes, Lincoln's forte in politics was the art and power of persuasion.[14] He appeared to relish political contestation in his senatorial struggle against Stephen Douglas. Regarding Vallandigham, however, Lincoln did not engage in political contest. Rather he invoked and channeled sovereign power—in order to disappear him.[15]

The more disturbing aspects and implications of Lincoln's sovereign decisionism exemplify Giorgio Agamben's concept of homo sacer. Through this disarming figure, Agamben theorizes the relationship between state and persons. Homo sacer (bare life) refers to human bodies that can be disposed of at will by the sovereign power of the state. These bodies can be arrested, questioned, and tortured to elicit useful information; they can be imprisoned indefinitely at made-to-order detention sites; they can be forcibly removed from the nation and relocated anywhere; they can be targeted and killed because it is expedient to do so. These are bodies that, whatever their precise fate, lack political recognition and thus protection—hence their disposability, their eliminability. The state is the entity that bestows the designation of bare life insofar as it can operate free from the law's interference when it declares a state of exception. For Agamben, the German death camp ably represents sovereignty's relationship to homo sacer. And while his claim that this abject space models the relationship between state and individual more broadly seems melodramatic, as Elisabeth Anker has persuasively argued, Agamben has nonetheless given a name to a menacing feature of democracy, and homo sacer works well as an analytical tool to dissect Lincoln's calculated reduction of human beings to nonexistence.[16]

In a chilling rhetorical move, when Lincoln addressed those who condemned his treatment of Vallandigham, he spoke on behalf of the military power of the Union, which, in turn, he equated with the latter's very condition of existence. According to Lincoln, to attack (his characterization) the army was to invite its counterattack. The military could legitimately wage war against a single democratic citizen exercising his rights, a decision that signaled the negation of his status: Vallandigham was reduced to bare life. His body could be seized, held, displayed, transported, signified, imprisoned, exiled, killed. Lincoln and Burnside assumed they could dispose of Vallandigham at will and that his disposition would lack any political significance or meaning. No one even knew how Confederate forces would react to Vallandigham's "transfer." Would they even accept him? Would they shoot him on the spot as a possible Union spy or saboteur? Would they imprison him? Would they also expel him from their territory? Why would they want him any more than Lincoln did?

When Union soldiers executed the exile order, it met with resistance. Meeting in Murfreesboro, Tennessee, "under a flag of truce to discuss the transfer," the South refused to accept Vallandigham. Undeterred, the Union officer in charge simply changed plans and dumped him near a Confederate camp, where he was quickly captured—by a private. Now the South was free to do with him as it pleased, the North having set the terms of his treatment. Vallandigham did his best to assert and achieve a different status: "I am a citizen of Ohio, and of the United States. I am here within your lines by force and against my will. I therefore surrender myself to you as a prisoner of war."[17] Lincoln, in short, disposed of one manufactured enemy by foisting him on another real enemy that could also treat him as disposable, eliminable. Vallandigham was utterly bereft, his status perhaps beneath the level of slaves (who, at least, were still recognized and considered of value).

Initially the Confederates didn't quite know what to do with him, but on orders from Richmond he was permitted to travel to Wilmington, North Carolina. From there he escaped (via Bermuda) to Canada, where he took up residence across the water from Detroit with a Union gunboat, cannons fixed on his home, assuming surveillance duty to make sure he made no move to return. The state assigned Vallandigham his own personal gunship to keep him in exile. The state disappeared him. It was going to make sure he stayed disappeared.

How did this situation arise? Lincoln suspended the writ of habeas corpus nationally on September 24, 1862, usurping congressional power.[18] Lincoln presented suspension as an act of military necessity, but it was fundamentally an antipolitical, antidemocratic measure. It created three categories of people: disloyal persons; Rebels and Insurgents; and those who aid and abet them.[19] It is the first category of person, which Lincoln introduced in the suspension's opening paragraph, that is "not adequately restrained by the ordinary processes of law from hindering" measures the sovereign deems necessary for the war's successful prosecution. More specifically, Lincoln was concerned these allegedly disloyal persons might discourage voluntary enlistments, resist the draft, or do something else ostensibly disloyal.[20] He was concerned, in other words, that they might practice politics.

Jennifer Weber would rescue Lincoln from any possible historical taint by arguing that suspension of the writ and the use of military tribunals to try civilians were "rational" decisions. Weber turns to the legal expertise of Mark Neely Jr., who, according to Weber, "concludes that most of the arrests in which habeas corpus was suspended would have taken place even had those protections been in place. Very few detentions were politically motivated." More importantly, Weber continues (apparently in her own voice), "the vast majority of arrests and military trials were in the border states, where civilian loyalties were uncertain. There is a logic during a civil war to putting defendants before a jury of uniformed loyalists rather than in a court where the judge and jury may rule against the government not on the evidence, but because they support the enemy."[21]

It's not just that Weber's defense of Lincoln suggests that the suspension of habeas corpus was both gratuitous and calculated, and that it enabled precisely the kind of politically motivated arrests that would otherwise have been impossible. It's not just that the logic of Lincoln's use of military tribunals was designed to confirm a result predetermined by the government's "uniformed loyalists" rather than allow a jury (any jury) to reach an impartial decision based on the evidence. Each measure reflected and contributed to the augmentation of sovereign power, articulated and exercised by the executive (later confirmed by the legislative branch), through the formation, detention, and disposal of suspect persons and their bodies.[22] Weber concludes, benignly: "The Civil War ended with a more powerful and centralized government than the country had ever known."[23] Because Lincoln proceeded incrementally and with (alleged) moderation, he succeeded where later presidents like Wilson and Roosevelt, who "target[ed] specific groups of people in a wholesale fashion, including political enemies," (supposedly) failed. Weber does not mention the possibility that Wilson and Roosevelt also succeeded in their endeavors precisely because of the centralization of sovereign power the Civil War made possible and over which Lincoln presided. His presidency made theirs possible. Weber does acknowledge Lincoln's shortcomings when it comes to the exercise of power (in instances where he overreached): "The obvious exceptions are a handful of high-profile cases involving politicians and newspapermen."[24] Yet Vallandigham was made one of these exceptions, a victim not of overreach but decisionism. Lincoln's treatment of him argues that he did more than merely suspend habeas corpus. Mere suspension of the writ still presumes there is a body to be produced. Vallandigham, however, named a body that, in the end, could not be produced. It was gone, disappeared. Lincoln, in effect, expunged habeas corpus when he exiled—and thereby erased—Vallandigham.[25]

IN ANDREW JACKSON'S SHADOW

Lincoln cites Andrew Jackson as a precedent for the legitimacy of his extralegal actions.[26] Jackson's example, however, discloses sovereignty's troubling dynamics, including its inherent tendency to mushroom. At the end of the War of 1812, then General Jackson presided over New Orleans. Assuming the British were about to attack the city, he imposed martial law. Once the war concluded, which was known before official word of peace arrived, Jackson continued martial law despite the expectation of citizens that it would be lifted. Facing criticism for this arbitrary decision, Jackson ordered the arrest of Louis Louallier for writing an article in a local newspaper condemning it as counter to American constitutional tradition. Jackson claimed he was concerned about the negative effect that the article would (allegedly) have on the army and its soldiers.[27] Louallier hired a lawyer to secure a writ of habeas corpus, which was quickly granted by U.S. District Judge Dominick Hall, who found the continuation of martial law unjustified.[28] Jackson had both the attorney and judge arrested. When someone rebuked Jackson for the escalation, he, too, was arrested, indicating the exercise of sovereign power had no logical terminus.[29] Martial law, at this point, was no longer the issue. Any citizen, for example, with a purely abstract concern about the scope of executive power became a potential state target.

Jackson's tribunal acquitted Louallier, but Jackson ignored the verdict and kept him imprisoned. What's more, Jackson presumed no court-martial would convict a federal judge, so he had Hall removed from New Orleans, taken four miles out of the city, and abandoned. Hall would not be allowed to return to the city and his office until peace was announced or the British departed the region. Not only did Jackson effectively eliminate one of the three branches of government in the American federal system. He also treated it with public contempt. His actions suggest he wanted to demonstrate an irresistible power. In this, Jackson's resort to (short-term) exile prefigured the treatment to which Lincoln would later subject Vallandigham. Perhaps Lincoln borrowed the idea from Jackson.

After official word of peace arrived, Hall returned to New Orleans and summoned Jackson to court—more than once in fact. Jackson refused to recognize the court's power to hold him accountable for his actions and therefore declined to answer questions regarding his contempt of its orders and imprisonment of the judge.[30] Hall eventually fined Jackson $1,000, which Jackson duly paid. More than a quarter-century later (1842), Congress took up a bill that would compensate Jackson for the fine.[31] This long-after-the-fact defense of Jackson and, more importantly, sovereign decisionism, signals a crisis for democracy greater than the original events that occasioned it. While an early version of the legislation made it clear that Congress was not passing negative judgment on Hall or the decision he rendered, the law that ultimately passed (1844) included no such provision.[32]

Jackson's unrepentant, autocratic conduct in the War of 1812 set a dangerous precedent –for himself. During the Seminole War of 1818, Jackson formed military tribunals to try two British subjects, Alexander Arbuthnot and Robert Ambrister, for their leadership roles in the conflict. The court found both parties guilty, but exile was not an option. These were deemed capital cases. The court ordered the execution of Arbuthnot but not, in the end, Ambrister. Both, however, were executed, the latter because of Jackson's personal intervention.[33] When the House Committee on Military Affairs looked into the matter in 1819, it could find no reason or justification for the trials (this determination was separate and distinct from the procedural issues that plagued the proceedings).[34] It voted to disapprove both the trial and the verdicts.[35]

Lincoln, to his discredit, never matched Jackson's symbolic deed in New Orleans. He never submitted himself to a court for judgment, however reluctantly or defiantly he might have done so. Lincoln also insisted that Jackson's actions in 1812 did no damage to the "permanent" rights of the people to speech, discussion, and press. He conveniently overlooked the only kind of damage that can be said to matter, that is, the "temporary" damage that Jackson inflicted at the moment when the exercise of those rights mattered most, when it might have stopped, or helped to stop, an abuse of power.[36] The permanent rights of the people exist in a series of temporary moments. To claim exception, to say that the exception is temporary, is effectively to say they (rights) do not exist. They have no standing of their own. They exist when the sovereign (or a local surrogate acting as sovereign) says they do.

VALLANDIGHAM'S RESILIENCE

Vallandigham, to his democratic credit, converted exile into a platform from which a political campaign could be waged, putting to shame Socratic presumptions that exile amounted to the end of an engaged life.[37] Vallandigham, as mentioned, eventually escaped from the South and maneuvered to Canada where he ran as the Democratic candidate for governor of Ohio in 1864.

Vallandigham did not win the gubernatorial race, but this was no foregone conclusion and was perhaps due to unexpected Union military victories, rendering Vallandigham's war criticisms less compelling. Americans love military success and tend to forgive anything in its wake. Either way, Vallandigham demonstrated his commitment to democratic politics by refusing to accept exile as political erasure and by taking great personal risk to leave the South, where, as a loyal citizen of the United States, he was an enemy alien, and elude Union blockades on his way to Canada—only to expose himself to possible retaliation from Lincoln's agents. His commitment to democratic contestation was greater than anything Lincoln exhibited in their confrontation.[38]

Though Lincoln did not know of or sanction in advance Burnside's suppression of Vallandigham, he did approve General Order No. 38, which Burnside cleared with the White House and which followed Lincoln's own precedent of suspending the writ of habeas corpus on his own authority.[39] Lincoln did, however, refuse to reverse Burnside and he took the occasion, when prompted, to defend Burnside's actions and articulate a (problematic) wartime political position. Democratic supporters of the war, meeting in Albany, New York, led by former Congressman Erastus Corning, passed a number of resolutions critical of the Vallandigham affair—while supportive of the sovereign's war to crush the rebellion. Given the national controversy the event generated, Lincoln penned a letter and sent a copy of it to the influential *New York Tribune*. It was later published as a pamphlet and sold roughly half a million copies, read by as many as ten million citizens. It may have been Lincoln's most successful public "address" while president.[40]

Lincoln opens the letter by complimenting the Albany authors for their patriotic undertaking. He reassures them that he has not taken—and will not "knowingly" undertake—any unlawful or unconstitutional measure to defeat the rebellion. This suggests that Lincoln recognizes the president is bound by certain limits, limits that he himself does not establish, and that he will do his utmost to adhere to them. Transgression would be inadvertent or incidental, thus no cause for (grave) concern. He even expresses a kind of regret for having to arrest and imprison Vallandigham and promises to release him at the earliest opportunity, namely, when public safety allows it (this was prior to exile). In addition, Lincoln claims that precisely because of his reverence for individual rights he has been slow to take the "strong measures" ultimately *forced upon* him in the name of public safety.[41] Lincoln seems to be practicing what John Burt calls "tragic pragmatism," honoring constitutional demands while respecting political necessity and hoping that his compromises don't compromise fundamental American ideals.[42] Lincoln relies on the constitutional provision regarding the suspension of the writ of habeas corpus to argue that exceptions to well-established constitutional practice and principle are possible and permissible. If anything, Lincoln insists, people are likely to criticize him for not doing enough—and doing it sooner—to win the war. Still, Lincoln's pledge of constitutional fidelity suggests that he believes the Constitution, by folding a wartime-peacetime distinction into its text, allows for a range of construals thanks to which the president enjoys, minimally, considerable license during wartime. Lincoln rejects the charge that any of his wartime measures, including the suppression of overtly political speech, are unconstitutional, belying Burt's tragic pragmatic claim.[43] Moreover, he portrays the principles of a democratic constitution as weaknesses that enemies exploit to pursue their deadly aims, which means they count on their opponents to (foolishly) adhere to these principles, thus guaranteeing their downfall. Lincoln refuses this self-annihilating double standard and thereby exemplifies the ambiguity for which he is famous: crush democratic dissent and deliberation while simultaneously signaling its affirmation.

LINCOLN'S LEGERDEMAIN

Lincoln denies he is silencing Vallandigham merely because he is criticizing the administration and Burnside's General Order No. 38. Otherwise, he agrees his action would be unconstitutional: "But the arrest, as I understand, was made for a very different reason. Mr. Vallandigham avows his hostility to the War on the part of the Union; and his arrest was made because he was laboring, with some effect, to prevent the raising of troops, to encourage desertions from the army; and to leave the Rebellion without an adequate military force to suppress it."[44] Lincoln offers an interpretation of Vallandigham that not only rejects the idea that he was practicing politics; it implicitly denies its possibility, at least when the subject is war and its successful conduct (Vallandigham's so-called laboring, a nefarious activity). Lincoln thereby conceals the antidemocratic, antipolitical bias of his wartime presidency while simultaneously suggesting that he still respects democratic contestation. Animus toward the war in general is problematic (it is the war, after all) but not necessarily actionable. Mere expression of opposition in general is to be tolerated, but opposition to the conditions of possibility of war is to be stifled—and prosecuted. Lincoln verges on arguing that citizens may give voice to political positions as long as they do not have consequences the sovereign deems unacceptable, that is, that might diminish its power to do as it wills.

In this muddied context, it is worth noting that Lincoln's characterization of Vallandigham's alleged labors cannot be sustained. Eyewitnesses that testified against him at trial, including two spies, both dispatched by Burnside, and a congressman, do not support Lincoln's account. There was no such "laboring." Lincoln may be defending his general, but he also attributes his response to Burnside. Lincoln's facts may be wrong, but he does not attempt to gather, let alone consider, the facts.[45] The sovereign creates and interprets facts. Besides, it doesn't matter that Vallandigham always counseled obedience to law and advocated for change only through the ballot box. The uncertainty Lincoln attributes to Vallandigham's arrest creates ambiguity. If he is wrong, a possibility left open, he will overturn Vallandigham's arrest given "reasonably satisfactory evidence." The concession reinforces Lincoln's claim that he would not knowingly do anything unconstitutional. It also suggests that Vallandigham's arrest is by definition a matter of interpretive contestation, which means there can't be agreement on the reason for his arrest. Lincoln sees it as a military matter requiring a sovereign decision. Opponents see it as a political matter.

According to Lincoln, criticisms of the war, calls for peace, condemnation of conscription, and summons to defend freedom of speech under government attack all discourage enlistment and encourage desertion, which is as destructive to Union war efforts as actually killing soldiers.[46] In a rhetorical question that resonated with much of the nation, Lincoln asked, "Must I shoot a simple-minded soldier boy who deserts, while I must not touch a hair of a wily agitator who induces him to desert?"[47] Lincoln's question suggests that shooting the simple-minded soldier boy amounts to a sovereign imperative over which he has no control. Simple-minded soldier boys who desert must be shot, at least on occasion, reducing them to bare life. This, in a phrase that marks the passive impersonality of the agency at work, is what is "called for." Desertion cannot be considered a political act either. A deserter is a body that refuses to fight and might induce other bodies to do likewise. The second part of Lincoln's question suggests its absurdity, from the sovereign's perspective: the wily agitator could never be considered a democratic citizen engaged in a quintessential political act. That is, when the sovereign conducts a war, citizens do not disobey—let alone counsel others to disobey—a conscription law on the grounds that it serves the democracy's best interests.

Lest this seem an overreaction, Lincoln holds Vallandigham responsible not only for what he says, but also for the violent, deadly resistance of others—to the war and conscription.[48] Lincoln renders him public enemy number one, even though he has to concede, two and one-half weeks after the first letter, that he "certainly [does] not know that Mr. V. has specifically, and by direct language, advised against enlistments, and in favor of desertion, and resistance to drafting."[49] According to Geoffrey Stone, "Lincoln did not argue that Vallandigham was guilty merely because he *should have known* that one effect of his speeches might have been to generate discontent and perhaps eventually 'cause' some listeners to desert or refuse induction."[50] Such an argument would make any criticism of Lincoln impossible and gut constitutional guarantees of free speech and press. According to Stone, Lincoln argued that Vallandigham was fully aware of "the danger he was creating [and] did not 'counsel against' unlawful resistance to the law."[51] This was all Lincoln needed—or wanted—to know. He condemned Vallandigham not for something he said but for something he did not say, as if he deliberately refused to say it. This approach would permit public criticism of government only as long as speakers "mitigated the danger" by stating clearly that they were not advocating law-breaking.

Stone finds this argument "ingenious," even though he knows it does not apply to Vallandigham.[52] Lincoln's regulation of public political speech would require democratic citizens to utter specific words, phrases, or sentences as disclaimers at governmental insistence as a condition of speaking in public. The logic is that such progovernment speech can be forced. If compliance is refused, speech can be silenced. The speaker brings it on himself. Lincoln has put citizens on (precarious) notice by rendering them uncertain as to what they may (or must) utter. For those actively engaged in politics, it is not clear whether their speech will run afoul of suppression. What kind of normalizing effect might this stricture have? The mere *possibility* of subversive speech must be policed by the state, and the state alone determines the nature of an individual's relationship to speech. Congress made this possible when it created the Provost Marshal General's Bureau to enforce the first draft law and monitor anyone who might interfere with it.[53] Indeed, the polity is modeled as a war zone where the demands of public safety require governmental surveillance—"mischievous interference" with the army, on whose existence the sovereign nation allegedly depends, can erupt anywhere.[54] For Lincoln, Vallandigham poses a (contagious) threat to the existence of the Union. Those who defend and support him become allies of an insidious enemy. Lincoln thus accuses the Ohio Democrats who rallied to Vallandigham's gubernatorial candidacy, and who also passed a resolution denouncing Lincoln for suppressing him and other war critics, of disloyalty. This places them in the crosshairs of Lincoln's suspension of habeas corpus. Anticipating their reaction to such a charge-cum-threat, he offers them an escape from the unpatriotic, potentially treasonous corner in which he tries to force them. They can continue to offer (some) criticisms provided they declare their loyalty—in advance, in Lincoln's terms.[55] He would even release Vallandigham, now a mere bargaining tool, if they publicly assent to his proposal and sign their names to his loyalty oath.

How does Lincoln come to his remarkable conclusion about Vallandigham's intent? Lincoln claims that Vallandigham had to know, given the volatile wartime context, the effect that his incendiary words were likely to have on conscription, enlistment, and desertion. If he were as innocent as he claims, he would have explicitly advocated against any effort to interfere with recruitment of any kind: "When it is known that the whole burthen of his speeches has been to stir up men against the prosecution of the war, and that in the midst of resistance to it, he has not been known, in any instance, to counsel against such resistance, it is next to impossible to repel the inference that he has counselled directly in favor of it."[56] Lincoln claims that to his knowledge Vallandigham did not counsel against resistance. Once again, Lincoln is wrong, though he apparently made no effort to determine the accuracy of his claim. But he leaves the question ambiguous (because he did not claim that Vallandigham had not counseled against resistance), allowing him room to offer an account of events convenient to the actions he wishes to take to suppress what he defines as disloyalty. Lincoln does not deny that Vallandigham has met his criterion; he deploys the phrase, "he has not been known . . . to counsel against resistance." Known by whom? Known by Lincoln? The Ohio Democrats he's writing? The American public he's engaging? It's unclear. Ironically, though Lincoln takes what would become a famous stand against ambiguity ("the man who stands by and says nothing when the peril of his Government is discussed, cannot be misunderstood. If not hindered, he is sure to help the enemy; much more if he talks ambiguously—talks for his country with 'buts' and 'ifs' and 'ands'"), it more rightly applies to him than Vallandigham.[57]

Lincoln rejects the claim that political rights such as freedom of speech attain greater significance during wartime. Rather, because it is the nature of war that it cannot be organized and waged seamlessly, Lincoln perceives numerous threats to its successful conduct. Instead of recognizing sovereignty's constitutive threat to freedom and rights, Lincoln sees sovereign power as a potential victim to undue limitations. Why does democracy's commitment to its fundamental principles take on additional significance during war (or other emergencies)? Democracy tends not to notice First Amendment rights when the order is untroubled. Rights are exercised and respected because they seem to be without consequences. Thus they don't need protection. Yet rights always need protection, as the American founders knew, because majorities are tempted to silence views with which they disagree or find objectionable, especially during war, when the sovereign routinely declares exceptions and pursues courses of action that augment its power. Lincoln, however, dismisses the objection that suppression sets a dangerous precedent and would continue during peacetime.[58] He insists that a patient who consents to necessary but unpleasant medical treatment (emetics) while sick would not continue such treatment once healthy. Lincoln, however, did not solicit the consent of the American people for his extraconstitutional measures. He imposed them unilaterally. And unlike emetics, Lincoln's prescribed course of action resulted in harm to the objects of his care: the Constitution and the people. An apt Civil War medical analogy might have been amputation. More importantly, Lincoln's analogy ignores sovereignty's logic of public safety, the logic by means of which the sovereign grants itself exceptions to the Constitution. That is, public safety is not solely a wartime concern, and wartime can exist absent armed conflict. Lincoln thus gives himself license to diagnose and treat the polity whenever he decides it is in need of it.

LINCOLN: AN APOLOGY

Benjamin Kleinerman finds new reason to admire Lincoln in the latter's wartime stewardship of the presidency. While Kleinerman steadfastly rejects any claim that Lincoln's four-year rule amounted to "a dictatorship, constitutional or otherwise," he appreciates the politically treacherous path Lincoln pursued to win the war.[59] Kleinerman makes a critical distinction in analyzing Lincoln's conduct. Lincoln did not assert that the inherent powers of the presidency enabled him to take whatever action he deemed necessary to save the Union. Rather, Kleinerman argues, "Lincoln actually suggests that the lawfulness derives from the indispensability of the action—did the president's action actually preserve the Constitution and the nation?"[60] The president, then, "cannot hide behind the legality of his intent."[61]

Kleinerman argues that Lincoln is making a political rather than a legal claim. This means that Lincoln must give reasons for why he thinks his actions are indispensable, making his claim conditional upon demonstration. This leaves Lincoln open to the judgment of Congress and the people, both of which might disagree with, even condemn him for his actions and remove him from office via impeachment or the ballot box.[62] Lincoln made no effort to override the constitutional checks and limitations that constrain power, as any actual dictator would do. If Lincoln had made a move to suspend elections, for example, he would have destroyed the Constitution "as a *constitution*," that is, with meaningful "structural checks on the powers of government."[63]

Kleinerman notes, in a discussion of Lincoln's "Letter to Albert Hodges," that to make the claim of necessity, one must also identify those actions that aren't necessary or indispensable to one's objectives. Lincoln did this when he overturned emancipation orders by his battlefield generals early in the war. This differentiates "the mere claim of necessity from its reality."[64] Lincoln did arrogate to himself rather than Congress the power to override fundamental rights, but he did so because the president can be held singularly accountable for his actions should he abuse the power.[65] Lincoln thus combines what Kleinerman calls aggressiveness and modesty.[66] He boldly exercises power with an understanding of its "accompanying restraints."[67] It is this distinctive combination that Kleinerman admires and can serve as a corrective to reservations that scholars, if not the American public, have about the greatness of Lincoln's administration.[68]

Kleinerman's account of Lincoln's exercise of war powers may conceal as much as it reveals about his conduct. Even assuming Lincoln did not tamper with (or even considered doing so) America's constitutional checks, whence the apparent need? As Kleinerman notes, Lincoln was more or less convinced that he would not win reelection, but this was not due to the controversial constitutional decisions he had taken. It was due to the lack of military success in the war, which was unrelated to Vallandigham. With military success, Lincoln became a new president. In other words, citizens tend to be forgiving of constitutional malfeasance if it pays off or they decide it doesn't matter. If the war is won, presidents can be forgiven a lot, assuming they need to be forgiven at all. Military victory can also induce selective amnesia.

In addition, citizens do not necessarily object when presidents sacrifice fundamental rights to provide security, largely because it usually involves the sacrifice of other people's rights rather than their own. This is why electoral mechanisms constitute a dubious limitation on presidential discretion.

The reason there is a Bill of Rights is that majorities cannot be trusted to respect them, especially in times of crisis. This is also the occasion for courts to defend rights against aggressive majorities and those public officials that act in their name. Kleinerman does not mention the role of the courts in his assessment of Lincoln. But he does make a suspect majority (the people) the ultimate guarantor of their rights when it is known that they are unlikely to be fit to play that role. This seems to be precisely what happened in the case of Vallandigham. Lincoln did not heed the national outcry (from elites in both parties) about Vallandigham's suppression by military tribunal. Rather, he turned to the newspapers to garner public support for his political persecution of Vallandigham—who had dared to enact democratic politics. The rights of those critical of the draft and the war were not of concern to the people who rallied to Lincoln.

Kleinerman needs to address a more fundamental problem that Lincoln (any president, really) faces. While he notes that Lincoln needs to make an argument for why it is necessary to override fundamental rights, how could he possibly demonstrate that an override was in actual fact necessary? What would proof look like? Rights can be violated and the war can be won, but how do you determine if the one contributed to the other? The same result might have come about in the absence of violation. What's more, for a president to submit himself to the judgment of the people every four years allows for considerable abuse in the interim. How do you undo the damage?

Kleinerman can claim an unlikely ally in George Kateb. Kateb assesses Lincoln's conduct of the war and the resort to military necessity to wage it on the terms he deemed indispensable. He pulls no punches when rehearsing Lincoln's problematic constitutional moves and measures (suspending habeas corpus, shutting down presses, imprisoning tens of thousands of political opponents, conducting military tribunals when civilian courts were in session, disregarding court orders, etc.).[69] "Perhaps to say that Lincoln disregarded the Constitution is too polite a way of putting it. One should say instead that he seriously violated it; or even that he destroyed it, by working on the conviction that the rights guaranteed by the Constitution and the limits it placed on governmental action could not be honored in an emergency as awful as secession and civil war. Much injury had to be done to the ideal of constitutionalism."[70]

Kateb is convinced that "Lincoln had to do what he did" to win the war.[71] This is a common position in patriotic discourse. Here Kateb's Lincoln comes across as brave and heroic. To do the right thing, to save the Union, Lincoln also had to do great wrong. His willingness to do great wrong even proves his love of the Union.[72] Kateb finds Lincoln's invocation of military necessity not only sincere but convincing.[73] Kateb may well be right, but how could this be known? Those who argue that necessity dictates the resort to certain problematic measures tend to rely on insistence rather than evidence or proof. Again, what would evidence or proof look like? Victory does not vindicate Lincoln. The South could easily have won the war despite Lincoln's maneuvers. More importantly, it's not as if Lincoln could simultaneously pursue two approaches to the war, one where he observed constitutional guarantees and one where he ignored them. Lincoln deemed the stakes too high to take the risk that things might not turn out well if he did not turn lawless. Politicians are always willing to sacrifice liberties for safety (or some other goal); politicians are not willing to risk lives (or their careers) to keep our rights intact by refusing to sacrifice them in time of emergency. Where are the citizens who are willing to die for rights untouched rather than sacrifice them? Where's the politician who will ask them to do so? Not Lincoln.

Kateb is also clear that Lincoln did damage that outlasted the war. The specters of Woodrow Wilson and George W. Bush, among others, haunt his book. Lincoln's "decisions to suspend or otherwise abridge certain rights meant that the Constitution he revered was grossly injured and endured the further injury of having precedents set for future presidents, who, we know, have acted not only in some approximation of good faith but also and more abundantly in bad faith. The injury of injuries that the Constitution experienced was that it was shown up as inadequate to the unprecedented emergency in which the Union faced destruction, and since that time has been treated, under such cover, as inadequate for much lesser emergencies or for spurious ones."[74] Again, Kateb's claim is appealing, but Lincoln never gave the Constitution a chance. So was it really shown up or were the public servants sworn to protect it, including Lincoln, shown up?

While Kateb writes that mistakes were made, he also argues that "for the most part [Lincoln] did not overreach."[75] Vallandigham, whom Kateb references but does not discuss, would not find such a formulation reassuring. As we have seen, to silence Vallandigham's opposition to the war and draft, Lincoln, following trial by a military kangaroo court, sent him not to prison but into exile in the South, effectively stripping him of his citizenship and reducing him to bare life. Lincoln seemed blind to the violence he inflicted on Vallandigham and his status, even suggesting that he was doing Vallandigham a favor. This kind of executive fiat did not unify the nation behind the war but further divided it.

Kateb writes that "Lincoln's formulation that what is 'otherwise unconstitutional becomes lawful' becomes ever more troubling the more you think about it."[76] Still, I'm not sure that Kateb is troubled enough. Having identified Lincoln's constitutional depredations and then ratifying them in terms of necessity, Kateb, like Lincoln, both disavows the damage done by arguing it was for our own good and effectively ignores the aftermath. What might Lincoln have done to become worthy of the offenses he committed? Taking responsibility for your actions is more than a grand rhetorical gesture. Lincoln, however, did not give repairing the Constitution a second thought because he believed the war's end would return the country to the status quo ante, just as a formerly sick patient, having taken his medicine, returns to health and resumes his normal life without it. Kateb, it could be argued, let Lincoln off the lawless hook too easily.

THE TRAGIC POLITICS OF RESIGNATION

Does Lincoln, then, possess or lack the tragic sensibility that Max Weber claims is critical to success in modern politics?[77] Weber insists the realization of worthwhile, even noble ends often requires resort to morally problematic means, violence in particular. It's critical that political actors not flinch in the face of this moral and political bind. To do what is right is also to do what is problematic, even objectionable and wrong. Doing the right thing, moreover, cannot render morally sound an evil (means) employed to secure it. The sovereign reduction of Vallandigham (and others) to bare life coupled with the rhetorical sleight of hand justifying it thus did double injury—to Vallandigham, to the democratic polity. Lincoln, apparently, is blind to this. What if, however, following Lee's formal surrender two years later, Lincoln had publicly acknowledged that he knowingly breached the Constitution and sacrificed American lives to save the Union, because slavery and the Slave Power represented such monstrous evils that they had to be eradicated by whatever means available? What then?

Following public admission, Lincoln would announce that, having accomplished his primary goals, he was resigning the presidency, effective immediately. His resignation would constitute an affirmation that his prosecution of the war had been both a success and failure, that success necessarily entails failure. Still, from a tragic perspective Lincoln succeeded without taking sufficient risk. A resort to necessity in wartime to justify problematic actions should not simply be accepted at face value or given the benefit of the doubt, however tempting. In doing terrible things to save the Union, Lincoln gambled with the Constitution and damaged democracy in the process. If Lincoln had refused to do terrible things in this cause, he would have taken a political risk that could have enhanced the democracy he did his best to serve. But Lincoln took the expedient route as he eliminated politics in his efforts to save the Union and destroy slavery. Democracy may (or may not) have survived, but (mere) survival is not enough. Democracy needs to demand more from itself.[78] Kateb claims that "the injury of injuries that the Constitution experienced was that it was shown up as inadequate to the unprecedented emergency in which the Union faced destruction."[79] Kateb may be right, but, as I argued above, we'll never know because Lincoln did not give the Constitution a chance to prove otherwise. Why must Lincoln resign? Thomas L. Dumm suggests that "resignation can be thought of as an experimental moment, a testing of the limits of the community."[80] Lincoln, in order to preserve and defend the Union, routinely violated its Constitution, which amounted to an experiment in the state of exception. His resignation would also constitute an experiment in political life, but in democratic recovery—daring citizens over whom he ran roughshod to retake their government—so it shall not perish from the earth from those bound and determined to save it.

Lincoln's resignation for crimes against democracy, especially to save it, would retroactively restore democracy's priority. The spirit of Andrew Jackson's surrender to civilian authority for wrongdoing while implementing martial law now becomes exemplary, but Lincoln often learned the wrong lesson from his most admired predecessors. Still, some might argue that resignation would amount to little more than abdication. As Dumm argues, a resignation "*is* the breaking of a promise, either by the person resigning or by the institution that has forced the resignation."[81] In Lincoln's case, resignation would constitute more than the breaking of a promise. It would also signify the keeping of a promise. The act of resignation would thus mimic his presidency. While Lincoln would not complete his second term or oversee Reconstruction, thereby breaking a promise to the democracy that twice elected him, he would take meaningful rather than rhetorical responsibility for his constitutional depredations, thereby keeping a promise to that same democracy that twice elected him to safeguard its fundamental values. Resignation is not redemption, however, nor does it pretend to be a cure-all. It is a fundamentally ambiguous act, as Dumm indicates: "resignations are evidence of the fact that there are no clean slates in life. A resignation, which can itself be thought of as an attempt to clean the slate, is never complete and never painless—only more or less so."[82]

Lincoln's resignation, then, would acknowledge and call attention to the messy slate he leaves behind. In short, Reconstruction was a national not just a Southern problem. Democracy was in dire straits everywhere. Why should Lincoln not perform this task himself? As with the appointment of the classical dictator, Lincoln's commissarial term expired with the cessation of formal hostilities. Insofar as Lincoln effectively appointed himself, his voluntary resignation closes the dictatorial circle. The wrongs he committed cannot be undone. They are a permanent part of the American political landscape. Lincoln's sovereign decisionism aspired to restore the Union to the status quo ante bellum, but given the morally and politically dubious actions taken on behalf of this goal—actions that distended the practice of presidential power and reduced the status accorded American citizens—restoration could not be achieved. The Lincoln effects perdure. This is why resignation needed to be one of them. As Dumm notes, "resignation . . . is carried out with a sense that the resignation may memorialize the broken promise but that a broken promise always lasts longer than a promise kept."[83] Lincoln's resignation would have stunned the nation and stuck in its collective memory as much as his assassination reverberates to this day, as the joy of victory in a fratricidal war more destructive than anyone ever imagined it would (or could) be was tempered by the reckoning it signifies, including the unexpected loss of the incomparable figure that engineered the victory. The cost was so great that Lincoln had to answer for it through an act of democratic self-expiation, a sacrificial ending to the war that victors do not usually experience.

RED MENACE IN THE REAR

A year before Vallandigham's public campaign against Lincoln's prosecution of the war, the Sioux Indians in Minnesota posed another challenge to sovereignty's prerogatives. Lincoln feared a so-called fire in the rear, the possibility of an insurrection in the northern parts of the Union that might compromise the war effort. Lincoln, as we have seen, never treated opposition to the war as a properly political phenomenon. He translated dissent into military terms and, as a result, a question of national survival. Dissent became a potential threat to be anticipated and an existential danger to be contained, controlled, managed, preemptively punished, and, if possible, eliminated.

Given the tone and content of Lincoln's second annual message to Congress, he did not anticipate disruption coming from an altogether different source: "the Indian tribes upon our frontiers."[84] In this formulation, which follows Jefferson in the Declaration of Independence, Indians are figured as a potential menace to "our" borders: what should be open and available is wild and obstructed. The Indians are present, but what are they doing there? Lincoln's concern focuses initially on the Civil War and the relationship of Indian tribes to the Confederacy. Whether various tribes "remained loyal to the United States" or they allied themselves with the insurgents, they were placed in an impossible position between two warring factions of a nation divided against itself. Those who remained "loyal" were driven from their land by Southern forces. Those who "defected" would be subject to reprisals by Northern Unionists.

An altogether different situation, however, erupted in Minnesota. After decades of dispossession, displacement, swindling, and starvation at the hands of the expansionist white American settler regime, the Dakota Sioux finally commenced a revanchist war of necessity, a last resort to fend off destruction of their way of life and perhaps their extinction.[85]

When the Sioux decided to reverse American colonialism, which combined military aggression and administrative exploitation in order to reduce and then erase them, they took up arms and attacked American settlements, waging their version of total war against them. Lincoln described the Sioux as having "manifested a spirit of insubordination," a behavioral departure from the norm of servility imposed on them. Lincoln's assumption-cum-assertion of authority effectively folds Native peoples into America's sovereign purview.[86] Indian peoples do not constitute separate and distinct nations equal in status to the United States and thus independent of its authority. Rather, Lincoln's tone suggests that he considers "Indian tribes" to be subalterns who "have engaged in open hostilities" and can be treated and disposed of at will. They may be in the United States, but they are not of the United States. Lincoln reports that they attacked white settlements "in their vicinity"—a formulation incompatible with an understanding of those settlements as existing on property once belonging to them.

Lincoln professes surprise at the attacks and ignorance of their cause, revealing an unconscious racial privilege. Perhaps he thought the two races were at peace, but peace and the treaties securing them amounted to little more than an interregnum between wars. As David Nichols argues, "treaties were almost always negotiated as a means of removing Indians from lands that whites wished to occupy, usually following armed conflict."[87] Appalled by the "ferocity" of the attacks, which Lincoln defines as an Indian war, especially given the killing of innocent men, women, and children caught unawares, he takes it for granted that the white settlers had no chance to defend themselves. Surprise is a sign of white innocence. It's as if a conquering race can expect to be immune from retaliation and revenge for its own successful campaign of expropriation and displacement. There's no other way to account for the high number of white casualties. Lacking the element of surprise, Indians could not have terrorized white settlers and taken hundreds of lives. Regardless, the balance must be restored to the political universe and the gravity of the crime matched by a fitting punishment. Lincoln's cursory recitation of events includes one numerical figure: "It is estimated that not less than 800 persons were killed by the Indians." He also mentions that "a large amount of property was destroyed." These are precisely the kind of harms routinely suffered by Indian tribes at white American hands, but Lincoln does not cite Indian casualties—then or in the past.

The shocking death toll led to calls for the elimination of Native peoples from the state—in the name of security. Monies stipulated by treaty to be paid to the Sioux would be used instead to pay property damage claims resulting from the war to white settlers and to force the Sioux from the state. America's Indian policy displays a cruel logic: it fosters a condition of insecurity for nonwhite peoples and attempts to redress this condition only worsen the insecurity. When Lincoln writes, "The people of that State manifest much anxiety for the removal of the tribes beyond the limits of the State as a guaranty against future hostilities," there is no awareness that the anxiety is self-induced, the result of their own relentless expansion. What's more, the cleansing of Minnesota was well under way and achieving its deadly results. By May of 1863 all but a few hundred Sioux had been forced from the state. Only those who assisted the settlers, that is, only those who cooperated in their own people's destruction, were allowed to remain. Michael Rogin notes: "The vision of Indian violence threatening the selfhood of young America reversed the actual situation. The expanding nation reiterated the claim of self-defense as it obliterated one tribe after another."[88]

NATIVE DISPOSITIONS

Lincoln would soon decide the fate of over 300 Sioux who participated in the war, sending to the gallows 38 pronounced guilty of murder. While Lincoln spared 265, commuting the sentences of those who "only" killed soldiers on the battlefield, thereby preserving a self-serving combatant-noncombatant distinction, it could be argued that what galls Lincoln is that the Sioux conducted themselves as if they were a sovereign people. Speaking not of concrete individuals but a political abstraction, Lincoln writes: "The State of Minnesota has suffered great injury from this Indian war." Depopulation, destruction of property, anxiety: Indians do not get to make war, not on white settlements, not on whites.

Before any executions could take place, however, trials were conducted by a special military commission. Before these trials could be staged, Indians had to be captured by any means necessary (force, deceit, etc.). And to be treated in this capricious fashion, they had to be reduced to bare life: those who kill defenseless whites unexpectedly, indiscriminately, and with "extreme ferocity" are not to be afforded the dignity of soldiers. On the one hand, Lincoln cannot see Indians as a sovereign people capable of agency or an act of war. On the other hand, he assigns Indians moral responsibility for their violent acts.[89]

Lincoln reviewed each death sentence, an evaluation required by law. He commuted more than 260 verdicts—which might suggest the dispensation of measured and thoughtful justice, but given that 300 trials were conducted in two weeks, with many lasting no more than a few minutes, Lincoln's exercise of generosity takes on a different cast. Each verdict could, even should have been overturned. Indians were provided no legal counsel and the vast majority did not understand the proceedings against them (they were conducted in English, a foreign language). It is also noteworthy that Lincoln's decisions took place within a military rather than civilian judicial system, which was designed to produce guilty verdicts expeditiously. In addition, over 1,000 Indians who had nothing to do with the attacks were herded into a relocation camp that, given its exposure to Minnesota's winter conditions, was a de facto death camp. This camp, in turn, was mere prelude to relocation outside of Minnesota to a site where it was known life could not be meaningfully sustained. The new life arranged for Indians signaled the intent to eliminate them—through an internal exile more brutal than Vallandigham's.

The Indians whose sentences were commuted were not released. Initially, they were subjected to indefinite detention as the government decided—or didn't decide—their ultimate disposition. In short, the sovereignty complex Lincoln managed could treat Indians in whatever fashion it deemed appropriate. The conversion of death sentences did not reflect a commitment to a justice fitting to the situation, but was a matter of sovereign convenience. Lincoln's commitment to the Union—not just the Union as it then existed but the Union coming to be as the country pursued its relentless westward expansion—meant that Indian resistance to colonialism did not slow, let alone stop it. If anything, Native resistance fostered imperial acceleration. Sovereignty denied is sovereignty energized, ready to flex its muscles and expand.

American exceptionalism finds a uniquely troubling voice in Lincoln, for whom the Indians were to blame for their inferior way of life and miserable fate, the one resulting in the other: "Although we are now engaged in a great war between one another, we are not, as a race, so much disposed to fight and kill one another as our red brethren."[90] It's not just that Lincoln seems to have forgotten the violent revolutionary origins of the United States and its subsequent ambition to expand into new territories. It's that America's imperial wars against Indian and Mexican peoples do not count in Lincoln's sovereign death calculus. His conceptualization of America's sovereign privileges means that its wars against others do not register as actual violence. Hence the American way of life, expansionary and brutal, grants itself an indemnity that enables its claim of racial superiority.

THE WORD OF LINCOLN

While Lincoln reports the Sioux attacks against white settlements in his message to Congress, he does not mention the impending executions. What does this silence signify? Does Lincoln ignore or omit the mass killings because they do not merit mention? Are they just one last logistical detail of a war already concluded and won (with the gallows a natural extension of the battlefield)? Does Lincoln sidestep the issue because he plans to reduce the number of hangings, which he knows will provoke outrage from a state critical to the war and his reelection? Or does the linguistic erasure anticipate the physical erasure of the tribes? In that case, Lincoln's silence would be part of a nation-building project.[91]

America's perpetual refounding, as it moves west, cannot rest on its inaugural violence against the British. If there is any violence involved in American expansion, responsibility for it must fall elsewhere. According to Lincoln, tribes only "occupy" Indian country. And it's only Indian country insofar as they (currently, contingently) occupy it. They do not (seem to) own or possess land. This would be impossible given Lincoln's nationalist political vision: "That portion of the earth's surface which is owned and inhabited by the people of the United States is well adapted to be the home of one national family, and it is not well adapted for two or more. Its vast extent and its variety of climate and productions are of advantage in this age for one people, whatever they might have been in former ages."[92] Here Lincoln is referencing secessionists, but the vision applies more fittingly to Indian peoples. Lincoln might prefer to anchor his racially exclusive political vision in the distinctive workings of geography, but this derivation merely deflects responsibility for the political facts on the ground that the United States creates. The North American continent is no more "well adapted to be the home of one national family" than it is to be the home of two, three, or more national families. The language of adaptation conceals the violence and eradication needed to bring about a single national family.

Despite Lincoln's official silence, he need not have worried. His treatment of the Sioux lends itself to the emergence of an American exceptionalism that refuses to idealize the nation in terms that simply deny its problematic political-historical record. The United States remains the world's moral exemplar, but not because it is miraculously without stain, blemish, or flaw. Rather, American exceptionalism Lincoln-style affirms its complicated record and folds it into an articulation of America's virtuous character and identity. Thus Lincoln is revered not despite but because he simultaneously dispenses considered justice and cold violence. He can deploy the full panoply of the terrible powers at his disposal. He can also exercise restraint. It's all in the decision. In the aftermath of the Dakota War he orders the largest mass execution in American history; he also spares over 260 Indians.[93] Of course, Lincoln had no more reason to hang the 38 than he did to let the 265 live.[94] But sovereign considerations dictated that some had to hang and the choreography needed to be perfect. As Bethany Schneider argues, "The deaths had to happen simultaneously in order to emphasize that this was the execution of a race, not of individuals, not of Dakota, and not of men; in order, in other words, to pleasure an audience that wanted to witness genocide."[95] Lincoln's political intervention may have aspired to a measure of justice, but even with the lives spared the rope, it still constituted a grave injustice. As David Nichols argues, "Lincoln, despite the lack of clear evidence, had concluded that a blood sacrifice was imperative but not on the scale sought by Minnesotans."[96] A little death goes a long way.

NATIVE AMERICAN MONUMENTS

In the temple of his war memorial, Abraham Lincoln stares into the distance toward the Washington Monument and beyond it to the Capitol, perhaps contemplating, if not fully comprehending, the possibilities that the exercise of sovereign power during his wartime presidency has opened up for his new republic. As we have seen, however, Lincoln succeeded in ways that no one anticipated and that we would do well to disavow. Daniel Chester French's regal statue thus projects a certain blindness, but Lincoln is not well positioned to appreciate the destructive nature of his creation. The Lincoln Memorial is less a testament to a Great Emancipator than to a Mortal God credited with saving, consolidating, and aggrandizing the Union. It is thus an expression of the sovereign power Lincoln enacted (see figures 1.1 and 1.2). Pace Kirk Savage, this renders Lincoln not so much a tragic victim but more a pyrrhic victor—or maybe both.[97] If so, Lincoln embodies a terrible ambiguity that haunts American democracy, especially insofar as the United States unthinkingly reveres him because of it. He represents great achievement secured at profound cost, commitment to high ideals coupled with exceptionally dirty hands (see figures 1.3 and 1.4). This does not mean there are two Lincolns but one ambiguous Lincoln—like the country he delivers and razes. The Mall requires a Lincoln Memorial to match this legacy.

Within the system of American national monuments, Native Americans have not fared well.[98] On the Mall in Washington, D.C., the Washington Monument dominates the skyline: the obelisk that celebrates the founding of the nation also denies the violence deployed to bring it about.[99] The Lincoln Memorial, the spiritual core of the Mall, likewise disavows the violence done to Native Americans as the nation refounded itself through the Civil War. While the National Museum of the American Indian opened in 2004, and signifies an architectural development that can be considered a monumental effort at redress, Native Americans remain largely invisible at the Mall's symbolic patriotic core.

Figure 1.1. Henry Bacon's Lincoln Memorial temple of sovereign power (from the southeast).
Courtesy of Robert R. Gerlits.

Figure 1.2. Henry Bacon's Lincoln Memorial temple of sovereign power (from the northeast).
Courtesy of Robert R. Gerlits.

Figure 1.3. Daniel Chester French's statue of Lincoln; Lincoln as war president.
Courtesy of Robert R. Gerlits.

Figure 1.4. Daniel Chester French's statue of Lincoln; Lincoln's war fist.
Courtesy of Robert R. Gerlits.

Monuments to Native Americans at the nation's periphery, however, can help reverse this white-privileged state of affairs. In Montana, the Little Bighorn Battlefield National Monument received a significant makeover, including a name change, starting in the 1990s.[100] Following Custer's defeat by Native American tribes opposing colonial expansion in 1876, the U.S. Army was determined to sacralize the site, especially what came to be known as Last Stand Hill where Custer was killed. In 1881 the War Department placed there a 36,000-pound granite obelisk with the names of the dead inscribed on it. The obelisk, which replaced a provisional memorial hastily concocted in 1879, sits atop a mass cavalry grave. As with the Alamo, a site of utter defeat was transformed into a site of heroic pride and ultimate victory. This (wounded) pride meant no recognition would be afforded the triumphant enemy, unsurprising given the logic of conquest behind the military action that resulted in defeat (only temporarily, of course).

In 1991 Congress, as part of the legislation that changed the name of the battlefield, called for an Indian Memorial to be built to recognize and honor the Native peoples (Lakota, Cheyenne, and Arapaho) who fought to defend their homelands against incursion. It debuted in 2003 and insofar as it supplements the first monument to the Seventh Cavalry, it can be productively compared to the Vietnam Veterans Memorial complex in Washington, D.C., which consists of four (so far) distinct elements. Designed by John Collins and Alison Towers, the Native peoples memorial has come to be known as Peace through Unity. It consists of a circular earthen and stone berm and a thick black wire sculpture just outside it. From within the confines of the berm, through what's called the Weeping Wall or Spirit Gate, there is a view of the Seventh Cavalry's obelisk. Water constantly trickling into a pool from the Weeping Wall represents tears for those—both Indian and cavalry—who died that day. The Spirit Gate is an invitation to the dead soldiers to join the dead warriors in friendship. This gesture of reconciliation is accompanied by the sculpture, which depicts ghost warriors riding out from their encampment to defend their people and their way of life against aggressors. Friendship may entail forgiveness, but it does not require forgetting. It's as if the victory of June 25, 1876, is relived again and again. The sculpture is a salute to those warriors who defended their people. They are forever riding, in perpetual motion. It has a vibrancy and animation that the Army's memorial obelisk lacks. The sculpture also evokes violence and death more viscerally than does the obelisk. To reinforce this point, Indian grave markers made of red granite have been placed in the area to signify the fallen warriors. This augments the dozens of white headstones on the slope of Last Stand Hill denoting fallen cavalry.

The literal and figurative reddening of the Little Bighorn Battlefield National Monument brings us back to the Lincoln Memorial in Washington,

D.C., which suffers, as mentioned, from some of the same death-denying flaws as the Washington Monument. The Mall needs re-covering—in the countermonument tradition. To build a new memorial in opposition to the Lincoln seems architecturally unfeasible. The west end of the Mall is rather crowded. What kind of innovation might be possible with the Lincoln itself?

Here a distinction might be made between a permanent and an annual augmentation. Serendipitously the Lincoln Memorial consists of thirty-six fluted Doric columns and two additional columns fronting the entrance to the temple inside the memorial—for a total of thirty-eight. This is the number of Dakota akicitas (warriors) who were sacrificed by Lincoln for political-cum-military reasons for defending their homeland against colonization. Borrowing from monumental developments at Little Bighorn Battlefield, what if the Lincoln's thirty-eight memorial columns were dyed granite red, one column for each state-sanctioned killing of a Dakota akicita? This visual transmogrification would signal the cost that America's (re)founding exacted from another people not party to the Civil War but still subject to a different war of gradual extermination. The new lurid Lincoln might be visually shocking, but that is the point. The juxtaposition of colors would highlight the constructed character of the memorial and its ideological functions. The Lincoln's majesty might now call critical attention to itself, raising suspicions rather than simply generating awe. What is this memorial profession of grandiosity hiding? Lincoln's participation in violence against Native Americans was not incidental. To de-deify the enormous Greek-inspired temple and its sole denizen, the name of one akicita could be inscribed on each column. Since Lincoln selected each one specifically to die for the Union, Lincoln is indebted to them, as is the country. They were killed so the Union could live. Thus, they already enjoy a personal political relationship to Lincoln. He may have executed them, but they would now stand guard over and (re)frame his memory. To visit Lincoln in his temple, which forever reminds people that he saved the Union for us, one would have to pass by them. One could not think or feel about Lincoln without confronting the full panoply of his deeds, the deeds he took on our behalf.

To supplement the architectural face-lift, each December 26 (execution day) the water in the reflecting pool could also be reddened, not so much as a rebuke but as a reminder: the United States is a multinational democracy the founding and refounding achievements of which are fundamentally ambiguous, a characterization that does not necessarily discredit but can dignify them through deromanticization. The blood pool makes it difficult to indulge or countenance national fantasies of America's purity. It would also deform the Washington Monument, the Lincoln Memorial's predecessor in nation-building crime. As its reflection "rests" in Lincoln's pool, its image no longer whitewashed, it points an accusing finger at Lincoln, who advanced the racial cleansing project Washington "started." Each opportunistically fought a "secondary" war against Indians to maximize the fruits of victory in the "main" action.[101] December 26 would convert the reflecting pool into sacred ground, a veritable watery necropolis that reminds us for a day of what Nietzsche, forever changing the status accorded them, wrote about our greatest accomplishments: "How much blood and horror lies behind all 'good things'!"[102]

NOTES

1. See Herman Belz's fine review essay, "Lincoln and the Constitution: The Dictatorship Question Reconsidered," in Belz, *Abraham Lincoln, Constitutionalism, and Equal Rights in the Civil War Era* (New York: Fordham University Press, 1998).

2. See, for example, George Kateb, *Lincoln's Political Thought* (Cambridge, MA: Harvard University Press, 2015), 143, 145, 151.

3. *Lincoln on War*, edited and with an introduction by Harold Holzer (New York: Algonquin Books of Chapel Hill, 2011), 2. See also 12.

4. Abraham Lincoln, "Message to Congress in Special Session," in *Lincoln: Political Writings and Speeches*, ed. Terence Ball (Cambridge: Cambridge University Press, 2013), 130.

5. I am deeply indebted to Geoffrey R. Stone's fabulous *Perilous Times: Free Speech in Wartime: From the Sedition Act of 1798 to the War on Terrorism* (New York: Norton, 2004), 91–119.

6. Carl Schmitt, *Dictatorship*, tr. Michael Hoelzl (Cambridge: Polity Press), 2013, 1–2, 12–13, 118, 150. For an excellent discussion of Schmitt, see Andreas Kalyvas, *Democracy and the Politics of the Extraordinary: Max Weber, Carl Schmitt, and Hannah Arendt* (Cambridge: Cambridge University Press, 2008).

7. Lincoln resembled Schmitt's sovereign dictator when he issued the Emancipation Proclamation, which declared slaves in rebellious states "then, thenceforward, and forever free." The temporality of the proclamation would seem to exceed its legitimacy as a war measure.

8. Stone, *Perilous Times*, 92.

9. Christopher Kutz argues: "the *nation* is rendered insecure only when its identity and existence comes under siege. The Civil War posed a threat of literal dissolution of the state. . . . Thus, the assessment of Lincoln's unilateral suspension of habeas corpus comes far closer (if not passes) the bar of real constitutional necessity." If the South had won the war the United States would have split into separate nations, but the South had neither the intention nor the ability to conquer and hold the northern parts of the Union. Military defeat would have had no democratic ramifications for the reconstructed Union. Southern victory would in many respects have mimicked the status quo ante bellum. Either way, the existential threat to the nation was to one version of it only. Kutz, "Must a Democracy Be Ruthless? Torture, Necessity,

and Existential Politics," in Kutz, *On War and Democracy* (Princeton, NJ: Princeton University Press, 2016), 155.

10. Burnside sent over sixty men to break into Vallandigham's home and arrest him. See Rick Beard, "The Fire in the Rear," *The New York Times*, May 8, 2013, http://opinionator.blogs.nytimes.com/2013/05/08/the-fire-in-the-rear/. Other estimates put the number as high as 150. See Jennifer L. Weber, *Copperheads: The Rise and Fall of Lincoln's Opponents in the North* (Oxford: Oxford University Press, 2006), 95.

11. Stone, *Perilous Times*, 106.

12. Merrill D. Peterson actually finds Lincoln's resort to exile funny, though he also writes of a "class of war victims with reason to remember Lincoln as both unmerciful and unjust." Still, Peterson lacks political empathy for the "notorious" Vallandigham and "his ilk." See Peterson, *Lincoln in American Memory* (New York: Oxford University Press, 1994), 107–8. Jennifer Weber, likewise, finds Vallandigham's exile "amusing." Weber, *Copperheads*, 98.

13. Weber, *Copperheads*, 96.

14. David Bromwich, "Lincoln and Whitman," in *Moral Imagination: Essays* (Princeton, NJ: Princeton University Press, 2014), 108–13.

15. Thus Eric Foner's comment on Vallandigham that Lincoln did not "possess a modern sensitivity to the importance of civil liberties" misses the democratic political point. Foner, *The Fiery Trial: Abraham Lincoln and American Slavery* (New York: W. W. Norton, 2010), 264.

More than constitutional issues are involved here. For one thing, war decisions are judgment calls made by political actors based on imperfect knowledge and information. A democracy may need to revisit such decisions, even if they are initially believed to be sound. See Stone, *Perilous Times*, 105.

16. Giorgio Agamben, *Homo Sacer: Sovereign Power and Bare Life* (Stanford, CA: Stanford University Press, 1998), and *State of Exception* (Chicago: University of Chicago Press, 2005); Elisabeth R. Anker, *Orgies of Feeling: Melodrama and the Politics of Freedom* (Durham, NC: Duke University Press, 2014), 216–19.

17. Quoted in Weber, *Copperheads*, 98.

18. Jennifer Weber notes that the founders located suspension of the writ in Article I, but claims they "muddied the waters by using the passive voice." She fails to mention that Section 9 specifies eight limitations on congressional power, one before and six after addressing the writ. How muddied is that? Jennifer L. Weber, "Was Lincoln a Tyrant?" *The New York Times*, March 25, 2013, http://opinionator.blogs.nytimes.com/2013/03/25/was-lincoln-a-tyrant/.

19. Lincoln, "Proclamation Suspending the Writ of *Habeas Corpus*," in Ball, 153–54.

20. Ibid., 154.

21. Weber, "Was Lincoln a Tyrant?"

22. Louis Fisher separates Lincoln from later presidents like Truman and George W. Bush insofar as Lincoln "did not invoke exclusive or inherent authority," which he importantly distinguishes from implied powers. Fisher acknowledges that Lincoln "claimed the right in time of emergency to act in the absence of law and sometimes against it, for the public good." But he insists that for Lincoln these were temporary,

exceptional measures for which he would ask Congress for "the authority he needed" (if after the fact). Congress's ready and generous compliance with presidential diktat when it comes to the public safety does not seem to trouble Fisher. Nor does the conversion of temporary, exceptional measures into anticonstitutional norms that can be trotted out by future presidents whenever public safety calls for it or politics (read: dissent) seems a nuisance. Fisher, "Invoking Inherent Powers: A Primer," *Presidential Studies Quarterly* 37, no. 1, 2007, 2.

23. Weber, "Was Lincoln a Tyrant?"

24. Ibid.

25. Douglas L. Wilson points to, however reluctantly, the ambiguity of Lincoln's presidency: "But even among many of his supporters, the steady employment of presidential war powers from the first days of the war—especially the suspension of habeas corpus and the detention of civilians—raised the specter of dictatorship." Wilson, "Lincoln Answers His Critics," *The New York Times*, June 12, 2013, http://opinionator.blogs.nytimes.com/2013/06/12/lincoln-answers-his-critics/.

26. Lincoln, "Letter to Corning," in Ball, 179–80.

27. Louis Fisher, *Military Tribunals and Presidential Power: American Revolution to the War on Terrorism* (Lawrence: University of Kansas Press, 2005), 25.

28. Ibid.

29. Lincoln, "Letter to Corning," 179.

30. Fisher, *Military Tribunals and Presidential Power*, 26.

31. See Wilson, "Lincoln Answers His Critics," http://opinionator.blogs.nytimes.com/2013/06/12/lincoln-answers-his-critics/?_r=0.

32. Fisher, *Military Tribunals and Presidential Power*, 26–27.

33. Ibid., 28–29.

34. Ibid., 30.

35. Ibid.

36. Not surprisingly, Lincoln does not mention Jackson's lethal conduct in 1818 when more than temporary damage was done to the people subject to sovereign decisionism.

37. James McPherson refers, without justification, to Vallandigham's campaign from exile as "strange." He also writes that "Lincoln's shrewd move failed in one respect: while in exile, Vallandigham rode to the gubernatorial nomination on a wave of sympathy from Ohio Democrats." From a democratic point of view, this is no failure, and he might (also) have ridden to the nomination on a wave of principled indignation. McPherson, *Battle Cry of Freedom: The Civil War Era* (New York: Ballantine Books, 1988), 597.

38. Lincoln's assault on Vallandigham was part of a broader Republican counterattack against democratic politics. McPherson precedes his narration of Vallandigham with a brief account of developments in Illinois and Indiana. The lower house in each state issued resolutions calling for an immediate cease-fire and peace conference. They also began work to strip their respective governors (Republicans) of control of state troops. The Illinois governor dismissed the state legislature, a move a state judge rejected as an abuse of authority, while the Indiana governor convinced Republican legislators to stay at home, thereby making a quorum impossible and

effectively abolishing the legislature. He then raised his own money and ran the government single-handedly. McPherson offers a benign characterization of these at best extralegal moves: "Republicans everywhere endorsed the principle of Morton's [the Indiana governor] action: the Constitution must be stretched in order to save constitutional government from destruction by rebellion." Stretching indeed. See McPherson, 595–96.

39. David Herbert Donald, *Lincoln* (New York: Simon & Schuster, 1995), 419–21.

40. Donald, *Lincoln*, 441–44.

41. Lincoln, "Letter to Corning," in Ball, 175.

42. John Burt, *Lincoln's Tragic Pragmatism: Lincoln, Douglas, and Moral Conflict* (Cambridge, MA: Harvard University Press, 2013), 4.

43. Lincoln's ostensibly principled position is problematic from a tragic perspective. It's as if Lincoln is claiming he will pursue a good end only through good means. This runs counter to a Weberian sensibility that assumes that in politics one must get one's hands dirty—at some point. If Lincoln thought saving the Union required unconstitutional measures, why wouldn't he knowingly employ them? How is it that under the circumstances of war he could even think anything else was possible?

44. Lincoln, "Letter to Corning," 177.

45. Stone, *Perilous Times*, 115. *The New York Times* offered a version of Vallandigham's speech that essentially supported Burnside's rendition of events. Vallandigham wrote a definitive letter of rebuttal and the *Times* published it.

46. Lincoln, "Letter to Corning," 175.

47. Ibid., 177.

48. Lincoln, "Letter to Birchard," in Ball, 184.

49. Ibid., 183–84.

50. Stone, *Perilous Times*, 116, emphasis original.

51. Ibid., 116.

52. Ibid.

53. See Weber, "Was Lincoln a Tyrant?"

54. Lincoln, "Letter to Corning," in Ball, 76–177.

55. Lincoln, "Letter to Birchard," In Ball, 184–85.

56. Ibid., 184.

57. Lincoln, "Letter to Corning," in Ball, 176.

58. Belz insists that "measures that depart from existing constitutional rules in the face of necessity do not establish precedents for future departures, regrettable though they may be." What's more, though prior departures may be cited as justification for new departures, an "individual whose action is subsequently taken as a political model has no control over this process of historical appropriation and cannot reasonably be held responsible for measures predicated on his example." Belz's claim seems to ignore the manner in which presidential power derives from a combination of text and practice, which means precedents are always being set. Moreover, because an individual has no control over the historical appropriation process, it is incumbent upon him to proceed with caution—since he knows others will invariably model their behavior on his. There is no way to avoid at least some responsibility in this process.

Belz, 41–42. Kateb is unsparing of Lincoln on this question. Kateb, *Lincoln's Political Thought*, 152.

59. Benjamin Kleinerman, "Executive Power and Constitutional Necessity," in *The Writings of Abraham Lincoln*, edited and with an introduction by Steven B. Smith (New Haven, CT: Yale University Press, 2012), 462.

60. Ibid., 463.
61. Ibid., 464.
62. Ibid., 465–66.
63. Ibid., 465.
64. Ibid., 467–68.
65. Ibid., 472.
66. Ibid., 473.
67. Ibid., 462.
68. Ibid., 461.
69. Kateb, *Lincoln's Political Thought*, 144–47.
70. Ibid., 139.
71. Ibid., 151.
72. Ibid., 154.
73. Ibid., 160.
74. Ibid., 152.
75. Ibid., 151.
76. Ibid., 155.

77. James E. Underwood considers Lincoln a "Weberian" political figure negotiating wrenching normative conflicts, but his account suggests that Lincoln did not think he faced tragic choices between equally compelling alternatives. Rather, Lincoln avoided or eliminated potential tragic conflicts of values, as well as the need to employ dubious means to achieve good, by positing a distinct hierarchy between them or by invoking the transformative power of circumstance: "I felt that measures, otherwise unconstitutional, might become lawful, by becoming indispensable to the preservation of the constitution, through the preservation of the nation." Underwood, "Lincoln: A Weberian Politician Meets the Constitution," *Presidential Studies Quarterly* 34, no. 2, June 2004, 355, 359. The Lincoln quote is from "To Albert G. Hodges," in Ball, 204.

78. Kutz credits Lincoln for effectively returning to the scene of his crime, as it were, when he looked for post hoc ratification for his use of extrajudicial authority, but such approval in wartime is rarely difficult to secure, especially when others are made to pay the price of any loss of rights or life. Kutz, "Must a Democracy Be Ruthless?" 151.

79. Kateb, *Lincoln's Political Thought*, 152.

80. Thomas L. Dumm, *A Politics of the Ordinary* (New York: New York University Press, 1999), 58.

81. Ibid., 58.
82. Ibid., 64, 65.
83. Ibid., 59.

84. Abraham Lincoln, "Second Annual Message to Congress," http://www.presidency.ucsb.edu/ws/?pid=29503.

85. See Scott W. Berg, *38 Nooses: Lincoln, Little Crow, and the Beginning of the Frontier's End* (New York: Pantheon Books, 2012), and David A. Nichols, *Lincoln and the Indians: Civil War Policy and Politics* (St. Paul: Minnesota Historical Society Press, 2012). Prior to raising the Indian question in the second annual message, Lincoln discusses the prosperity of America's territories, some of which possess "immense mineral resources . . . to be developed as rapidly as possible," and looks forward to their incorporation into the federal union as states. Following two paragraphs on Indian troubles, he reports on the construction of the Pacific Railroad.

86. Lincoln, "Second Annual Message," http://www.presidency.ucsb.edu/ws/?pid=29503.

87. David Nichols, "Lincoln and the Indians," in Richard W. Etulain, ed., *Lincoln Looks West: From the Mississippi to the Pacific* (Carbondale and Edwardsville: Southern Illinois University Press, 2010), 217.

88. Michael Rogin, "Liberal Society and the Indian Question," *Politics & Society* 1, no. 3, June 1971, 285.

89. Rogin might unduly simplify matters when he writes, "Liberating Indians from their land, whites offered them paternal assistance. But the paternal relationship was insisted upon most persistently precisely at those moments when Indians by their behavior were denying its validity—expressing genuine independence, real power, or legitimate grievances." Lincoln did not imagine that he was putting children to death in Minnesota. Rogin, "Liberal Society and the Indian Question," 297–98.

90. Abraham Lincoln, *The Annotated Lincoln*, ed. Harold Holzer and Thomas A. Horrocks (Cambridge: Cambridge University Press, 2016), 487.

91. See Kennan Ferguson's superb "Silence: A Politics," *Contemporary Political Theory* 2, no. 1, March 2003. Compare Lincoln's silence with regard to the Indians on trial with the generosity expressed toward the South in his Second Inaugural. How did secessionists like Jefferson Davis and Robert E. Lee—whom Lincoln considered traitors and had infinitely more blood on their hands than Sioux leaders—escape the hangman's noose? One might invoke Lincoln's famous generosity in the Second Inaugural, but how was what we now call the ethnic cleansing of Indian tribes any less a national crime and responsibility than slavery? Instead Lincoln assumes the dispensation of "justice" to the Sioux as little more than the collateral damage of war.

92. Lincoln, "Second Annual Message," http://www.presidency.ucsb.edu/ws/?pid=29503.

93. See, for example, David Von Drehle, *Rise to Greatness: Abraham Lincoln and America's Most Perilous Year* (New York: Henry Holt, 2012).

94. http://www.winonadakotaunityalliance.org/education/1862-exhibit/. The 265 Indians Lincoln "spared" were sent to a concentration camp, an administration of justice that resulted in an additional—and predictable—88 death sentences. Blind to the cruelty he inflicted, Lincoln contributed to the conditions that would guarantee future outbreaks of Indian resistance to American colonialism.

95. Bethany Schneider, "Abraham Lincoln and the American Indians," in Shirley Samuels, ed., *The Cambridge Companion to Abraham Lincoln* (Cambridge: Cambridge University Press, 2012), 91–92.

96. Nichols, "Lincoln and the Indians," 217. Though the Sioux were formally defeated in the Dakota-U.S. War, Lincoln might have declared that their war was just, that American expansion had rendered resistance inevitable. We would have done likewise if placed in the same situation. Thus, unlike their Southern counterparts, the Sioux had every reason to go to war. They, too, had suffered as a result of the conflict, and he was therefore canceling the verdicts of a misbegotten military commission out of respect for an enemy brave enough to fight what it could only believe was a righteous war of survival it knew it could not win but had to wage nonetheless. This does not mean Lincoln would criticize, let alone oppose, American expansion. It does mean that he appreciates its horrific cost to others. And to acknowledge cost is to open the possibility for something more, later on.

97. Kirk Savage, *Monument Wars: Washington, D.C., The National Mall, and the Transformation of the Memorial Landscape* (Berkeley: University of California Press, 2009), 217–28.

98. See, for example, Rebecca Solnit, "The Struggle of Dawning Intelligence: On Monuments and Native Americans," *Harvard Design Magazine*, Fall 1999, 52–57.

99. See Steven Johnston, *The Truth about Patriotism* (Durham, NC: Duke University Press, 2007), 142–43.

100. The site used to be named for General George Armstrong Custer.

101. Fred Anderson and Andrew Cayton, *Dominion of War: Empire and Liberty in North America, 1500–2000* (New York: Viking), 2004.

102. Friedrich Nietzsche, *The Birth of Tragedy and the Genealogy of Morals* (New York: Anchor Books, 1956), 194.

Chapter Two

Democratic Ironies of Lincoln's Cinematic Exceptionalism

> Why, if the old Greeks had had this man, what trilogies of plays—what epics—would have been made out of him!
>
> —Walt Whitman, "Death of Abraham Lincoln"

In American cinema three noteworthy films memorialize Abraham Lincoln as an exceptional figure of American democracy and thereby problematize them both, however inadvertently: John Ford's *Young Mr. Lincoln* (1939), John Cromwell's *Abe Lincoln in Illinois* (1940), and Steven Spielberg's *Lincoln* (2012). Though separated by more than seven decades of social and political turmoil, profound technological developments, and distinct directorial styles, the films share a certain affinity insofar as they are steeped in ambiguity: while displaying the finest in American politics and promising even greater things to come as the country ostensibly struggles to make itself a more perfect union, they also expose its constitutive relationship to violence, self-destruction, and death.

The cinematic Lincoln invites, even demands reflection on the American polity—not only as it is idealized in narratives of heroic self-overcoming and self-realization in the pursuit of life, liberty, and happiness but also as it reveals the brutality that animates America's democratic institutions; the indispensability (and risk) of political participation by extraordinary individual citizens; the possibility of violent death that threatens those who challenge established power and prerogative; the internecine bent of civic contestation over basic democratic principles; and the temptation of state actors to ignore or violate constitutional norms in times of crisis—and then be celebrated for it. The assumption of these films is that democracy does not possess the resources it needs to sustain itself, especially in times of stress, and that it must turn to and rely on extra- or undemocratic forces and figures to perdure. In each of them, accordingly, Lincoln lives in ambiguity. He stands apart from and watches over democracy in order to save it from itself, from its excesses and insufficiencies, but in the process he necessarily contributes to and exacerbates them. He is loved on screen because he can (seem to) rescue democracy even while fatally injuring it. He is loved, that is, for doing in the name of democracy what no democracy should (have to) tolerate, let alone solicit and welcome.

In consequence, I read these Lincoln films as if they formed an ancient Greek trilogy. Why turn to the tragic poets? There are a number of structural similarities between the movies and plays. In Sophocles the mythical Oedipus leaves home and initiates a daring contest with Apollonian prophecy to prevent a criminal miscarriage of justice. He succeeds, but at an unbearable price. The cinematic Lincoln leaves home and commences an epic engagement with democratic politics to promote the realization of justice. He, too, succeeds, but at a terrible price. Just as Oedipus's odyssey discloses tragic aspects of the human condition, in which actions taken bring about results contrary to what was intended, Lincoln's exploits document tragic aspects of the democratic predicament, in which actions taken in good faith on behalf of democracy irreparably damage it. Just as Oedipus simultaneously enjoyed stunning success and startling failure in life and politics, Lincoln simultaneously engineered unrivaled goods and unprecedented evils in national public affairs. Just as Aeschylus's *Oresteian* trilogy exposes justice's deadly, precarious, ambiguous dimensions, the Lincolnian trilogy reveals democracy's violent, fragile, equivocal aspects. If Oedipus models the contingency of the human condition, Lincoln models the ambiguity of democracy, especially its underside.

The films' storylines do not form a linear narrative. Nor do they overlap much as they flirt with and move inexorably toward Lincoln's (un)timely death. Each film succeeds as a self-contained political drama revolving around Lincoln, but given democracy's turbulent nature each remains incomplete and points to a sequel, including the third and final installment, which leaves democracy triumphant but also traumatized thanks to that triumph. This indeterminacy reflects the fraught character of America's democratic experiment, as well as Lincoln's contributions to it, which unfolds on a brittle edge between good and evil, and can lead to either one—or both simultaneously.[1]

A tragic trilogy, of course, calls for a satyr play as a finale—to add a dose of levity to the proceedings so the audience doesn't perish from the weight of potentially crushing truths. Such a conclusion might seem a tall order when it comes to Lincoln, but Timur Bekmambetov's 2012 fantasy-action-comedy-horror film, *Abraham Lincoln: Vampire Hunter*, based on Seth Grahame-

Smith's novel of the same name, fills the role admirably. Contrary to the sober, pensive, and melancholy Lincoln who seems unbearably trapped by the forces of democracy in each of the first three films, Bekmambetov presents a hard-drinking, swashbuckling, joyful Lincoln who relishes his trade as a stone-cold killer in a righteous cause. This secret assassin of the already dead, whose trademark long black coat conceals his signature axe repurposed as a weapon of war, first works behind the scenes and then in the public arena to rid America of its own evil parasites and render it a less infested union. *Abraham Lincoln: Vampire Hunter* differs from the prior three films by virtue of the pornographic violence it depicts and the gruesome killing it affirms: its mayhem amounts to a bacchanalian orgy sanctioned by the contemporary political condition, ultimately making war and death a diverting spectator sport on the road to national redemption effectively indifferent to—or perhaps selectively unaware of—the price paid for it.[2] Isn't that the stuff of Lincoln's greatness?

LINCOLN'S HOMEGROWN FOREIGNNESS

Young Mr. Lincoln, *Abe Lincoln in Illinois*, and *Lincoln* have structurally similar openings. *Young Mr. Lincoln* begins in New Salem, Illinois, in an election year with John T. Stuart, a Whig politician running for reelection, making a speech denouncing the evils of the Jackson administration, which he promises to eradicate if returned to office. He quickly segues to his main, but also related, purpose: the introduction of Abraham Lincoln as a candidate for state legislature. Lincoln, played by Henry Fonda, is offscreen for the introduction.[3] The staging is deliberate, but not because the identity of the candidate is a mystery. The staging is designed to produce an effect—to give us an image to remember. The spatial suggestion seems to be that Lincoln is a foreigner, someone who hails from elsewhere, which, in turn, harbors the implication that he could also be a source of much-needed renewal, reinvention, or rescue, which only someone from the outside can offer.[4] Of course, this can render him a source of tumult and controversy as much as inspiration and salvation, for what he has to offer might well be unsettling, disruptive, or dangerous—in a word, foreign—and come replete with potentially tragic consequences, especially if the gift should become an imposition or demand.

As Lincoln ambles into view with a rather elongated, belabored gait, a physical peculiarity to match his existential standing, he offers himself to the assembled electorate for office. It seems, however, that his electoral success is of little or no concern to him. For one thing, running for office was not his idea. Friends asked him to do it. Either way, he states his political principles in a couple of short sentences, the remarks of an antipolitical politician. The people will have to decide for themselves whether they want to take advantage of whatever it is he has to offer them. Whether they will recognize the gift that lies before them is thus left an open question.[5]

The film audience, of course, assumes it knows Lincoln, but the sequence suggests otherwise. By having Fonda enter the frame from beyond its initial parameters, we are invited to reconsider our settled perspective and take a second look at what is supposedly familiar. Lincoln says he presumes he is known to everyone, but the directionality of his entrance subtly calls the presumption into question. He is not exactly one of us. Lincoln's first appearance thus indicates that we may be strangers to ourselves, living in close proximity but dangerously ignorant of and unlike one another, a set of circumstances ripe for political division and conflict and a portent of death in a riven world—which seems to be America's ontological condition.

From its opening credits *Abe Lincoln in Illinois* also announces Lincoln's foreignness. With a chorus singing "Old Abe Lincoln Came Out of the Wilderness," we are encouraged to believe that his origins are a source of mystery. The wilderness is an uncultivated, uncivilized, alien place located somewhere else—but with no precise location. As the film opens in Macon County, Illinois, we encounter an outsized Lincoln stretched across his living room floor in front of the fireplace reading poetry, more specifically Shakespeare, a decidedly foreign author this poor, backward Southern family. As far as his father is concerned, Lincoln's preoccupation with poetry is incomprehensible and, what's worse, unmanly. No son of his will write it, let alone build a life on it. Lincoln ignores his father's angry prejudices, and even his stepmother's encouragement seems to matter little to him. His alien identity is cast. Lincoln crowds and dominates the frame. It can barely contain him, as if he does not belong there. Lincoln is out of place in his own home with his own family. At the same time, the wider world entices his entry into it, where he is likely to be equally alien. Given an opportunity (any opportunity) he leaves home—for other things, for better and greater things. How far he goes in the world is more than a question of self-making, but whatever greater success awaits him apparently revolves around his peculiarity, his foreignness, which will govern the mark he makes on things. Nothing is likely to be the same afterward, for better or worse—or both.

Lincoln's opening sequence presents a ghastly image of the Civil War: a black Union regiment and white Southern rebels engage in vicious hand-to-hand combat in mud, water, and muck. This is America's race war, as Spielberg's signature Stars and Stripes flashing across the otherwise gray screen indicates, filled with the brutality and hatred one would expect in a war of mutual annihilation. This depiction of savagery sets the stage for Lincoln's emergence: a kind of godlike figure that, once again, seems to appear out of nowhere, he alone can put an end to the sufferings that flesh and blood humans locked in fratricidal political contest inflict on one another.

Spielberg's Lincoln also arrives offscreen, heard before he is seen. A black soldier, Private Harold Green, has been recounting his recent battlefield experience. After rebel forces murdered every black soldier they captured at the Battle of Poison Springs, black Union soldiers returned the barbarous favor at the Battle of Jenkins' Ferry. Finally Lincoln appears, but the camera is positioned behind him, at an angle. The camera's focus on Green ironically renders Lincoln the focal point of the shot. It's as if he is holding court and granting audiences. Again, though his voice can be heard, he is not seen speaking. The conversation between strangers is idle, stilted. He does not discuss the war, the politics of war, not even race war, with Green. A god does not discuss such matters with (mere) mortals, however well they serve him. Rather, Lincoln asks him his name and how long he's been a soldier. He does compliment the colored troops who fought at Jenkins' Ferry for their bravery, but it feels more like a statement of fact. Corporal Ira Clark, who accompanies Green, presses Lincoln on issues of inequality in the military, but the most Lincoln will do is acknowledge that he's aware of them. What else is there to do with one's lessers but make do with small talk? This awkwardness reflects and enhances Lincoln's authority. When we finally see him face on, he is seated on a makeshift throne made of wooden boxes. The pose he strikes mimics the position he enjoys at his memorial in Washington, D.C. Lincoln observes the action in front of him, troops massing and organizing to descend on Wilmington, North Carolina, for a crucial assault he has ordered in January of 1865. The mortal god on earth does not seek supplicants. Rather soldiers approach him, awed, which means they keep a respectful distance when he grants them an audience. He commands and they obey.

The introductions to these films intimate Lincoln's otherness, his foreignness—to his family, to his fellow citizens, to his soldiers, to his country—and thereby raise the question of American democracy's inherent foreignness to itself insofar as it is constituted by differences: of peoples, cultures, practices, dialects, ideas, norms, values, ways of life. The democratic condition is thus bound to entail strife, volatility, and conflict, which renders violence, tragedy, and death more or less inevitable under the right circumstances. Lincoln's involvement in politics, then, rooted in contested principles, policies, and positions, is destined to engender its own successes and failures. His initiatives will be both apposite and inapposite for the country—at the same time. No wonder that Lincoln appears to represent America at its best but also at its worst. On one hand, he stands for the rule of law, the power of political discourse, and the rejection, ultimately, of violence in public affairs. On the other hand, he signals that even fundamental law is a precarious achievement to be discarded at a moment's notice, that political discourse can be used on behalf of coercion as well as persuasion, and that violence enjoys everlasting appeal and legitimacy in politics. These films celebrate Lincoln as emblematic of American greatness, but Lincoln's conduct and the images of democracy in them dampen, even defeat the celebration.

DEMOCRACY AS MOB RULE: *YOUNG MR. LINCOLN*

John Ford's *Young Mr. Lincoln* is a conservative piece of filmmaking.[6] It opens with a rendition of "Battle Cry of Freedom" and concludes with "Battle Hymn of the Republic" and a close-up of the Lincoln Memorial in Washington, D.C. The framing provided by the opening and closing sequences suggests that the greatness of the canonized president can be discerned in his low-born beginnings and that these beginnings in turn led to the towering political figure, a second founding father, worthy of our worship. Lincoln was made—and made himself fit—for greatness, which would be prompted and then revealed by events. Still, as the editors of *Cahiers du Cinéma* argue, *Young Mr. Lincoln* suppresses Lincoln's political aspects, especially his engagement with slavery, in order to construct the mythical figure of Lincoln whose morality raises him above politics and serves as a source of unification.[7] Perhaps, but even if it does suppress politics along one register, the film also offers a troubling portrayal of the American polity: democracy as (little more than) mob rule. The image suggests not only that democracy discredits itself as a political form through its very exercise. It also suggests that democracy offers an antidemocratic remedy for its own ills by producing a figure of singular distinction who can substitute his superior judgment for the people's impassioned will, which, ultimately, the people seem all too ready to embrace, even at their own expense.[8]

The film's narrative drama revolves around a murder trial for a killing that took place during New Salem's annual Independence Day celebrations. The civic event designed to unite the community around founding accomplishments and patriotic sentiments turns into an occasion for the people to exercise their collective power. Two brothers, strangers in town, stand accused of slaying Scrub White, a no-account deputy sheriff looking for trouble. The arrest takes place almost immediately after White's death. From the crowd's reaction, people are in the mood for a helping of impromptu violence. Men are seen drinking to excess and talking themselves into an indignant rage. This, in turn, leads to a desire to take the law into their own hands, which they assume to be their right. Leaving the crime site, they rush to the jailhouse hell-bent on hanging the obviously guilty prisoners.

As this scene unfolds, Lincoln is no part of it. Rather, he is seen observing it on the outskirts of the crowd. We see Lincoln watching events transpire as if he were an outsider—in New Salem but not of it. It's not just that he has no taste for exacting an arbitrary, thoughtless public revenge. It's that Lincoln, by virtue of his distance, dress, and affect, does not belong in this human, all-too-human happening. This alienation enables Lincoln's view of democracy to form. He understands the crowd's bloody intent and follows the people into town. As they storm the jailhouse, endeavoring to smash through the front door, the sheriff has already made defensive preparations, having deployed the jailhouse door's considerable defenses to keep the people at bay. That the town has devised a jail where the most impressive fortifications are designed not to prevent prisoners from escaping but to keep aroused democratic citizens from breaking in to implement their own brand of frontier justice reveals the threat that the people themselves pose to the legal and political order. The film thus pairs a dangerous people with a fearful, weak, ineffective state.

Though repeatedly pounding a tree against the door, the enraged crowd cannot gain entrance to the jail. It's as if New Salem has learned from painful experience how to protect the accused from an angry, agitated mob to ensure they get their day in court. The civic architecture of New Salem reflects the dangers that the people themselves represent—not just to others but also to each other, thus to themselves. As the crowd rams the door with the tree pole, we can see the entire building rattle from inside. The people cannot be seen from this angle. Here democracy represents a kind of permanent, invisible threat, something you know is always already there whether you can see it or not. This suggests not only that democracy poses a great risk to itself. It also suggests that democracy lives perpetually on the edge of its own self-destruction. Given the proper context—some kind of crisis, emergency, or unexpected event—democracy's elaborate institutional arrangements, including its ability to defend and reproduce itself, can unravel at its own hands. Democracy is a veritable suicide always potentially in the making. No precautions can protect it with any degree of certainty or effectiveness.

As the people assail the jailhouse, it is obvious they will eventually succeed. The sheriff remains behind the barred door, but once it gives way there's no reason to believe he'll offer the crowd any formal resistance. He will not take life to protect life—not in these circumstances. If the people are determined to harm others, even if it also means harming themselves, he will not (be able to) stop it—certainly not by employing any means necessary. The rule of law does not run deep, it seems. No one from within the crowd raises a dissenting voice, including the very best, highly respected citizens who form part of it. It is one with itself. The people themselves do not possess the ability to pause, reflect, and rethink or reconsider what they are doing. They act—more or less unthinkingly. This scenario sets the stage for an inevitable rescue.

Lincoln fights his way through the mob. From a perspective immediately in front of the jailhouse looking out, we spot Lincoln irrupting into the frame. Similar to Liberty Valance's abrupt entrances in *The Man Who Shot Liberty Valance*, it gives Lincoln an air of menace.[9] Lincoln's facial expression and bodily energy convey angry resolve as he crashes through tightly packed bodies to get to the jailhouse door: democracy might need violence to combat violence. Discourse is not irrelevant, but it may be necessary to turn to violence and wield it effectively in order to get a hearing.[10] Democracy necessarily suffers in comparison to Lincoln, whose conduct points to the limitations of democracy and the need for an antidemocratic agent to oppose it—even one who also affirms democracy.[11]

The images of Lincoln in this scene between the crowd and the jailhouse reiterate his foreignness. Facing the assembled people, he is not (quite) one of them, even if they all know him by name. With his back to the jailhouse door rather than inside the jail itself, Lincoln is not of the state either. He invokes no authority, though he does exercise it. Citizenship is not only about rights and responsibilities but also about risks and dangers. If the people are convinced not only of their legitimate power but also of their righteousness, this combination of power and conviction makes for a potent and deadly entity that does not necessarily listen to reason, if it listens at all, especially when inspired or inflamed.

This can place citizens in an antagonistic relationship to each other, one that can turn deadly. Anyone who intervenes in such a civic dynamic takes a great chance. When Lincoln places himself in harm's way in an effort to prevent a (possible) miscarriage of justice, the outcome is radically unknown, contingent. Though a friend and neighbor, the people could easily kill him insofar as he's in their way. Fortune, it seems, governs the outcome. Lincoln uses a combination of macho bluster, folksy humor, civics lesson, public shame, and divine threat to (literally) silence the mob. Once muzzled, he dismisses them and sends them home. They need to know their place.

Lincoln becomes something of a local folk hero for his derring-do at the jailhouse, but American democracy can take little comfort in his heroics. Lincoln's exceptionalism presupposes not just American democracy's ordinariness but its inherent ugliness and dangerousness. Since Lincoln is unique, what happens when the democratic crowd swings into action elsewhere in his absence? No one will be there to challenge, let alone stop it. What's more, American democracy cannot take credit for Lincoln. He is not the result of a system that cultivates the citizens it needs to sustain itself. Rather, Lincoln effectively comes out of nowhere, even if he also comes from the American heartland. American democracy tends to produce citizens who adhere to the norm and follow the crowd. Lincoln's exceptionalism, then, raises the specter of dictatorship rather than establishing a new standard of civic engagement for citizens. How can they be entrusted with sovereign power given how they exercise it under routine conditions? *Young Mr. Lincoln* discloses that the people might take a potentially innocent life to satisfy their blood lust following a murder. What might they do when the country is at war, when their fellow citizens are being slaughtered by the tens or hundreds of thousands, and someone is accused of a political crime related to the war? What kind of extralegal force might be necessary to direct and discipline democracy then? What happens when a political actor emerges who feels an overwhelming commitment and sense of responsibility to do what he thinks best to preserve the political order he genuinely loves? Isn't this the kind of warning Lincoln issued in his speech to the Young Men's Lyceum of Springfield, Illinois, in 1838?[12]

For all of Lincoln's heroics, however, the two boys still face trial in a hostile environment, which means Lincoln may have done nothing more than delay the inevitable. He suffers from no illusions, of course, requesting of the mob he defuses that if an execution is going to take place, it could be done with a little "legal pomp and show." This is not the principled defense of law that one might hope for from a man like Lincoln. It could be taken to mean that the spontaneous execution does not do justice to the heinous nature of the crime it punishes. Something more extravagant, more spectacular is required for such an occasion.[13] Lincoln may be appealing to the lowest common denominator, which is suggested when he invokes their self-interest. Once a people get in the habit of taking the law into their own hands, it can be difficult to break. Hanging becomes a reflex easy to indulge and hard to resist. Such violence could turn on those who practice it now with a sense of impunity: hang someone today; get hanged tomorrow.

Lincoln may have "convinced" the people to retreat, but this does not mean the people are to be trusted. Democracy empowers the people, but it must also find ways to circumvent their exercise of power. It's tempting to conclude that the people must be made to do what they will not do themselves—for their own good. Lincoln was able to stop the mob without the use of violence—this time. The issue here is not just that violence might have to be used against the people in another setting that plays out differently. The issue is that the people regularly discredit themselves, which means others have to act on their behalf and despite their objections—because they do not know the right or best thing to do and there is no time to explain it to them or the explanation can come only after the fact. At the end of the jailhouse sequence, with the people properly shamed, Lincoln, as I mentioned, dismisses them—with a curt "good night." He remains in front of the jailhouse door. The image of Lincoln as civic sentinel says: leave the dispensation of justice to your betters.

Lincoln also comes to the rescue at trial and saves democracy once more from perpetrating a grave injustice. The mob that tried to storm the jailhouse has reconstituted itself in the jury and stands watch in the courtroom. The trial scenes are claustrophobic. Depending on the proceedings, the people could transmogrify themselves and intervene if they think justice is not being done. They are just feet away from Lincoln and the defendants. The bar that separates them could be breached in an instant. Significantly, it's not through legal skill that Lincoln prevails. Nor do the people play any role in it. If anything, the jury must be excluded, their unreliability already proven. Democracy's vaunted jury system is at best an irrelevance. Rather, Lincoln proves to be an astute detective (and a lucky one at that) who discovers the actual killer of Scrub White.[14] The people now set their sights on him.

After the surprise ending to the trial, Lincoln is about to leave the courthouse when one of his friends insists that he meet the adoring crowd waiting outside ready to celebrate him and his victory, which is their victory, too—but not because of the verdict itself. They have a leader. Lincoln hesitates but complies. The film concludes with a shot from just outside the courthouse door. We look inside and see Lincoln standing alone. This angle reverses the kind of shot for which Ford later became famous in *The Searchers* (and other films). In the latter, Ethan Edwards (John Wayne) makes possible a world from which he is excluded. The film closes with a shot from inside the home that Ethan has restored but that he cannot enter. He threatens the very place that cannot exist without him. The door closes and Edwards is left out in the cold. In *Young Mr. Lincoln*, on the other hand, we see Henry Fonda emerge alone from an interior world (the courthouse, the locus of justice) where "we the people" do not belong. The crowd that awaits him is heard but not seen. Lincoln is an exceptional figure. It is the people's place to recognize and appreciate him. Democracy needs him, but as a nondemocratic supplement. Democratic form triumphs over democratic substance. Lincoln does not seek or welcome the adulation bestowed on him, but he does not reject it either. Perhaps he fears the danger it poses. After all, the people represent an unstable force that can turn in an instant on those it favors. This scene, importantly, indicates that the legal arena cannot contain Lincoln. A wider public, political world and life await him.

As the film closes, Lincoln says goodbye to the people he saved. Rather than return to town, he tells a friend he'll walk on a bit, perhaps to the top of the hill on the horizon. The scene isolates Lincoln from society and suggests not just his uniqueness but also his queerness. Once he makes it to the top of the hill, what then? Ford seems to be suggesting that New Salem, Sangamon County, and the state of Illinois can no more contain Lincoln than the courthouse where he made the legal system work for two brothers and one family. Like Oedipus, Lincoln must leave home, haunted not by a prophecy of cosmic obscenities to come but by the reality of gross earthly crimes here and now. What, then, does the film's denouement mean for American democracy? The country is in need of justice as much as New Salem, but what must be done—and what price must be paid—to secure it, especially if the people themselves obstruct it? Lincoln, apparently, is setting himself on a collision course with American democracy, which offers no guarantees for grand political adventurism other than fraught possibilities. To engage this political monster at its worst involves risking life and limb—and not just your own. Thus a film that seems to offer an inspirational ending concludes on a somber note. Death stalks young Mr. Lincoln and thus American democracy. In later life, Lincoln will reverse the relationship and stalk them both.[15]

DEMOCRACY AS PRECARITY: *ABE LINCOLN IN ILLINOIS*

Abe Lincoln in Illinois doesn't gather narrative momentum until Lincoln arrives in New Salem. Like *Young Mr. Lincoln*, it exudes a generous myth-making sensibility on the subject of Lincoln's inauspicious beginnings. His political birth coincides with a crisis in New Salem, as one local democracy finds itself on the verge of extinction. When Lincoln first moves to New Salem to make it his home, the town is holding an election, as in *Young Mr. Lincoln*. Here, though, Lincoln is not running for office. Here Ben Mattling, an old-timer from the Revolutionary era, is giving his annual election-day speech bemoaning the decline and fall of founding ideals. The current generation consists of nothing but milksops, which is one reason the country has "gone to the dogs." As if to prove Mattling's point, Jack Armstrong, a good-for-nothing bully, has decided to subordinate the town to his drunken will. He runs roughshod over the tavern, helping himself to drink because he has no money to pay for it. In the center of New Salem he dares anyone to stop him. Town officials are too timid to resist. No citizen challenges him. Lincoln, who has just arrived, also looks the other way, refusing a taunt from Armstrong (who addresses him as stranger) to fight him for effective control of the town. It is only when Armstrong accosts Ann Rutledge, whom Lincoln had met earlier in the film when he passed through New Salem on a boat bound for New Orleans, that Lincoln is moved to action.[16] Rather than rally the citizens, who greatly outnumber Armstrong, with words, Lincoln turns to violence. After he defeats Armstrong and saves the town, Ann Rutledge speaks for everyone when she says, "Mr. Lincoln, you're the man we've been waiting for."[17]

Rutledge's (misplaced) compliment and Lincoln's (eventual) courage notwithstanding, the picture of democracy disconcerts. While the people in *Young Mr. Lincoln* are portrayed as a mob, in *Abe Lincoln in Illinois* they are portrayed as passive, fearful, and weak. Despite Rutledge's praise of Lincoln, there is no real "we" in New Salem. Participation, however, is critical to democratic institutions. Citizens have to be willing (and able) to do more than attend meetings, discuss issues, and cast votes to make them work. They also have to defend democratic institutions when necessary—not so much against external enemies but against fellow citizens. Not everyone in a democracy believes in it. Some may become frustrated by and impatient with its practices and procedures and usurp both, often cloaking their actions in a rhetoric of the common good, but sometimes in a simple power play designed to serve their naked self-interest. The domestic threat to democracy is the most difficult to counter because people mistakenly believe that rights and liberties are to be enjoyed rather taken and retaken, or that someone else will protect and preserve their rights and liberties for them. These assumptions are long-standing threats to freedom and democracy. In *Abe Lincoln in Illinois*, not even Lincoln seems ready to do civic battle at first, as if he can live the life he chooses regardless of New Salem's political condition. The film states repeatedly that his greatest desire in life is to be left alone. Ironically, the personal makes him move toward the political.[18] The political, in turn, is the domain where an exceptional figure can distinguish himself, even and perhaps especially at democracy's expense.

Lincoln's implication in politics is long and slow. He never aspired to become a politician and even considered it disreputable, unlike those who treat politics as a means for personal enrichment or party aggrandizement. Ironically, Lincoln thinks of politics, at least in theory, in grander—and thus more ominous—terms. Early in the film, as his efforts to succeed in business fail, he rejects the idea of politics as a vocation since it would involve life in a city. By way of explanation, he recounts his trip to New Orleans, a notorious center of slavery, where he developed a fear that people wanted to kill him. While this story might seem like a heavy-handed foreshadowing of his assassination, it can also be read as a condemnation of American democracy. Insofar as New Orleans represents the embodiment of gross injustice, what would it mean for an ambitious man such as Lincoln, with a keen sense of right and wrong, to enter public life? Like Socrates argued, those who pursue justice in an unjust order are likely to be killed by it. Entrenched interests do not appreciate challenges. He remained silent about the evils of slavery during his trip, but what would have happened if he had spoken against it? For Lincoln, to think about politics as a vocation is a life-and-death matter.

Not surprisingly, then, the more involved Lincoln becomes in politics, the more his demeanor darkens. He serves briefly in the state legislature and scorns the very idea of reelection.[19] Lincoln resists a political career in part because he finds the ambitions others possess on his behalf—and try to force on him—offensive. Yet this only strengthens one of the larger impressions the film leaves, namely, democracy needs most those most reluctant to serve it. It is people such as Stephen Douglas who fervently seek public office that democracy should fear. The citizen to trust is the one who eschews the pursuit of power, including when he actually holds office and expands the powers entrusted to him in the name of the greater good. Since self-interest and aggrandizement are not involved, the people can allow, even affirm it. It must be necessary.

Abe Lincoln in Illinois is not just playing on the audience's knowledge of Lincoln's ultimate demise. The point is a broader existential one. Politics in the antebellum American democracy was a deadly contest, denial of which the Kansas-Nebraska Act, the Dred Scott decision, and John Brown's raid on Harpers Ferry made impossible. Nothing less than the Union was at stake with Southern factions determined to preserve their wicked way of life regardless of the cost inflicted, including the Union itself. Lincoln, then, ultimately pursues the highest national office in a context where the fate of millions of enslaved people—and the peace of millions more—hangs on the outcome. The specter of mass internecine warfare haunts Lincoln's trajectory in public life. While that life cannot be reduced to nothing but violence, violence haunts its every move.

The film peaks with the final Lincoln-Douglas debate, severing it from a losing Senate campaign and tethering it to his victorious presidential campaign, thereby signaling the inevitability of a mortal conflict over slavery.[20] The depiction of the debate disconcerts. While it takes place in the public square, it consists of alternating monologues. The public is present but does not participate. It is mere spectator. The Illinois state legislature will decide the Senate election. American democracy affirms an arrangement that excludes the people in favor of their alleged betters. They speak and the people, or at least white people, are allowed to listen. None of them, apparently, has an independent view on slavery—or any other issue. Their job is to identify with and support a candidate that others will select (to act) on their behalf.

Stephen Douglas, deeply concerned that Lincoln has finally decided "to come out and fight," associates Lincoln with abolitionism—thus revolution and lawlessness. He insists that the current racial order can endure in perpetuity—as long as Supreme Court decisions (Dred Scott) remain the law of the land and neighbors mind their own business regarding slavery. Lincoln, on the other hand, embraces the ideal of equality articulated in the Declaration of Independence, which "admits of no exceptions." He refuses to be indifferent to the "monstrous injustice" of slavery and combines two beliefs—that the Union must not be dissolved and that it cannot live half free, half slave but must become all one or the other—that secessionists cannot mistake for anything other than a promise of war. Indeed Lincoln values America as an "encouragement" rather than a "terror" to the world, America as a model of republican freedom that its enemies cannot dismiss because of its hypocrisies, and though he doesn't say so explicitly, the South is one such enemy of freedom: it has placed itself on the wrong side of justice, morality, and history in an eternal power struggle in which some claim the right to rule others as their property.

By the time Lincoln is elected president (at the end of the film), victory constitutes a dreaded outcome more than a desired result. He seems resigned, if not quite depressed.[21] This reaction, which means that Lincoln will have to leave home again in search of a bigger stage for his epic encounter with American democracy, mystifies his campaign managers, who apparently do not understand that Lincoln's victory means war, a war over which he must preside. There will be blood and it will be, in part, on his hands. Yet the prospect of a wartime presidency alone does not quite account for Lincoln's mood. Other presidents have been wartime presidents. Is there something different about this war? Given its civil and thus divisive nature, Lincoln will inevitably face resistance from the North and likely turn to problematic measures to achieve Union war aims, thereby magnifying the damage inflicted on the country. These decisions will be his responsibility, too. He takes neither pride nor pleasure in winning the White House. It's as if he knows that to do what (he believes) is right regarding the Union and slavery will put him in the position of having to commit great wrongs, making him the agent of destruction of what he loves most. This is what civil war does.

Thus, rather than greet and address a boisterous crowd gathered outside his campaign headquarters, Lincoln decides to exit through the back door and go home to tell his wife the news, as if he were a condemned man who had just received his sentence. Before he can leave the building, a military escort arrives to accompany him. This is not a ceremonial guard accorded the new president-to-be, the highest elected official in the country. This is a bodyguard tasked to protect his life from the threats that shadow his impending assumption of the presidency. He is a walking target in an undeclared war, one for which the South has been preparing for years. To serve American democracy, as Henry Fonda learned in *Young Mr. Lincoln*, is to risk everything. Democracy routinely feeds on its own. If a murder case can bring democracy to the brink, as it did in *Young Mr. Lincoln*, what about a civil war featuring contending forms of life?

Lincoln departs for Washington by train at film's end, at night, and disappears into the darkness, a beacon of light eventually swallowed whole by it. Before leaving he addresses his fellow citizens seeing him off: "We have gained democracy, and there is now doubt whether it is fit to survive." This is not just a comment on democracy's moral incompatibility with slavery. It also points to one of the principal challenges facing democracy, namely, whether it possesses the wherewithal to deal with not just difficulties and dilemmas but threats and perils endemic to it—in this case dissolution and civil war by Southern secessionists. Democracy's mettle, then, is uniquely tested by existential challenges to its basic tenets, especially its ability to defend itself without also destroying itself in the process. Lincoln's terrible somberness as he leaves can be attributed to a presumption that the tasks facing him must exact a terrible toll. The images surrounding the departure scene mark Lincoln's revered—because martyred—status to come, but democracy is characterized by reversals of fortune that complicate the construction of heroic political narratives. What might happen when an exceptional politician arrogates extraordinary power to himself to deal with an unprecedented crisis rather than trust democratic norms, institutions, and practices? Democracy, it seems, fosters dubious solutions to solve its problems. Not even Spielberg's *Lincoln*, to which I now turn, can fully obscure this dynamic—despite, even because of, its hagiographic efforts.

DEMOCRACY AS CIVIL WAR

Steven Spielberg's *Lincoln* completes the trilogy. It covers the president's last months in office, culminating with his assassination by a disaffected fellow citizen bent on vengeance for social and political betrayal. Like ancient Greek audiences familiar with their founding myths, everyone knows Lincoln must be killed. Death here is complicated, however, insofar as there is no shortage of crimes with which to charge this president—from his many constitutional transgressions to his responsibility for the destruction of another way of life. They form part of the political backdrop animating the film's visceral registers: a country about to conclude a four-year civil war is not about to enjoy the peace it anticipates. Thus the film offers another troubling portrait of the American polity: democracy as a state of civil war, declared or not, sometimes cold, sometimes hot. Reversing von Clausewitz's famous dictum, this image of democracy means that politics is the continuation of war by other means, reflecting deep-seated conflicts between Americans that basic institutions address but cannot resolve. The American civil religion proclaims that anyone is welcome to join the republic, regardless of their place of origin or metaphysical commitments, as long as they profess allegiance to the constitutional regime.[22] Yet the official ideology faces intractable impediments. Differences of race, region, religion, culture, class, ethnicity, party, political prejudice all contribute to mutual suspicion, distrust, resentment, hatred, and disgust. Deep divisions lie just below the surface of public life poised to erupt with sufficient provocation. Democracy is combustible, leading to citizen squaring off against citizen, neighbor against neighbor, family against family, section against section, state against state.

Lincoln's challenge is to present the president's death in distinctive fashion. The Civil War is grinding to a conclusion. Rebel defeat following Sherman's devastating victories in the South is inevitable. The timing and terms of defeat, however, remain uncertain, and it is in this context that the film's events unfold. Lincoln focuses his administration's energies on passing a Thirteenth Amendment to the Constitution, which would put a formal end to slavery. In addition to a resolute military figure waging total war, then, Spielberg's Lincoln is also the consummate party politician with a shaky relationship to the rule of law, a twist on the undemocratic identity on display in *Young Mr. Lincoln*. This authoritarian characterization departs from his august one-dimensional reputation and informs the determination of Southern conspirators, unseen in the film, aspiring to kill Lincoln for what they take to be a betrayal of the country's racial heritage as well as its constitutional traditions. In this assessment they cannot be said simply to be wrong. The United States founded a republic whose crowning achievements of independence and liberty were grounded in chattel slavery. Blindness and arrogance led (some of) its founders to believe that they could combine incombinables. Their political, social, and economic project was bound to produce tensions that would one day erupt and turn back on themselves, leaving untold destruction in their wake. The civil war of 1861 originated in the Philadelphia peace accord of 1787.

Lincoln combines elements of the first two films. Like *Young Mr. Lincoln*, Spielberg's homage finds Lincoln in confrontation with the people, here represented by Democratic House members, an angry, determined mob bent on opposing the racial justice of the Thirteenth Amendment. There is no reasoning with it. As in *Abe Lincoln in Illinois*, Lincoln must manipulate an unduly timid, weak-willed people, represented by conservative House Republicans grown weary by years of war and eager to see it come to an end as quickly as possible regardless of slavery's fate. Lincoln believes the interregnum between Congresses offers an opportunity to reintroduce the amendment. The Democrats ousted in the 1864 election that were instrumental in defeating the amendment months earlier will be looking for work, and Lincoln plans to put the party patronage system to good use, enticing them to switch their votes in sufficient numbers to win passage. This amounts to thinly veiled bribery and Lincoln, via Secretary of State Seward, dispatches Republican operatives to "persuade" the soon-to-be ex-legislators. When the pace of persuasion slows to a crawl, thus endangering passage, Lincoln becomes directly involved. The film shows America a president who does not hesitate to maneuver, manipulate, and dissemble to achieve a political objective. This is American retail politics at its ingeniously corrupt best and Lincoln is a master of subterfuge, possessing invaluable local knowledge that his lieutenants do not enjoy. Rather than continue to orchestrate from a covert distance and leave the details to others, he takes the reins of this stealth campaign himself. His reputation can withstand a little taint in behalf of a greater good, especially when many of his fellow citizens are indifferent or blind to the wrong they would perpetuate and cannot be persuaded to do what is morally and politically right. There are circumstances in which waiting for people to see what is right cannot be tolerated. One way or another right must be secured, even imposed on those not (quite) ready for or opposed to it.

The film reveals, as did *Young Mr. Lincoln*, the dangers attending this tack. Fernando Wood, Democrat from New York and a menacingly gifted orator, takes to the House floor when debate over the Thirteenth Amendment begins and denounces "His Highness, King Abraham Africanus the First—our Great Usurping Caesar." Wood catalogs Lincoln's constitutional offenses and military ineffectiveness, portraying him as a "tyrant" who claimed "the war's emergencies permitted him to turn our Army into the unwilling instrument of his monarchical ambitions."[23] Wood is one sentence short of soliciting a contract on Lincoln's life.[24] Upon hearing the heinous charges cited, would it not be the freedom-loving citizen's duty to save the republic from the grip of this horrid dictator? Lest this bloody possibility seem like an exaggeration, one indignant House Democrat tries to murder the Lincoln agent who approaches him to change his vote on the Thirteenth Amendment—not so much, presumably, because he is insulted by the pecuniary offer but because of the racial cause behind it. After all, no one takes such violent offense at a financial inducement unless it acts as a trigger for a larger grievance. The civil war raging between the Union and Southern rebels over slavery is also raging between Northern factions. If Lincoln's lieutenants are at risk as they practice the art of politics, then what of Lincoln himself, their boss, who officially bears responsibility for slavery's demise? Here it is worth noting that Spielberg shoots the would-be murder scene just mentioned for laughs, as if to suggest that lethal violence is a routine part of American democracy. Regardless, the validity of Wood's political accusation gets lost in the melodrama on the House floor.

That he is a Democrat opposed to the war and the Thirteenth Amendment does not mean, as Spielberg would have us believe, that his charges are baseless. Images of Wood suggest that he might even kill Lincoln himself.

Lincoln's constitutional scheming also generates opposition at home. Following her husband's reelection, Mary Lincoln objects to spending precious political capital to pass an amendment doomed to failure. Secretary of State Seward agrees. Given the godlike status Lincoln has achieved with the American people through his conduct of the war and decisive electoral triumph, there must be grander projects to pursue. Lincoln, however, is resolute—if his dreams are any indication, that is. He sees himself on the bow of a ship hurtling into unknown waters. Lincoln may well be a visionary, able to chart a course previously unimagined, but the dream also suggests that Lincoln has undertaken a solo suicide mission. The ship on which he travels is empty but self-powered. Mary reminds him of a recent assassination attempt (which Lincoln ignores), fearing further murderous attempts on her husband's life. Though Lincoln lives in the nation's capital under armed escort, he is anything but secure. In a democracy at war with itself, there are no safe havens.[25]

Lincoln's own cabinet is ambivalent about pursuing the Thirteenth Amendment, adding to the tension over its fate. Interior Secretary John Usher thinks it's an "unwarranted intrusion by the Executive into Legislative prerogatives," part of what Usher deems a disturbing pattern of executive conduct by Lincoln, thus echoing Fernando Wood's excoriation.[26] Lincoln, on the other hand, wants to win passage of the amendment because the Emancipation Proclamation might be revoked in the postwar world. The idea of free men ordered to return to slavery, especially after taking up arms to fight for their freedom, is unthinkable to Lincoln, and he would no longer be in position to ignore a court order since his war powers, even assuming their legitimacy, would no longer be relevant.

In the course of this cabinet conversation, Lincoln effectively admits he has been acting much like the dictator the Democrats denounce. He *acts* with the confidence of the all-knowing Oedipus, asserting, "*I decided* that the Constitution gives me war powers, but no one knows just exactly what those powers are. Some say they don't exist. I don't know. *I decided* I needed them to exist."[27] The profession of agnosticism is a cover for a dangerous resort to decisionism. This, in turn, means that Lincoln's justification for war powers amounts to little more than rationalization. The decision comes first, justification follows. *Lincoln* has no interest in constitutional argument, however. The film takes it for granted that Lincoln's exercise of extraconstitutional war powers, rooted in claims of military necessity, have been critical in deciding the war's outcome. This supposedly excuses him. Remarkably, Spielberg's film does not distinguish between Lincoln's self-assumed war powers aimed at Southern insurgents and those same powers directed at loyal Northern states and citizens, as if the targets of his actions were all of a piece. What's more, Spielberg's often comedic depiction of Lincoln's seedy Thirteenth Amendment campaign implicitly works to render his unseen constitutional offenses harmless or irrelevant.

In Spielberg's benign telling, a vote on the Thirteenth Amendment enjoys new life in the aftermath of Lincoln's reelection, which had been in grave doubt one year earlier. Lincoln's electoral success, however, flowed from stunning battlefield victories, which were anything but ordinary. Sherman's total war on Southern infrastructure left the South unable to fight, perhaps even survive. The war to save the Union was destroying much of it, both land and lives. Lincoln feels compelled to travel to Petersburg near the close of the war (and film) to meet with Grant to survey the destruction the two of them have unleashed on the rebels. They are partners in crime, the crime of war, and this is perhaps (some of) what Raymond Massey foresaw in *Abe Lincoln in Illinois* when he could take no joy in winning the presidency. In Spielberg's *Lincoln* Grant comments on how much Lincoln has apparently aged (ten years) since their last meeting (twelve months prior). Lincoln's suffering not only becomes the affective center of the film. It proves that he understood the consequences of his decisions throughout the war and that no one would do this to himself if not absolutely necessary. Lincoln's suffering is the guarantee that he did only what he had to do and that it was right. Patriots knowingly suffer for their country.

Lincoln, it turns out, is also prepared to have America suffer any price for victory. He informed Confederate Vice President Alexander Stephens that if the war proved nothing more than democracy wasn't tantamount to chaos, it would be justified. Why? Because democracy would remain in position to aspire to and become worthy of its ideals. Thus, in Lincoln's last scene, he discusses the volatile issue of "Negro voting." It looks as if the project to realize American ideals and honor Northern dead—as promised at Gettysburg—is alive and well. He will not live to see the day, of course, and his last words in the film reflect this painful truth: "I suppose it's time to go—though I would rather stay."[28] Referring to his date at Ford's Theatre and thus his execution, the audience would rather he'd stayed home that night, too.

While it's tempting, because comforting, to believe that if Lincoln had lived postwar American democracy would have more closely approximated its ideals with Lincoln at the helm, this is the kind of speculation that works to conceal his problematic record. Lincoln compromised his own Gettysburg aspirations. He may have promised a new birth of freedom, but the one thing he delivered was the most empowered national state in American history. What's more, he failed to fully understand the Southern enemy just defeated. As the war came to an end Lincoln appeared ready to compromise Gettysburg's racial promise, a prospect revealed after he took the oath of office for a second time. How is the Second Inaugural handled in the film? As George Kateb observes, the Second Inaugural, "in an inspired displacement," is heard after Lincoln's shooting has been announced and death witnessed. Kateb writes: "One thing that Lincoln did not do in the Second Inaugural Address was to give way to unqualified anger toward the South, an anger that he would have been entitled to feel on behalf of the North, and that many people of the North did feel, and not only Union soldiers, not to mention slaves."[29] Lincoln makes the magnanimity ("with malice toward none, with charity for all") he recommends possible, as Kateb notes, by holding God ultimately responsible for slavery and the war.[30] Nevertheless, the assignation indicates that Lincoln did not appreciate that extending generosity to an angry, defeated, and hateful enemy requires reciprocity to work. Otherwise it is likely to be interpreted as weakness and suggest that there is an opportunity to reverse intolerable losses. While the South also welcomed the formal end of war, for them it meant only the end of actual fighting. The Second Inaugural's rejection of malice and embrace of charity inadvertently signaled, in advance, the ultimate defeat of any meaningful version of Reconstruction, the defeat of which would return African Americans to a condition much like the slavery that was formally abolished. The South may have been beaten on the battlefield, but it harbored dreams of restoration and revenge that would not rest until satisfied. As Lincoln stalls for time to win passage of the Thirteenth Amendment, Alexander Stephens declares that he would agree to immediate surrender if it meant rebel states could reenter the Union in time to defeat it. Stephens even mocks Lincoln for being unable to save the Union through democratic means after Lincoln upbraids him for losing faith in the democratic process. Stephens and his fellow peace commissioners remain unrepentant, true believers in racial hierarchy, domination, and exploitation. Defeat in war and pending ratification of the Thirteenth Amendment constitute setbacks, but they are prepared to take the long view in this struggle even if they do not quite openly admit it in the film. The Second Inaugural's ethos of reconciliation contravenes the promise made to the honored dead at Gettysburg. They will die in vain.

 Lincoln, then, remained tragically blind to the intransigent, unrepentant nature of the South—as if the Thirteenth Amendment could resolve America's race problem. His reliance on constitutional politics encourages the resumption by other means of the race war glimpsed in the film's opening. Here it is worth recalling that *Lincoln* begins with black soldiers fighting and thus freeing themselves, followed by a scene in which two awestruck white soldiers try to recite the Gettysburg Address for Lincoln. They fail, and it takes a black soldier to complete it—because whites can't follow through. The new birth of freedom heralds a biracial condition. The Confederacy, of course, understood the significance of blacks fighting (and fighting effectively) in uniform, which is why it tried to annihilate every last one of them it could in the war. That failed, but a Southern agent enjoyed unforgettable symbolic success when he murdered Lincoln, their commander-in-chief, instead.

John Wilkes Booth, however, is denied a scene in the film and silenced, which means it mimics Lincoln's presidency when it comes to critics. Booth disconcerts. The political claim, sic semper tyrannis, he makes after shooting Lincoln is erased, though it has a long history as an epithet hurled at those who abuse power dating back to Rome and the killing of its dictator, Julius Caesar, a renowned soldier who also betrayed the republic. Giving Booth voice would have linked his charge to Congressman Wood's speech on the House floor denouncing Lincoln for his Caesarism and converted the assassination into a national as well as a Southern killing. To take Booth's claim seriously would call attention to Lincoln's long list of high crimes and misdemeanors, from closing newspapers and suppressing speech, from forming military kangaroo courts to locking up tens of thousands of political prisoners, from suspending habeas corpus to ignoring lawful court orders. With the film located almost entirely in Washington, D.C., in early 1865, it's possible for Spielberg to ignore Lincoln's systematic decimation of American democracy, which is happening elsewhere. In fact, Spielberg must erase that history in order to sanctify Lincoln. He is thus killed offscreen.

As for Lincoln's new birth of freedom, one reason American democracy never quite realizes its ideals, that it always seems long on aspiration and short on realization, is that it routinely fails to confront an uncomfortable truth at its core, namely, that its commitment to democracy is always already partial. It contains and engenders constituencies and forces antithetical to it, including ostensible friends. This means that those who would make America a more perfect union may be unlikely to live to see it—in part because of their efforts (for good and ill) and the backlash they generate. Lincoln, then, can be considered one of the last casualties of a political war, killed by one of American democracy's mortal enemies for simultaneously subverting and reinventing it (Spielberg's film minimizes his role in the first and exaggerates the second). Booth and Wood were not altogether wrong.

Lincoln's romanticization of its subject as America's political guardian angel is a reminder that enemies of democracy invariably make democratic agents pay a high price for their efforts, especially if those agents are successful, knowing that the project of democratization is always incomplete and that others will try to complete it. Killing Lincoln was not just about settling an "old" score. It was also a warning shot regarding the country's future. Radical change will not simply be accepted, let alone imposed, without resistance. Insofar as Lincoln represented the democratization of America, he was killed for it. This speaks to democracy's tragic condition as civil war.[31] Contestation over America's fundamental identity, including its racial identity, is an existential question.

Spielberg's biopic also points to a more tragic treatment of its subject, if inadvertently. Booth's vigilantism cannot be reduced to racial ressentiment. When he jumped to the stage he hurled a political accusation not a racial epithet at the audience. He unwittingly presented the republic a second occasion for a new birth of freedom. Lincoln, American democracy's defender, was also its enemy.[32] Booth managed to secure an outcome that those officially charged with protecting the Constitution never considered: Lincoln's removal from office for his problematic wartime conduct. Booth is not to be congratulated for his violent act. Yet the effect of what he did contains an essential ambiguity. It took an assassin to get the Constitution some justice. Perhaps, then, it's time to treat Lincoln's death not just as a cause for mourning but also as a reminder that no one, including the president, is above the law, particularly during wartime, and that those who place themselves there, even in a noble cause, can face a terrible comeuppance. Welcome to the life and times of American democracy—in a Dionysian world, anyway.

ABRAHAM LINCOLN: VAMPIRE HUNTER

The New York Times's Manohla Dargis summed up much of the critical reaction to Russian director Timur Bekmambetov's *Abraham Lincoln: Vampire Hunter*: "[This] is such a smashing title it's too bad someone had to spoil things by making a movie to go with it."[33] Dargis's wisecrack is understandable. Nevertheless, if the movie is placed at the end of the Lincoln trilogy just assembled, it can serve as an antidote to its collective solemnity. Though Lincoln was known for telling jokes and stories and telling them well, cinematic treatments of Lincoln tend toward the (unduly) reverential, not to mention grim. There is no such problem with *Abraham Lincoln: Vampire Hunter*. Revolving around a cosmic battle between clearly identified forces of good and evil, it is a celebration of righteous, necessary, excessive violence leavened by enough gallows humor to keep the frontier machismo from spiraling completely out of control. Or not.

Still, *Abraham Lincoln: Vampire Hunter* feels decidedly respectful—with a twist—or perhaps I should say chop. In a letter to Albert Hodges in April 1864, Lincoln insisted, "I am naturally anti-slavery. If slavery is not wrong, nothing is wrong. I cannot remember when I did not so think, and feel."[34] Likewise, six years earlier, responding to Stephen Douglas's opening 1858 Senate campaign speech, Lincoln declared, "I have always hated slavery, I think as much as any Abolitionist.... I have always hated it, but I have always been quiet about it until this new era."[35] According to *Abraham Lincoln: Vampire Hunter*, however, Lincoln does not quite do sufficient justice to his antislavery credentials.

The film credits him with an understanding that the institution of slavery requires a response commensurate to it. In other words, there can and will be no quarter given. The evil is too great, the enemy too fanatical. Though Lincoln is seen giving a speech or two, the film contains no politics whatsoever (other than Lincoln's patriotism, of course). When Stephen Douglas claims that slavery is a complicated issue, Lincoln retorts that he could not disagree more (so much for their famous debates). This is a war of elimination, which means that it is a guilt-free struggle for survival. The violence that is depicted on screen is meant to satisfy, to be enjoyed. Slaughter is what the enemy deserves. It has earned it. It is fitting, ontologically speaking. The enemy represents death. Death is what it receives. What's more, Lincoln is doing God's work. His axe is washed in silver, the one substance against which vampires are helpless. Since Judas was paid his thirty pieces to betray Jesus, silver has been the curse of the cursed. Seriously.

How long has Lincoln actually been antislavery? In the film's first sequence, young Abraham witnesses his (fictional) black boyhood friend Will beaten and whipped by a plantation owner, Jack Barts. Though Abe's father Thomas urges him to look away (his father's solution to most problems), the prepubescent young Mr. Lincoln decides to intervene instead. With hatchet in hand, Abe runs headlong toward the slaver to strike him dead, only to fail in his simultaneously brave, heroic, and ludicrous rescue attempt. Before the slaver can turn his whip on Abe his father intercedes, forced into action by Abe's example. Young heroes cannot suffer for their great deeds. Though the confrontation dissipates, the slaver feels insulted, even humiliated, and takes his revenge against the Lincoln family by breaking into their home in the middle of the night and attacking Nancy, Abe's mother, in front of him. As he later watches his mother die, Thomas again advises Abe to look away. He declines. This is not the usual Lincoln biography backstory.

Some ten years later Lincoln is ready to exact his revenge for his mother's death. Determined to kill Barts with a single pistol shot, Lincoln's plan unravels when the gun misfires. While Lincoln manages, eventually, to get off another shot, one that he thinks completes his task, it fails to kill Barts, who then thrashes Lincoln until he is rescued by a stranger, Henry Sturges. It is Sturges, a vampire himself, who educates Lincoln not only about the existence of Southern vampires but also about the true dimensions of the slavery problem in the United States. Southern heritage will never be the same.

Sturges trains Lincoln to be a vampire hunter, a role that carries grave responsibilities, and for which serious personal sacrifices must be made—one way or another. Vampire hunting as patriotic calling. You cannot save the world and the ones you love, Henry intones. Saving the world creates enemies that will target your family. Henry informs Lincoln that vampires have been in the new world for centuries. They targeted Indian tribes and early settlers, but it was not until Europeans started importing slaves that the vampire presence in America exploded. They sensed a unique opportunity and proceeded to build an empire in the South.

Does *Abraham Lincoln: Vampire Hunter* thus relieve the South of its responsibility for slavery? Can it be attributed to an alien presence in the country? Is there anything American about it? No, no, yes. The two worlds have been living side-by-side in peaceful coexistence for generations, each exploiting black human beings in order to live. The South's perfidy provided the vampires with the perfect cover. The two factions mimicked each other so perfectly that no one could tell them apart. Each was insatiable. In short, the South's slave empire gave birth to even more and greater evils than its own peculiar institution. The vamps, tracing their inspirational lineage to other slave-based orders such as ancient Egypt and imperial Rome, become a threat unprecedented in human history. More than the fate of the United States, then, hangs in the balance. Lincoln is fighting for all of human being.

When the war goes badly for the South, Jefferson Davis turns to his neighbors, the vampire empire, for assistance. In a deal of mutual support, the vamps will provide the Confederacy with all the dead soldiers it needs to win the war. The alliance mocks Southern pretensions to superior military talent and skill. Davis relies not on Robert E. Lee's strategic and tactical genius to invade the North and save the Confederacy but on legions of gray-clad leeches supposedly impossible to destroy. This turn gives new meaning to Southern bravery, honor, and tradition.

To fight the good fight, however, Lincoln must be trained. He is not the self-made man of frontier legend who can invent and reinvent himself at will. Rather he is an eager apprentice who cannot wait to put his newly acquired skills to good violent use. (In fact, he'll put them to such good use that he will fall asleep on dates with Mary; when she complains, he apologizes and informs her that he's been working nights—hunting vampires.) Lincoln thus undergoes nearly a decade of rigorous vampire combat instruction from Henry. In this film the awkward, ungainly, homely Lincoln commonplace in American cinema morphs into an aesthetic wonder to behold. Still tall, of course, he's also agile, quick, graceful, and beautiful. The long black coat that conceals his axe is the uniform of a cold-blooded assassin who performs his lethal civic virtue in the dark. This Lincoln is also a babe magnet, certified as such by the enticing Mary Todd as soon as she lays her lustful eyes on him. Who better than this young stud to fight evil and ensure that America remains "a nation of men, not monsters"? This Lincoln, moreover, will not have to resort to any extra- or unconstitutional measures to save the Union. Just waste vampires.

Abraham Lincoln: Vampire Hunter is also, self-consciously, a racially feel-good film. There is no existential angst about Northern complicity in the institution of slavery. It is a purely Southern phenomenon that is trying its best to make Northern inroads. This becomes abundantly clear to Lincoln when his childhood friend Will tracks him down in Springfield in need of legal assistance to prove his free status so he is not kidnapped by bounty hunters (and shipped south to feed hungry vampires). Will is abducted nevertheless. Given Lincoln's growing success—and reputation—as a hunter, Adam, the vampire's leader in the South, forces him to make a command appearance at his plantation (to save Will), determined to turn Lincoln and enlist him in their cause for a national home. Lincoln, alongside Joshua Speed, rescues Will and they return north to wage the war they now know is coming.

As Lincoln's political career advances, Will is by his side, ultimately accompanying him to the White House, though his role there is not identified.[36] Nevertheless, Lincoln's home prefigures the biracial society he wages war to create. The South initiated hostilities, but Lincoln will put an end to them. Gettysburg is to be the decisive battle of the war, and Jefferson Davis thinks he has a winning hand with the vampires at his disposal. There's just one thing they had not anticipated: silver. Lincoln is told that the war is going badly, but rather than retreat or seek a truce, he escalates. He throws everything he has at the vampire army, but it is not enough. He remembers that they can only be destroyed by silver. He thus organizes the fastest silver drive on record to send the melted-down proceeds from Washington, D.C., to the front lines in a last-gasp effort to win the war.

The plan, however, is little more than a vehicle for a great train robbery sequence in which Adam meets his well-deserved death. Confident that they are on the verge of victory, the vampires do not realize that Lincoln has lured them into a lethal trap. This sequence may represent Lincoln at his iconic best: taking the fight directly to the enemy by effectively inviting them to a rendezvous, he does not have to rely and thus wait on all-too-passive generals to carry out his orders as instructed. Lincoln may have possessed sovereign authority, but this did not always translate into action. If it had, the war would have been over much sooner, as the train sequence in the film (mis)leads us to believe. Adam, moments before learning the truth about Lincoln's trap, boasts that the country will soon be his and that he will destroy the myth of Abraham Lincoln and history will forever know him as a monster. Adam's inadvertently hilarious threat falls short, however, since Lincoln can only become a myth once Adam and his allies are destroyed and lose the war.

While Lincoln and Will fight alongside one another on the train, the Civil War's now decisive confrontation is being decided elsewhere, on an altogether different kind of railroad, the Underground Railroad. African Americans deliver the silver goods Union forces need to prevail. This deceit allows downtrodden African Americans to make an indispensable contribution to the triumph at Gettysburg, despite not fighting in the three-day battle themselves. The Union that Lincoln is saving has already constituted itself as a biracial nation. This vindicates the Emancipation Proclamation that Lincoln had signed earlier in the film. Blacks earned their freedom and future place in the American society they helped save.

As the film grinds to a halt, Lincoln delivers the Gettysburg Address. There is a quick follow-up the day of his assassination when Henry offers to make him immortal so together they can continue the struggle for freedom for all eternity. Lincoln declines, insisting that vampires aren't the only things that live forever. Earlier in his film, Lincoln, retiring the axe, did his best to fight with words and ideals, which he believed to be stronger weapons. These proved insufficient, but he also understood that "history prefers legends to men. It prefers nobility to brutality, soaring speeches to quiet deeds. History remembers the battle, but forgets the blood." Lincoln represents both, of course, but American memory fixes its attention on the softer side of sovereign power. In *Abraham Lincoln: Vampire Hunter*, the record is corrected with plentiful helpings of gore. This means that there is no conceptual room for the Second Inaugural, with its rejection of malice and its call for charity for a defeated enemy. This film's Lincoln could not imagine being in the South's position regarding slavery and acting no differently. "Whatever history remembers of me, if it remembers me at all, it shall only remember a fraction of the truth. For whatever else I am—a husband, a lawyer, a president—I shall always think of myself first and foremost as a hunter."

Because the film effectively ends with the Gettysburg Address, Lincoln's assassination becomes irrelevant. Though he departs for Ford's Theatre with Mary in the closing shot, his eternity has already been established. The issues that plagued the nation ended when the war ended. Violence cleansed and regenerated the country, so there is no aftermath to be confronted, as the Second Inaugural suggests. Here America's future has already been guaranteed. No one, including Lincoln, died in vain. Lincoln could be said not to have died at all. He will outlive all of us—thanks to his aptitude for violence and our appetite for triumphalism. *Abraham Lincoln: Vampire Hunter* is the patriotic slasher film a haunted icon needs to restore himself and a nation beleaguered by his ambiguity.

NOTES

1. To borrow from the editors of *Cahiers du Cinéma*, who were writing about John Ford's Lincoln film alone, the ambition in this chapter "is to make [the trilogy] say what [it] has to say within what [it] leave[s] unsaid, to reveal [its] constituent lacks . . . the unsaid included in the said and necessary to its constitution." A collective text by the editors of *Cahiers du Cinéma*, "John Ford's *Young Mr. Lincoln*," Screen 13, no. 3, 1972, 8.

2. As mentioned, while *Abraham Lincoln: Vampire Hunter* differs from *Young Mr. Lincoln*, *Abe Lincoln in Illinois*, and *Lincoln*, this doesn't mean that the latter don't also enact problematic relationships to violence, which means the violence they do countenance is not so far removed from *Vampire Hunter*. In short, these films are close relatives in the Lincoln family.

3. John Ford said, "The idea of the picture was to give the feeling that even as a young man you could sense there was going to be something great about this man." Joseph McBride and Michael Wilmington argue that Ford "gives a strange gravity to Lincoln's character, a far-away look to his countenance, a self-absorbed equanimity to his bearing." This points to what I am calling Lincoln's foreignness. Joseph McBride and Michael Wilmington, *John Ford* (New York: Da Capo Press, 1975), 26–27. The Ford quote is from the book.

4. Here I am indebted to Bonnie Honig's splendid *Democracy and the Foreigner* (Princeton, NJ: Princeton University Press, 2003). See also Julia Kristeva, *Strangers to Ourselves* (New York: Columbia University Press, 1994).

5. While Brian J. Snee refers to Lincoln as "the Great Commoner," I suggest to Lincoln's foreignness. Snee examines how Ford's film reconciles the tensions between "plain Abe" and "the Great Emancipator." The need for this project seems less compelling to the degree that Lincoln's plainness and greatness are both resisted and refused from the get-go. See Brian J. Snee, *Lincoln before 'Lincoln': Early Cinematic Adaptations of the Life of America's Greatest President* (Lexington: University of Kentucky Press, 2016), chapter 4. When Snee writes about the distinctive dialectical ways in which Ford's film resolves the potential incompatibilities of Lincoln's dual nature, I would suggest placing resolves in square quotes. Snee, *Lincoln before Lincoln*, 80.

6. Merrill Peterson does not take Ford's film seriously because he does not think Ford takes Lincoln seriously: "Without any pretensions to historical accuracy, Ford plays Lincoln for laughs." Merrill D. Peterson, *Lincoln in American Memory* (Oxford: Oxford University Press, 1994), 345.

7. A collective text by the editors of *Cahiers du Cinéma*, "John Ford's *Young Mr. Lincoln*," 16–19. The editors articulate an economic, political, and ideological analysis of the film that focuses on its contexts of creation and looks beneath the surface for underlying infelicities. This approach is invaluable and can be extended, it seems to me, if it is also posited that *Young Mr. Lincoln* transcends these contexts and speaks to the problems of democracy across time and place.

8. *Young Mr. Lincoln* can also be read along more democratic lines, especially since Lincoln is not a government official of any kind. Citizens serving democracy—to defend basic rights and liberties, to pursue common goods—not infrequently court, even invite retaliation or revenge. Democracy tends to prey not so much on those who violate its ideals but on those who enact them, especially insofar as democracy suffers from a kind of blindness that prevents it from seeing what the maintenance of those ideals, especially when they're under duress, requires. Those who defend them can come to seem like enemies, and political action in a democracy can effectively convert citizens into agents of their own destruction. Lincoln takes great risks, but security, being at risk, does not concern him. His efforts appear heroic, but it could be argued that they represent the everyday performance of citizenship, some of the results of which can prove tragic.

9. See Robert B. Ray's *A Certain Tendency of the Hollywood Cinema, 1930–1980* (Princeton, NJ: Princeton University Press, 1985).

10. The editors of *Cahiers du Cinéma* note the role the threat of violence plays in this scene, but they do not address the risk and danger posed to citizens who assume Lincoln's position. Instead they focus on the realization of the Lincoln myth, which comes at the expense of democracy. We know Lincoln will not be killed here, but he doesn't know it. A collective text by the editors of *Cahiers du Cinéma*, John Ford's *Young Mr. Lincoln*, 28–29.

11. Again, if read democratically or aspirationally, Lincoln's intervention should not be deemed exceptional. He does what good democratic citizens should do—and should be expected to do—in such conditions. They must be able to put themselves at risk not only to protect others, but to guarantee democracy itself.

12. See Michael Rogin, "The King's Two Bodies: Lincoln, Wilson, Nixon, and Presidential Self-Sacrifice," in *Ronald Reagan the Movie and Other Episodes in Political Demonology* (Berkeley: University of California Press, 1987) and Edmund Wilson, *Patriotic Gore: Studies in the Literature of the American Civil War* (New York: W.W. Norton, 1962).

13. Lincoln certainly did his part to deliver pomp and show when he sanctioned the mass execution of thirty-eight Dakota Sioux Indians for violently resisting American expansionism during the Civil War in Minnesota, as we saw in the last chapter. See Scott W. Berg, *38 Nooses: Lincoln, Little Crow, and the Beginning of the Frontier's End* (New York: Pantheon, 2012).

14. Like the jailhouse scene, the trial sequence could be read more democratically. The citizen-lawyer who defends unpopular clients, including accused killers, by definition places himself at risk. What if the state is unable to prove its case? What if in the people's judgment Lincoln enabled a killer to go free? What happens to him?

15. Cf. Scott Eyman, who unknowingly appreciates a tragic dimension in Ford's work: "Many writers have opted for a simplistic view of Ford, noting how his work progressed from optimism toward disillusion as the director aged. But Ford always qualified the optimism in even his early work with a sense of loss. In any case, Ford's celebrations of community and the future are always set in the past, never the present. The greater the optimism, the further in the past the story. Filmmaking, not alcohol, was Ford's primary narcotic, and nostalgia his primary emotion." Scott

Eyman, *Print the Legend: The Life and Times of John Ford* (New York: Simon & Schuster, 2015), 193.

16. Pace Snee, who does not address the presence of violence at work in democracy in the scene, this is Lincoln's first political involvement. Snee, *Lincoln before 'Lincoln,'* 95, 102.

17. As if to prove the point, town officials immediately enlist Lincoln to preside as clerk over the local election; his outside status guarantees impartiality. Lincoln's foreignness solves a critical democratic problem: electoral integrity.

18. Snee refers to Lincoln as a reluctant hero. Snee, *Lincoln before 'Lincoln,'* 93.

19. Despite what the film seems to suggest, he actually served four terms.

20. The cinematic version of Lincoln's speech in the Senate campaign borrows from his House Divided speech and several of the debates. It proceeds John Brown's Raid on Harpers Ferry, which wouldn't take place until the following year. Brown is included as a prophetic voice of violence, warning Colonel Robert E. Lee, the officer who arrested him, that the elimination of slavery will require the spilling of blood.

21. Snee argues, surprisingly, that "the election night scene is devoted to demonstrating Lincoln's apathy toward the contest." Snee, *Lincoln before 'Lincoln,'* 104.

22. See John Schaar, "The Case for Patriotism," in *Legitimacy in the Modern State* (New Brunswick, NJ: Transaction Publishers, 1981).

23. Tony Kushner, *Lincoln: The Screenplay* (New York: Theatre Communications Group, 2012), 45–49.

24. In Wood's denunciation, it's virtually impossible not to be reminded of John Wilkes Booth's public political statement after assassinating Lincoln: sic semper tyrannis (thus always to tyrants).

25. Lincoln is right, democratically speaking, to ignore Mary's concerns. Democratic citizens cannot make personal safety in public life a condition of participation. A risk-free civic life is impossible and citizens seeking absolute assurances for their well-being have no business living in a democracy. As we saw in *Young Mr. Lincoln*, to be a democratic citizen is to be at risk, if not now, then at some point. Lincoln's best moments in the film do not necessarily revolve around his majestic orations; they occur when he rides around the republic's capital in an open carriage with minimal protection. This is not mock heroism. Lincoln is a citizen who does not live in fear. For him democracy and violence coexist.

26. Kushner, *Lincoln*, 34.

27. Ibid., 35–36. Emphases mine.

28. Ibid., 160, 161.

29. George Kateb, *Lincoln's Political Thought* (Cambridge, MA: Harvard University Press, 2015), 201.

30. Ibid., 202.

31. A. O. Scott thinks *Lincoln* is "among the finest films ever made about American politics," at once a "political thriller" and a "civics lesson." In short, "the genius of 'Lincoln,' finally, lies in its vision of politics as a noble, sometimes clumsy dialectic of the exalted and the mundane." Yet Scott's astute review somehow ignores or misses the violence inherent in American politics. A. O. Scott, "A President Engaged

in a Great Civil War," available at http://www.nytimes.com/2012/11/09/movies/lincoln-by-steven-spielberg-stars-daniel-day-lewis.html.

32. Cf. Walter Berns. For Berns, Lincoln "used the occasion of the war to cause us to love the Union . . . because of what it stood for, and in the process we came to love him because he saved the Union and embodied what it stood for." Berns's Lincoln is heroic, democracy's martyr. Magically, he understood the need for dead patriot-heroes he now meets, though the Union and Lincoln would come to stand for more (other) than Berns could admit. Walter Berns, *Making Patriots* (Chicago: University of Chicago Press, 2001), 97–98, 100, 94, 97.

33. Manohla Dargis, "Slaying with Silver in the 19th-Century South," *The New York Times*, June 21, 2012.

34. Abraham Lincoln, "Letter to Albert G. Hodges," in *Lincoln: Political Writings and Speeches*, ed. Terence Ball (Cambridge: Cambridge University Press, 2013), 203.

35. Abraham Lincoln, "Speech at Chicago, Illinois," *The Writings of Abraham Lincoln*, edited and with an introduction by Steven B. Smith (New Haven, CT: Yale University Press, 2012), 141.

36. William Johnson was Lincoln's valet in Springfield. He brought him to Washington.

Chapter Three

A "Humble Offering"
The (First) Lincoln Memorial

> The race to which we belong were not the special objects of his consideration. Knowing this, I concede to you, my white fellow-citizens, a preeminence in this worship at once full and supreme. . . . To you it especially belongs to sing his praises, to preserve and perpetuate his memory, to multiply his statues, to hang his pictures high upon your walls, and commend his example, for to you he was a great and glorious friend and benefactor. Instead of supplanting you at his altar, we would exhort you to build high his monuments; let them be of the most costly material, of the most cunning workmanship; let their forms be symmetrical, beautiful, and perfect, let their bases be upon solid rocks, and their summits lean against the unchanging blue, overhanging sky, and let them endure forever! But while in the abundance of your wealth, and in the fullness of your just and patriotic devotion, you do all this, we entreat you to despise not the humble offering we this day unveil to view.
>
> —Frederick Douglass, "Oration in Memory of Abraham Lincoln"

The Lincoln Memorial's erasure of Native Americans by no means exhausts its racial shortcomings. Though the memorial itself, a parvenu, is not the focus of this chapter, its defects can be appreciated from another racial angle by juxtaposing it to the first Lincoln memorial, an unassuming structure that makes the democratic case that its follow-up need not have been built—it was gratuitous. What underpins such a conclusion?

Dedicated in 1922, the Lincoln Memorial sits on the western edge of the Mall in Washington, D.C. Despite the earlier arrival of the Washington Monument in 1885, it has dominated the nation's most sacred civic landscape for nearly one hundred years. Henry Bacon's classic Greek temple and Daniel Chester French's regal sculpture have received great and widespread praise from critics and visitors alike. Thus, the Lincoln Memorial reflects and fortifies Lincoln's exalted place in American public memory.

Glowing receptions, however, do not necessarily make *this* Lincoln Memorial the most fitting remembrance of Lincoln and his presidency—if the purpose of public memorialization involves something other than mere canonization, that is. The Lincoln Memorial is a supremely patriotic architectural appreciation of the sixteenth president—it ignores, denies, and forgets as much as it signifies—but this kind of preferential civic treatment obscures Lincoln's complex constitutional legacy.[1] From a democratic perspective, fortunately, it is not the only Lincoln memorial in Washington, D.C. The Freedmen's Memorial Monument to Abraham Lincoln, dedicated nearly fifty years earlier in 1876, offers a modest and, however inadvertently, even more apt commemorative tribute to Lincoln. Though it is located on the margins, then and now, of Washington, D.C.'s ceremonial geography, *this* is the Lincoln memorial that makes a pertinent and noteworthy contribution to American democracy. If anything, Lincoln himself is more likely to have approved of this human-scale tribute than the gargantuan deification three and a half miles west of it (see figures 3.1 and 3.2).[2]

AN ACCIDENTAL DEMOCRATIC MEMORIAL

The Lincoln Memorial received over seven million visitors in 2014.[3] This is not surprising. Sheer self-celebrating grandiosity is one reason for its success. In honoring Lincoln we also pay tribute to ourselves and to the nation. It's not just that he died so we could become great. His death means we are (and were) great already. Assassination presumes and confers greatness. Another reason relates to the memorial's democratic recovery by the civil rights movement, which art historian Albert Boime describes as a "process by which a conservative, mainstream public monument was appropriated and repatriated by the wider community." Boime refines this assessment a few pages later when he writes of the movement that it managed "to divest the monument of its original ideological trappings and reframe it for a different constituency." This resulted in a "redefinition of the public space of the monument, wherein the site was claimed by groups whose ideologies were more consistent with the historical memory of the descendants of the emancipated."[4] Lincoln came to signify emancipation more than union.

The Lincoln Memorial's transformation was anticipated, even encouraged by Robert Moton, principal of the Tuskegee Institute, who offered dedication remarks as a representative of his race when the Lincoln opened in 1922. Moton characterized the United States as a nation at war from inception, divided

A "Humble Offering" 85

Figure 3.1. Thomas Ball's Freedmen's Memorial Monument to Abraham Lincoln; Lincoln de-deified, if not deromanticized.
Courtesy of Robert R. Gerlits.

by "two great forces," freedom and bondage. Inevitably, this conflict, at once philosophical and practical, would find its way to the battlefield. Lincoln represents the final, costliest casualty of the Civil War. While he worked primarily to save the union, his "claim [to] greatness" derives from the Emancipation Proclamation, which "gave freedom to a race, and vindicated the honor of a nation conceived in liberty and dedicated to the proposition that all men are

Figure 3.2. Thomas Ball's Freedmen's Memorial Monument to Abraham Lincoln.
Courtesy of Robert R. Gerlits.

created equal." With "this newly consecrated shrine of liberty" it remains for the American nation and its people to complete the work that Lincoln began. Otherwise the memorial becomes "a hollow mockery, a symbol of hypocrisy." Drawing on Lincoln's Gettysburg Address, Moton calls for collective dedication to the "lofty task" for which Lincoln died. Moton's address is tantamount to a clarion call. What's more, it effectively invites citizens to consider the Lincoln Memorial and its surroundings as a place where decisive action might unfold, with Moton's own speech paving the way for others to follow. Lincoln saved the union, and this made dissenting politics both possible and legitimate. It also authorizes a politics that eschews violence (that is the legacy of the South). It is not surprising that one day his call would be heeded. That said, Moton's invitation is a conservative one. It asks that American citizens demand that the country live up to its own ideals, not that it change them or adopt new ones. Match word to deed, Moton insists. When he calls on America to finish Lincoln's undertaking, he suggests that the country would have realized its ideals if only Lincoln had not been murdered. Moton never doubts the possibility, in theory, of realizing Lincoln's vision for the country. Lincoln stands for an ideal already achieved. The people need to arrive at the place where Lincoln awaits them. Should the nation fall short, the problem is always assumed to be one of political will. We know what has to be done. The only question is whether we will unite to do it. This is a dangerous assumption. The Freedmen's Memorial, on the other hand, represents an ideal always already violated and transgressed. It suggests not only that the country has more work to do, but that it will always have more work to do because ideals cannot be realized. The very effort to bring them about also subverts them, as here.[5]

Insofar as Boime's account of the (second) Lincoln Memorial resonates, then, it constitutes grounds for democratic concern. Why? It means that much of Lincoln's problematic legacy has been lost, forgotten in a wave of populist enthusiasm that misreads the political possibilities available in American democracy. Fortunately, as I said above, there is another significant memorial to Lincoln in Washington, D.C., a site that does not need to be recovered but one that functions as a permanent provocation for democracy to overcome itself. While Frederick Douglass advised white America to spare no expense, imaginative or financial, in building the most grandiose monuments to Lincoln, he may have been shaming or embarrassing them into doing no such thing, knowing that the memorial he was dedicating, whatever its shortcomings, would more than suffice for his departed friend.

No visitation records are kept for the Freedmen's Memorial in Lincoln Park, which seems to be enjoyed mostly by people who live in the Capitol Hill neighborhood where it is located. The discrepancy in attendance between the two memorials is perhaps understandable but nonetheless undeserved.

This is not to say that the Freedmen's Memorial is unknown—anything but. It could be considered notorious, which is one reason it is instantly recognizable to so many, including to those who have never seen it in person. At first glance, it appears to be, at best, a misguided contribution to the country's national memorial landscape. Depicting a standing Lincoln and a kneeling (if also freed) slave, it seems to sabotage from inception any meaningful symbolic purpose it might have served. Insofar as the statuary group reproduces the racial hierarchy it supposedly transcends, the Freedmen's Memorial is a brazen affront to the new birth of freedom it ostensibly salutes. As is often the case with civic memorials, however, things are more complicated than they seem initially. That which is set in stone (or bronze) rarely is.

The origins of the Freedmen's Memorial inspire and disconcert. In the immediate aftermath of Lincoln's assassination, Charlotte Scott of Marietta, Ohio, conceived the idea of a memorial to the memory of Lincoln. For this purpose, she set aside five dollars, which, at the suggestion of her former owner, she entrusted to a local minister.[6] A local newspaper learned of the magnanimous gesture and ran a story about it, word of which soon spread. As other African Americans, especially war veterans, also contributed money, the funds began to accumulate and an unlikely idea looked like it would become a reality.[7] Not surprisingly, perhaps, as the project for a memorial tribute to Lincoln gained serious momentum and attention, it would soon be commandeered by what Kirk Savage refers to as "larger forces." One of these included the Western Sanitary Commission of St. Louis, Missouri, a humanitarian war relief organization. Notified of the Lincoln effort by Union General T. C. H. Smith, the commission stepped into a power void and took control. Simply put, blacks would raise the money, but whites would gather it and allocate its use. Thus, when it came to questions of memorial design, the actual founders of the memorial would have no say in it. This decision-making structure led to deeply problematic aesthetic and political consequences.

MEMORIAL TWINS

At first glance, the Lincoln Memorial and the Freedmen's Memorial to Abraham Lincoln appear profoundly alien to each another. One treats Lincoln as a secular god in his temple whom supplicants approach with awe and devotion; the other brings him down to earth as a mere mortal trying, however belatedly, to right the gross wrongs of his people. One sanctifies him as the nation's second founder responsible for victory in war and reconciliation in peace; the other presents him as a statesman taking a decisive political action whose broader effects remain unknown. One sits grandly elevated on the nation's most sacred civic ground and dominates everything around it; the other, nearly a dozen blocks east of the Capitol, barely registers when you first approach it from the west. One presides over a public space filled with a bevy of monumental counterparts marking the nation's glorious and gory history; the other stares at the architecturally anodyne Mary McLeod Bethune Memorial, the kind of insipid structure that usually sits in front of a city government office building.

Nevertheless, for all of their evident differences, the Lincoln Memorial and the Freedmen's Memorial to Abraham Lincoln nicely complement one another in ways that a democracy should find disconcerting, at the very least. The argument advanced here is that the two memorials share a certain conception of democracy that finds expression in their respective architectures. Given the grandiosity of the Lincoln Memorial and the repressive racial dynamic in the Freedmen's Memorial, this should come as no surprise. Yet the problematic design and character of the latter, however inadvertently, discloses troubling aspects of democracy in practice that might engender a democratic renewal. That is, it just might take a long-neglected and disrespected 140-year-old memorial to identify the undemocratic, even antidemocratic metaphysic that undergirds American democracy. This would render the Freedmen's Memorial not just an insult to recently liberated slaves, signaling the limitations and restraints they will inevitably face in a polity (supposedly) experiencing a new birth of freedom. It would also reveal the controls and regulations that non-elite white citizens have accepted and embraced as part of the democratic order of things, a reality previously obscured by the deplorable condition of millions of blacks in bondage.

The position of Archer Alexander, a former slave and model for the memorial, vis-à-vis Lincoln troubles the viewer. The recently freed slave seems to have adopted—or had imposed—a new position of subordination. Resting on one knee and gazing into the distance, it does not look as if he is about to rise and claim, that is, take his future. If anything, it looks like the slave might have been standing and Lincoln has returned him to this inferior position. While one set of chains has been broken, this does not mean that others are not already in position to replace it. The moment of emancipation is captured by Alexander's pose, but it is also a moment of uncertainty. The promise that it holds feels unknown, precarious. Things could easily be reversed, undone. Maybe they have been already. Lincoln towers over the newly freed slave, one hand on the Emancipation Proclamation, the other extended over the slave as if to restrain him should he try to rise too quickly. The downward extension of Lincoln's left arm and hand, with the index finger slightly raised and separated from the middle finger, suggests unease, as if Lincoln is about to offer words of caution. Or perhaps something more ominous (see figures 3.3 and 3.4).

Figure 3.3. Thomas Ball's Freedmen's Memorial Monument to Abraham Lincoln (from the south).
Courtesy of Robert R. Gerlits.

Figure 3.4. Thomas Ball's Freedmen's Memorial Monument to Abraham Lincoln (from the north); the moment of emancipation: Lincoln's "new birth of freedom" compromised from the very beginning.
Courtesy of Robert R. Gerlits.

Let it be emphasized that Thomas Ball depicts Lincoln issuing the Emancipation Proclamation, one instance—but only one instance—of Lincoln's arrogation of extraordinary war powers to suppress rebellion in the South. These war powers were highly controversial across the political spectrum. Lincoln himself was not fully convinced of their legitimacy, which is one reason he insisted on bringing the Thirteenth Amendment to a vote shortly after his reelection (the liberation secured through the proclamation might be reversed, as we saw in the previous chapter). Thus the act of emancipation, however it might be portrayed, presupposes exceptional sovereign power, a power that does not dissipate when it has achieved its objective. Lincoln's bold stroke enhanced the power of the presidency, in part by making it self-aggrandizing, which means that American freedom also suffered as a result. The freedom of slaves, then, was accompanied by a loss of freedom for citizens, which would eventually affect the status of the recently freed people themselves. Thus Lincoln's successful exercise of sovereign power also constitutes a threat to the very people that have just been liberated. The Lincoln Memorial may physically dwarf the Freedmen's Memorial but not necessarily in the political symbolism of power. In the latter freedom is also something granted or bestowed from on high, not something struggled for and taken from below.

Lincoln's extralegal assumption of power is manifested in his posture toward the ex-slave. He looks down on him with a stern gaze. It's as if the president and commander-in-chief, who freed human beings for reasons of military necessity, must first inform Archer Alexander that his liberation may only be temporary. Either way, he must then explain to Alexander the terms of his emancipation before he can actually enjoy it. He might have been liberated, but freedom is not his to exercise as he—and he alone—sees fit. There is still an order to things and Lincoln sits at the top of it. Ball's grouping might appear patronizing, at a minimum, but it also embodies the proper relationship in American social and political life, a formal rhetoric of equality notwithstanding, between leaders and the citizenry. There are those who possess the right qualities to govern the country for the benefit, to one extent or another, of everyone else. The citizenry is not formally disempowered, but it needs to know and keep its place, as the founders imagined and arranged it. That the moment of emancipation is chosen for depiction, and then depicted with a statesman-like Lincoln and a nearly naked slave, suggests that the world is divided between those who possess the mind and spirit required to rule and those who, largely defined by the body, must be ruled.[8]

Ball's depiction of the ambiguous, even precarious status of the freed slave resonates with Giorgio Agamben's account of bare life. The moment of emancipation in the Freedmen's Memorial does not anticipate passage of the Thirteenth Amendment outlawing slavery, let alone the Fourteenth or Fifteenth Amendments. Any such anticipation would have been more dramatic but also specious. Dramatic because liberation constituted a first step in a process unlikely to end with the mere breaking of chains, so to speak, specious because liberation was going to involve aspects that often rendered it more apparent than real, more formal that substantive. The freed slave of 1863 was liberated from bondage and thereby made available for military service—the former reduced human beings to use as personal property by whites, the latter reduced them to use as military property by the government. Liberation, in other words, was predicated on use by the state. Liberation was not a moral question; it was a military and thus instrumental question. What would it take to defeat Southern rebels in war? More bodies. Uniformed. Armed. Disposable. In the Emancipation Proclamation Lincoln "declare[s] and make[s it] known" that "such persons of suitable condition, will be received into the armed service of the United States." As of January 1, 1863, the date of issuance, Lincoln seems content to deploy newly freed people away from the front lines in noncombat positions. This suggests that they will be used as the Military Power sees fit, but also in such a way that no reciprocal obligation is created. Those who serve can be used but they can make no claim on their own behalf that must be honored as a result of service. Lincoln states that he "sincerely believe[s this]" to be an act of justice," but emancipation is an act of political and military expediency.

The war that freed slaves also reduced citizens, the newly freed included, to a condition of bare life. Lincoln's articulation of executive power links the two identities. Liberation thus amounts to an ambiguous achievement. Citizenship doesn't have the implications regarding rights and responsibilities reasonably expected given the liberal self-conceptions of American political discourse because it *can't* have the implications reasonably expected. Liberation leaves one set of constraints and restraints behind, but it simultaneously involves the introduction of a new set of controls and regulations. This means that Ball's statue accurately depicts the condition of liberated slaves. It also means the depiction enjoys a wider, more general applicability beyond slaves. The subservient posture assumed by Ball's slave can apply to bodies of any color. Thus newly freed slaves join still ascendant white citizens in established relations of social and political control, and those relations can amount to a new form of domination for them. During war the state can and does treat its own citizens with an arbitrariness resembling that with which slave owners treat their property.

The look of surprise on Archer Alexander's face now takes on new meaning. Savage writes: "the Freedmen's Memorial offered a stark lesson. Instead of representing a new order, it reasserted the old racial structure and power relations of slavery." Savage recognizes the conceptual failure of Ball's artistic scheme. "In Ball's world—which in many respects is still our world—equality is not simply a long way off; it remains outside even the imagination." Savage, however, does not push the political point far enough, for equality (and freedom) is more than a racial question. Who knew that the era of liberation would entail novel forms of subjection, some as total in their own way as slavery? Savage observes the problematic conception of politics at work in Ball's sculptural embodiment of emancipation: "not everyone can dominate. Some men must sink to their knees if others are to stand up and assume power."[9] Ball's creation is naturally focused on the question of slavery. As Frederick Douglass reminded his white audience members at the dedication of the Freedmen's Memorial, citing Thomas Jefferson, one hour of slavery "was worse than ages of the oppression your fathers rose in rebellion to oppose."[10] Still, whatever truth is contained in Jefferson's sweeping comparative judgment may conceal as readily as it reveals, which the plight of Clement Vallandigham demonstrates. Lincoln subjected Vallandigham to a kind of treatment he would not have considered inflicting on slaves in the South who aided and abetted the enemy.

The Western Sanitary Commission's decision to affirm Ball's selection of 1863 for a tribute to Lincoln is telling, especially since the design was probably commissioned not long after 1871.[11] The memorial was unveiled in 1876 as Reconstruction was collapsing. Why this particular rendering of emancipation? Doesn't it feel dated upon arrival? Why not depict a freed slave in military uniform standing next to Lincoln, especially since the Western Sanitary Commission had a model for what a more democratic representation of emancipation might look like? Initially, the commission was committed to a design by Harriet Hosmer. While Hosmer's scheme was ultimately dropped because of its cost, it included among its many elements "a sculptural cycle of African American history, featuring four standing black male figures" delineating the life of blacks in America from the imposition of enslavement to the donning of uniforms and the bearing of arms in the fight for freedom. Though Lincoln appears reclining in a coffin, his martyrdom does not dominate the memorial because of the centrality of the African American cycle. Hosmer's arrangement amounted to a "decisive break with the iconography of manumission. Though Lincoln is represented up above the black figures to maintain the hierarchy of heroism, he is in the horizontal position while they stand erect. His power and agency have been drained from him by death, as if to reemerge in the emancipated slaves beneath him."[12] Hosmer's cyclical scheme, as Savage argues, documents the radical change in status of the black male, something not fully accounted for in Ball's conception. Here the well-armed black soldier consolidates a newfound masculinity that not only overcomes the passivity and helplessness for which he was (allegedly) known, but also takes the fight to the very institution responsible for his captivity and domination. Rather than being forced to accept the overwhelming violence that was slavery, the black soldier can now return violence with violence of his own, putting so much self-serving Confederate dogma about the inherent inferiority of slaves to rest for good.[13] Emancipation enacted means the acquisition of equality. Hosmer's sculpture embodies emancipation as a taking; Ball's sculpture embodies it as a gift bestowed.

Savage argues that Ball's composition makes no sense. He notes the tension between recognition (the slave's surprised look of freedom somehow realized) and resistance (the slave seems to have broken his chains himself).[14] Ball's original design did not incorporate any element of black agency, upon which the Western Sanitary Commission insisted. This accounts for the incoherence Savage discerns. The problem, according to Savage, is that Ball left the slave in the original position, kneeling, but tried to add resistance to the figure by extending his right arm and clenching his fist, a gesture expressive of self-determination. The resistance offered here is out of place with Lincoln standing right behind him supposedly delivering him from bondage. Why the need for self-assertion when freedom has already been bestowed on you? Ball needed to reconceive the slave's entire body, not just one part of it. The child-parent relationship of the original prevails, with Lincoln playing the role of the anxious parent and the slave the child who does not seem to understand what is happening. Savage rightly wonders, if the slave has worked to break his chains, how can he also be surprised at having done so? This is what reduces the slave to an infant.[15] Contra Savage, however, this may be what accidentally saves the memorial from obsolescence.

Ball's combination of recognition and resistance might be compatible after all—if we expand the temporal frame of the scene depicted. What if emancipation is conceived not as a single moment in time but as a process that unfolds? Thus, when it comes to resistance, we could believe that a specific goal is impossible, incapable of realization right now, with circumstances being what they are. Still, we often strive for things that we don't believe are really going to happen anytime soon but are worth struggling for since they might happen one day. Later, while seemingly trapped in perpetual overcoming, we might receive (unexpected) assistance. Now a goal that seemed always on the horizon suddenly materializes. The (im)possible happens. In such a scenario, we could be surprised at having accomplished something we were trying to achieve all along (recognition and resistance joined). On this reading Lincoln does not have to be thought of as an anxious parent, but he can be an ambivalent politician who wants to proceed with caution not despite what he's done but precisely because of the contingencies surrounding what he's set in motion. Here Lincoln acts as commander-in-chief, which means that he is comfortable with blacks as would-be soldiers because he enjoys the power of life and death over them. He will use them as he sees fit for military purposes, which renders the inferior kneeling position apt. If the ex-slave had been depicted as a fully clothed citizen, the kneeling position might have raised uncomfortable political questions—not that it would have been any less apt. In short, it's not that I disagree with Savage's astute reading. It's that the relationship depicted in the memorial might be more problematic than he indicates insofar as it is a dire commentary, however inadvertent, on the basic tenets of American democracy.

MY FRIEND FREDERICK DOUGLASS

On April 14, 1876, the eleventh anniversary of Lincoln's assassination and two days prior to the fourteenth anniversary of the abolition of slavery in Washington, D.C., Frederick Douglass delivered the dedicatory address for the Freedmen's Memorial Monument to Abraham Lincoln. An impressive number of political luminaries assembled for the occasion just blocks from the Capitol: the president of the United States, Ulysses S. Grant, and his cabinet; the chief justice and the Supreme Court of the United States; and various members of the Senate and House of Representatives. The sizable crowd was also filled with ordinary citizens, including many recently freed African Americans. As the featured speaker at the unveiling, Douglass's oration would give him the opportunity to fix a definitive, lasting interpretation on this brand new piece of public commemorative architecture and thus also on Lincoln's presidency, already the stuff of American historical legend. Douglass was alert to the politically fraught situation in which he found himself speaking. Patriotic memorial occasions generate expectations in the audience for a rousing tribute and impose obligations on the speaker to deliver fitting accolades. To fail, let alone refuse, to perform one's civic duty in the face of such pressures would require consummate rhetorical courage and skill. Who better than Frederick Douglass to execute such an assignment? More importantly, what kind of political effect might a contrarian performance by Douglass generate? Could it constitute an alternative approach to cultural politics that contributes to a new understanding of democracy?[16] The selection of a black speaker such as Douglass in front of a multiracial audience guaranteed there would be many layers to the oration.[17]

Douglass's oration begins inauspiciously. While he declares, as if to reassure the audience, that "this is no day for malice," Douglass offers a characterization of the contemporary national condition that surely must have confounded those hearing it. "I congratulate you . . . upon the very favorable circumstances in which we meet today. They are high, inspiring, and uncommon. . . . Few facts could better illustrate the vast and wonderful change which has taken place in our condition as a people than the fact of our assembling here for the purpose we have today. Harmless, beautiful, proper, and praiseworthy as this demonstration is, I cannot forget that no such demonstration would have been tolerated here twenty years ago."[18] Douglass does make a quick reference to "the spirit of slavery and barbarism . . . which still lingers to blight and destroy in some dark and distant parts of our country," but this hardly suffices as a rendering of the dire straits of Reconstruction in 1876. It is effectively, if not yet officially, dead. Douglass thus spares Grant and his cabinet officials the profound public embarrassment of a full accounting of the campaign of Southern terrorism and sabotage accompanying America's new birth of freedom.[19] For the South, the Civil War never ended. The guerrilla war they had been waging since its formal conclusion would soon take a decisive turn for the better (for them) thanks to the negotiated results of the 1876 election.

Douglass's disavowal of malice may have comforted the audience, but any sense of consolation would have been short-lived. For Douglass malice was irrelevant. On this kind of public occasion, where a slain president is being honored and made into a heroic figure for generations to come, speaking truth to (memorial) power was mandatory, a civic obligation. Douglass appreciates that much of what he is about to say will be met with disapproval from much of the audience, especially but not exclusively the white audience. But he insists that "truth compels me . . . *even here* in the presence of the monument we have erected to his memory" to speak candidly of Lincoln. With this assertion Douglass not only signals to his audience that the Lincoln they are about to receive will not simply be praised, let alone flattered; that his memory is not fixed but fluid, a subject of ongoing political contestation. He also reveals that the design and purpose of traditional patriotic ceremonies are about to be re-covered, a process aided and abetted by a memorial Douglass dislikes. Ordinarily it would be considered de rigueur to overlook a figure's flaws and failings at the very moment he is being publicly saluted. Critique can wait for another more appropriate occasion. Douglass will have none of this.[20]

This is not to say that Douglass ignores the spirit of the commemorative moment, especially since it includes a "blood-bought freedom."[21] What's more, Douglass conceives of this instance of monument building and the rituals and ceremonies attending its unveiling as an opportunity for freed blacks to prove their commitment and express their devotion to the United States as equal citizens—in case, perhaps, fighting in the war had not (sufficiently) proven it. He thus acknowledges the unveiling of the memorial as an occasion for gratitude and appreciation. The nature of public approbation, however, derives not from an objective consideration of Lincoln and his accomplishments. It flows from the position a person occupied in the American republic during the Civil War, a position governed by, among other things, race. This position, in turn, informs the perspective one is likely to take on Lincoln's (alleged) greatness. Thus Douglass makes a distinction that enables him to proceed with a critique that fits in with the diplomatic protocols of the event. Lincoln was not the president of a unified people or nation. He was first and foremost a white man and the white man's president. He made it clear before and after he became president that his primary ambition was to save the Union. Slavery's fate, then, would hinge on that ambition, meaning that it could continue indefinitely. Douglass reminds the white members of his audience that Lincoln was prepared to defend and protect the interests of white America despite the fact, again citing Jefferson, that "one hour of [slavery] was worse than ages of the oppression your fathers rose in rebellion to oppose."[22]

This kind of instrumentalization was not Lincoln's only offense against his fellow (black) Americans. He was prepared to defend the Fugitive Slave Act and return freed people to their chains. He was prepared to suppress any slave rebellion for freedom. He was prepared to use the violence of the American state to defend these positions, even though the masters of slavery had already taken up arms against the government. Perhaps this is why Douglass offers the strangely qualified formulation that people who see the memorial now and in the future may appreciate "*something* of the exalted character and great works of Abraham Lincoln, the first martyr president of the United States."[23] Either way, Douglass allows the audience to see Lincoln as he appears from the perspective of a black man who was not just a slave who had escaped into freedom but a political force in his own right during and after the war. Douglass is here to praise but also appraise. After a short recitation of Lincoln's credentials as a defender of the white nation and constitution, Douglass reminds everyone of the irony at work in today's ceremony: "The race to which we belong were not the special objects of his consideration."[24] Lincoln may have been president but he was not equally the president of everyone.

Douglass thus sets the stage for the idea of a contested public memory. Forget the Southern enemy, still a force in American politics. Those well-disposed to Lincoln, Union, and abolition do not share an understanding of the slain president. With Douglass's assistance, the memorial designed to honor Lincoln will not just bring people together to honor him. It will also divide them. There is not one Lincoln—nor can there be. There are many Lincolns, depending on position and perspective. This is not the kind of reception that national monuments and memorials want to have built into their basic structure of remembrance. Memorial controversy might seem all too familiar to us today, but even with such controversial designs as Maya Lin's Vietnam Veterans Memorial, the dedication and subsequent ceremonies usually aspire to overcome difference and division, if only by rhetorical fiat. Douglass's oration signals that Lincoln must be a contested figure and the new memorial a contested site. He thus qualifies his feelings of gratitude and appreciation: "Knowing this [Lincoln's ambivalent record], I concede to you, my white fellow-citizens, a preeminence in this worship at once full and supreme." In what seem to be the most quoted words from the oration, Douglass continues: "First, midst, and last, you and yours were the objects of his deepest affection and most solicitude. You are the children of Abraham Lincoln. We are at best only his stepchildren; children by adoption, children by forces of circumstances and necessity."[25]

The upshot of Douglass's oration leads to the inevitable conclusion that Lincoln can and must be recognized and "celebrated" differently by different peoples. The Freedmen's Memorial to Abraham Lincoln is perfectly adequate to its modest purposes. Others will find its modesty unacceptable, even objectionable, especially if and when Douglass's dedication places an indelible interpretive stamp on it.[26] This means that other constituencies will have to build their own memorials to Lincoln. The Freedmen's Memorial thus announces, with Douglass's assistance, the need for its own supplementation. Not because of any flaw or failing in the memorial but precisely because of its success. Some citizens will see the memorial and conclude that this is not their Lincoln—this is not how they want to remember him. Some (whites in particular) will have to play the hagiography game: "To you it especially belongs to sound his praises, to preserve and perpetuate his memory, to multiply his statues, to hang his pictures high upon your walls, and commend his example, for to you he was a great and glorious friend and benefactor. Instead of supplanting you at his altar, we would exhort you to build high his monuments; let them be of the most costly material, of the most cunning workmanship; let their forms be symmetrical, beautiful, and perfect; let their bases be upon solid rocks, and their summits lean against the unchanging, blue overhanging sky, and let them endure forever!"[27] Ingeniously Douglass has called for new and more Lincoln memorials and simultaneously undermined their legitimacy insofar as they reflect white patriotic worship. This will make them white memorials, built on racial myopia and exclusion. Their nationality will arrive stillborn. The Lincoln Memorial on the west end of the Mall could be said to have fallen right into Douglass's invitation-cum-trap, as it reveres Lincoln for saving the union and effectively erases the question of slavery, its Second Inaugural inscription notwithstanding.

Douglass, then, assumes the Freedmen's Memorial will not meet with the satisfaction of those assembled (or much of the nation) given its modest scale and (apparently) narrow focus on the single act of emancipation rather than the grand sweep of Lincoln's presidency. Other than describing the Freedmen's Memorial as a "humble offering," Douglass studiously ignores the sculpture's configuration. Later in life he mentioned that he would have preferred a manlier pose for the freed slave, one that better reflected his newfound condition of freedom.[28] If Douglass had addressed the memorial's design, based on his long-standing engagement with Lincoln, how might he have developed his critique? Douglass's analysis of Lincoln's first inaugural address seems pertinent here. It suggests Douglass would have expressed reservations not only about Archer Alexander's posture but Lincoln's as well. In other words, it would not have been sufficient merely to raise Alexander. Lincoln's dominating comportment would also have to be adjusted. Douglass signals a possible memorial revision in the opening to his essay on the first inaugural: "The circumstances under which the address was delivered, were the most extraordinary and portentous that ever attended any similar occasion in the history of the country. Threats of riot, rebellion, violence and assassination had been freely, though darkly circulated, as among the probable events to occur on that memorable day. The life of Mr. Lincoln was believed, even by his least timid friends, to be in most imminent danger."[29]

Douglass notes Lincoln's bravery, blasts the Buchanan administration, and holds it responsible for this appalling state of affairs. On the other hand, he praises General Winfield Scott for the "elaborate military preparations" that allowed the inauguration to take place peacefully and thereby secure the republic's continuation. Douglass then notes the stealthy manner in which Lincoln had to make his way to Washington, D.C., to be able to assume office and offers a provocative comparison: "He reached the Capital as the poor hunted fugitive slave reaches the North, in disguise, seeking concealment, evading pursuers, by the underground railroad, between two days, not during the sunlight, but crawling and dodging under the sable wing of night. He changed his programme, took another route, started at another hour, travelled in other company, and arrived at another time in Washington."[30]

Douglass makes it clear he is not being critical of Lincoln for the measures to which he resorted to make it to his own swearing-in ceremony: "We have no censure for the President at this point. He only did what braver men have done. It was, doubtless, galling to his very soul to be compelled to avail himself of the methods of a fugitive slave, with a nation howling on his track."[31] In Douglass's skilled rhetorical hands, Lincoln and a fraction of the slave population share a moment of rough equality. The memorial not only ignores but rejects the possibility of this kind of identification. That is, the memorial fails to acknowledge Lincoln's dependency on the very people he freed. Black Americans helped Lincoln solidify the power that he used to win the war, including the act of emancipation. While he is shown freeing them, they helped save the union and thereby freed themselves. The memorial's depiction of emancipation gets it wrong. By reducing and simplifying it to a single moment in 1863, it distorts the history surrounding it. Most of the white audience can recognize themselves in the memorial, however disappointed they might also be, but for the black audience it is a different story.

Nevertheless, Douglass offers a piece of civic advice to white attendees: "Despise not the humble offering this day unveiled to view," he entreats them. Though Douglass, as I mentioned, would later reveal his dislike of the memorial, here he observes a discreet but noticeable silence on its architectural aspects, its embodiment of passive subordination in particular. This reticence no doubt enables Douglass to offer the respectful treatment the occasion demands and the audience expects. Douglass accomplishes this ceremonial duty by taking Lincoln in the round, by adopting what he calls "a comprehensive view of Abraham Lincoln."[32] Of what does this view consist?

Douglass recites many of the great things that happened while Lincoln was president. Before enumerating them, however, he notes that "our faith in him was often taxed and strained to the uttermost, but it never failed." Thus, before paying tribute to Lincoln's presidency Douglass resumes his critique of Lincoln. He blamed slaves as the cause of the war. He worked to remove them from their homeland through colonization. He refused to deploy them in the war and, once he did, he refused to respond (at least initially) to Southern atrocities against them. He revoked the regional emancipation proclamation of one of his generals, John Frémont. He failed to move quickly to sack the ineffective head of the Army of the Potomac, a Southern sympathizer. He kept insisting that if he could save the union with slavery he would do so.[33] When Douglass writes that "the President had bribed the rebels to lay down their arms by a promise to withhold the bolt which would smite the slave-system with destruction," he comes perilously close to accusing Lincoln of lying down with the enemy.[34] Nevertheless, Douglass insists, "when we saw all this, and more, we were at times grieved, stunned, and greatly bewildered; but our hearts believed while they ached and bled." They were able to take a comprehensive view because they were willing to "make reasonable allowance for the circumstances of his position."[35] This move puts Lincoln in context, placing him "at the head of a great movement" that would bring about the termination of slavery in the United States.[36]

Douglass recites a list of developments that occurred in America while Lincoln held office. He does not ascribe direct agency to Lincoln for the many transformations that took place. Rather, Lincoln emerges in Douglass's oration as a presiding force. Thus, under Lincoln's rule, African American slaves moved from a condition of bondage to liberty. Under Lincoln's rule, the country uniformed and armed two hundred thousand black soldiers. Under Lincoln's rule, Haiti's independence was recognized and its minister received in Washington. Under Lincoln's rule, the internal slave trade was abolished, as well as slavery in the District of Columbia. Under Lincoln's rule, the prohibition against the foreign slave trade was enforced and a slave trader hanged. Under Lincoln's rule, the racist Confederate States were dismembered and destroyed. Under Lincoln's rule, an Emancipation Proclamation was signed, making "slavery forever impossible in the United States." Such developments were all a long time coming, but come they did.[37]

Douglass notes in particular the delirious effect on blacks everywhere of the Emancipation Proclamation, the highly awaited blow to slavery and Southern war prospects. Caught up in the excitement of that event, it was possible to momentarily forget and forgive Lincoln's many shortcomings. As Douglass continues his oration, however, he develops one dimension of his contextual analysis to surprising and ironic effect.[38] Lincoln was a man of his time and race, which means that he shared many of the prejudices of his day and people. Given that he was also president, however, these failings might well have worked to good political advantage. Insofar as Lincoln had to rally the loyal part of a fractured nation behind an unpopular, controversial war, the fact that they could identify with him because of his prejudices meant that one of their own was asking them to sacrifice—not some stranger possessed of beliefs foreign to them. If Lincoln had been an abolitionist, Douglass surmises, surely he would have failed either to save the union or kill slavery. When the South fired on Fort Sumter, Northern whites and the loyal Border States were not prepared to fight a war against slavery. He needed the sympathy and cooperation of the people and he could secure them because they recognized themselves in him. This leads to a nuanced assessment of Lincoln, both damning and complimentary: "Viewed from the genuine abolitionist ground, Mr. Lincoln seemed tardy, cold, dull, and indifferent; but measuring him by the sentiment of his country, a sentiment he was bound as a statesman to consult, he was swift, zealous, radical, and determined."[39] Douglass does not say that either of these perspectives corresponds to the black perspective. Perhaps not even the abolitionist perspective could do justice to the grievances and demands of the enslaved. From their perspective, tardy, cold, dull, and indifferent would be polite characterizations of Lincoln's deliberateness.

Noting that while Lincoln was alive he was morally and politically assailed from every conceivable direction, from passionate friend and bitter enemy alike, Douglass suggests that time, because it is "impartial" and "just," will take good care of Lincoln: "it is a great worker, and often works great wonders."[40] Douglass has made his own unique contribution to this wonderful work, as has the Freedmen's Memorial, something that cannot be said of the

Lincoln Memorial on the Mall. It is anything but impartial and just. It does not aspire to either quality, of course, so perhaps its prejudices cannot be held against it—or not too much, anyway.

Douglass concludes the oration with remarks on Lincoln's assassination, stressing its gratuity. It could serve no (political or military) purpose but malice and revenge. The war was over and lost. The Southern states had been battered and crushed by Grant's and Sherman's armies. The nation was already moving toward peace. Douglass will not deign to speak the foul murderer's name. He is not worthy. Not only did he accomplish nothing. Ironically, Lincoln's assassination "has done some good after all. It has filled the country with a deeper abhorrence of slavery and a deeper love for the great liberator."[41] Assassination was the final narcissistic criminal act of the Slave Power, itself a criminal force. If Lincoln had died from natural causes in his old age, his memory would not be what it is today, "doubly dear" and "precious forever."[42] In other words, absent his murder, there would in all likelihood be no secular cult of Lincoln. Martyrdom trumps an ending where "the solemn curtain of death come[s] down but gradually."[43] Violent death conferred a status on his presidency that it apparently did not achieve on its own. Lincoln's timely death meant that commemoration would focus on the last moments of his administration, victory in war and union in peace. Not yet built, would there be a Lincoln Memorial on the west end of the Mall without Booth? Douglass does not say it, but it seems that the country, or at least white America, owes a debt of gratitude to John Wilkes Booth. His act enables the United States to remember Lincoln selectively, to focus exclusively on creating a memory of what he is said to have accomplished, but this is precisely what Douglass, for the most part, refuses to do.[44] While Booth can be considered one of the founders of the Lincoln Memorial on the Mall, he has no role to play in Lincoln Park.[45]

In presenting an ambiguous Lincoln to the crowd of honored guests, attendees, and onlookers, Douglass reinvents formulaic patriotic commemoration, converting it into a productively ambivalent democratic reckoning. As he said the day Lincoln was assassinated, "republics have proverbially short memories." Douglass delivered an oration that, in remembering the Lincoln regime in its totality, documented its many misdeeds—despite the tendency to willfully forget inconvenient political truths deemed expedient or necessary in the heat of political crisis. The transformation effected by Douglass calls into question the very ritual at which he speaks. After all, it might turn out, once Douglass has finished his oration, that the subject being honored merited some other kind of recognition. Thus, rather than the speech serving as an introduction to the memorial that then becomes its capstone, the speech works to subvert the very reason for being of the memorial. Ironically, the problematic configuration of the Freedmen's Memorial precludes this outcome. If the Lincoln Memorial (or something like it) on the western edge of the Mall had been unveiled in 1876, following Douglass's oration it would have been necessary to dismantle it. However inadvertently, the Freedmen's Memorial to Abraham Lincoln fits him perfectly and Douglass's oration in turn complements it. While Douglass claims for black citizens "no superior devotion" to Lincoln because they have made possible a monument dedicated to his memory, it might be appropriate to ask whether Douglass, with the unwitting assistance of Thomas Ball, renders devotion of any kind to Lincoln more or less impossible. Douglass seems to possess an ambiguous appreciation for Lincoln, but to what does such an appreciation amount? What if Lincoln had not been assassinated, would he be the subject of the kind of unqualified admiration that public commemoration requires?

From a democratic perspective, the Freedmen's Memorial works well, even to this day—as a countermonument. Representing and affirming the fiction that Lincoln freed the slaves with a stroke of the commander-in-chief's pen, the memorial embodies the nation's still very real and problematic racial conceits and shortcomings. In denying blacks effective agency in their own emancipation, it also denies blacks the moral, social, and political equality they have supposedly gained as a result of emancipation. It is a monument to enduring white racial superiority even if that superiority has been formally abolished. It now operates in different guises. The memorial thus posits an ideal and depicts the violation of that same ideal in its moment of triumph. Lincoln becomes a figure that simultaneously signals pride and shame, achievement and defeat. It fosters an understanding that despite, even because of this or that accomplishment, it is now possible to see how much work there is to do as the nation continues to insist that it believes in (its) ideals. The memorial's ambiguity means that self-satisfaction is impossible. If read suspiciously, it might foster a sense of angry dissatisfaction and disappointment and thereby function as a spur to action. Because of the ineradicable gap between what is and what might otherwise be, it induces the feeling that things cannot be allowed to stand as they are. And not just for blacks, but for virtually all democratic citizens.

NOTES

1. Christopher Thomas reads the Lincoln Memorial as a product of the age of Roosevelt (Theodore), arguing that it "barely resembles the Abraham Lincoln of history; 'he,' rather, was a confection of a cultural and political elite bent on stripping Lincoln of his earthly imperfection and his war of its bloodiness, to make him

into prototypes of the progressive and (for some) imperial nation that Republicans of 1901–1912 hoped to shape. Sitting in effigy inside the regal memorial is the ideal American president, not Abraham Lincoln." This intriguing architectural conspiracy theory misunderstands both Lincoln and American fealty to him. Lincoln is the ideal (progressive and imperial) American president precisely because of his imperfections, which the memorial recovers as strengths and affirms through its idealization of him. Whatever erasure or denial of America's problematic history this might entail is not blind but knowing. Christopher A. Thomas, *The Lincoln Memorial and American Life* (Princeton, NJ: Princeton University Press, 2002), xv.

2. I refer to the Freedmen's Memorial as the first *national* Lincoln memorial. Washington, D.C., commissioned the first Lincoln monument, designed by Frank Pierson and sculpted by Lot Flannery, not even two weeks following his murder. It was dedicated in 1868. Pietro Mezzara of San Francisco fashioned the first Lincoln statue in 1865. My thanks to Eric Lamar regarding the Pierson-Flannery memorial.

3. http://www.theatlantic.com/politics/archive/2015/05/15-most-visited-national-landmarks-in-washington-dc/451941/.

4. Albert Boime, *The Unveiling of the National Icons: A Plea for Patriotic Iconoclasm in a Nationalist Era* (Cambridge: Cambridge University Press, 1998), 253, 257.

5. Robert Moton, "Draft of Speech at the Lincoln Memorial," *The Lincoln Anthology: Great Writers on His Life and Legacy from 1860 to Now* (New York: Library of America, 2008), 428–34. President Warren Harding delivered the official dedication. Harding, however, stressed that the Union was Lincoln's great accomplishment, emancipation a means to it. Washington was the founder of the country, Lincoln its savior. While Harding insisted "there are neither supermen nor demi-gods in the government of kingdoms, empires, or republics," he went on to compare Lincoln to "The Child of Bethlehem." Warren Harding, *President Harding's Address at the Dedication of the Lincoln Memorial*, Washington, D.C., 30 May 1922, Washington, Government Printing Office, 1922.

6. "Final Report of the Western Sanitary Commission from May 9th, 1864 to Dec. 31st, 1865," 133, https://babel.hathitrust.org/cgi/pt?id=uiug.30112049382978;view=1up;seq=141.

7. Throughout this section, I am indebted to Kirk Savage's marvelous *Standing Soldiers, Kneeling Slaves: Race, War, and Monument in Nineteenth-Century America* (Princeton, NJ: Princeton University Press, 1997), 89–93, 113–22.

8. The memorial's sculptural depiction of Lincoln, despite what Douglass calls its humbleness, did not incite controversy. Lincoln appears statesmanlike, exercising the awesome powers at his disposal to free the slaves as he conducts a successful military campaign to win the Civil War. The Emancipation Proclamation, it must be remembered, was first and foremost, at least in Lincoln's thinking, a war measure. Not all representations of Lincoln were so lucky. In 1917 George Grey Barnard's Lincoln was unveiled in Cincinnati to great contention. Barnard's Lincoln gave new meaning to the word humble. Part of a struggle over the status and standing of the sixteenth president, it offered a "realistic" interpretation of Lincoln that embodied his common origins and meager beginnings. Looking more

like a hobo than a statesman, Lincoln was truly one of the people themselves, which enabled him to identify with the lower orders of American society. If anything, it de-deified him. Barnard's Lincoln is eminently approachable, a mere eleven feet tall standing on a pedestal of roughly two feet. It was not built as a destination, and when visiting Cincinnati's Lytle Park one could easily walk by it, not even recognizing the beardless, somewhat disheveled-looking Lincoln. As a work of art, there is nothing exceptional about it, which seems to be precisely the point. This reduction of Lincoln stood in contrast to the idealization of Lincoln that stressed his transcendental qualities. What made Lincoln great was that he surmounted his inauspicious start and become an internationally recognized statesman who saved and refounded the Union, thereby becoming a source of universal inspiration. The Lincoln Memorial on the Mall, where he presides over the nation like a god, perfected this understanding of Lincoln. A terminus, people go the Mall to pay all manner of respects to him. He cannot be missed. One's Lincoln of choice tended to be governed by the politics of class. Ironically, however, both incarnations of Lincoln glorified him; they just did so from different directions. His enduring greatness was never in question in either representational approach. This means that the contest between the transcendental and the realist Lincoln obscures the deceit operative in his commemoration. See Boime, *The Unveiling of the National Icons*, 269, 274–82.

9. Ibid., 119.

10. Frederick Douglass, "Oration in Memory of Abraham Lincoln," *Frederick Douglass: Selected Speeches and Writings*, ed. Philip S. Foner (Chicago: Lawrence Hill Books, 1999), 619.

11. Savage, *Standing Soldiers, Kneeling Slaves*, 114.

12. Ibid., 95, 96.

13. Ibid., 97.

14. Ibid., 118.

15. Ibid.

16. Boime argues that when Douglass identified Lincoln as a "son of toil," he "courageously attempted to recuperate Lincoln for the less privileged sectors of American society." *The Unveiling of the National Icons*, 256. Given the overall thrust of Douglass's oration, this conclusion seems unwarranted.

17. James A. Colaiaco writes of the challenge confronting Douglass: "to deliver a speech that both praised what should be praised and criticized what had to be criticized." Colaiaco, *Frederick Douglass and the Fourth of July* (New York: Palgrave Macmillan, 2006), 194–95.

18. Douglass, "Oration," 616.

19. Boime argues that Douglass is reminding the Grant administration about the effect of "lingering discrimination" on full emancipation. If so, it's a gentle reminder. Boime, *The Unveiling of the National Icons*, 256.

20. Colaiaco notes: "As the nation paused to give honor to a revered president, Douglass was saddened by the limitations of Lincoln's legacy." *Frederick Douglass and the Fourth of July*, 198.

21. Douglass, "Oration," 618.

A "Humble Offering"

22. Ibid., 619.
23. Ibid., 618.
24. Ibid.
25. Ibid.
26. Merrill D. Peterson's account of the memorial attends to Douglass's ambivalent oration, but doesn't appreciate that Douglass's narrative of Lincoln's presidency might affect an overall assessment of his "greatness." Douglass's oration involves more than "pierc[ing] clouds of sentimental rhetoric" for "Negroes." See Peterson, *Lincoln in American Memory* (Oxford: Oxford University Press, 1994), 59, 60.
27. Douglass, "Oration," 618–19.
28. Colaiaco, *Frederick Douglass and the Fourth of July*, 195.
29. Douglass, "The Inaugural Address," *Selected Speeches and Writings*, 432.
30. Ibid., 432–33.
31. Ibid., 433.
32. Douglass, "Oration," 619.
33. Ibid.
34. Ibid., 620.
35. Ibid, 619.
36. Ibid. Douglass's historically sensitive analysis reveals an aspect of contextualization that may not receive much attention, especially regarding the commemoration of great political figures. Assessments of such figures may be explained, even enhanced by contextualizing them, that is, by not holding them to current standards or expectations. But insofar as great figures are to be considered great because they overcome or redefine the contexts in which they find themselves placed, contextualization can also diminish them. After all, even if they are reflections of their time and place and thus should not be expected to be anything more, others in the same circumstances found the wherewithal to transcend the norms and standards of their day, even reject them, and push the country in a new direction.
37. Ibid., 620.
38. Colaiaco observes that "Douglass had come to see Lincoln in a better light, cognizant of the important distinction in politics between the 'is' and the 'ought.' Political limitations had constrained the president. . . . Douglass understood that politics, especially in a democracy with a multitude of interests, is the art of achieving the possible." But Douglass does more than recognize the roots of Lincoln's pragmatism, as we will see. Colaiaco, *Frederick Douglass and the Fourth of July*, 200, 201.
39. Douglass, "Oration," 621.
40. Ibid.
41. Ibid., 623. This claim is consistent with what Douglass said in extemporaneous remarks at the Rochester City Hall eleven years earlier on the day Lincoln was murdered.
42. Ibid., 624.
43. Ibid., 623.
44. Douglass concludes his oration by asserting that Lincoln was killed—refining what he said just sentences before when speaking of the pointlessness of the

assassination—"because of his fidelity to union and liberty." Douglass does not address, except along racial lines, Lincoln's great ability to sacrifice liberty for the cause of union.

45. In the Rochester City Hall speech Douglass reminded his audience that Lincoln's death was a moment to recall the treason of Robert E. Lee and his cohorts and call to mind the blood on their hands. Douglass did so given what he took to be Lee's inordinate and inexplicable popularity at the time of Lincoln's killing: "We were manifesting almost as much gratitude to Gen. Lee for surrendering as to Gen. Grant for compelling him to surrender!" Douglass, "Our Martyred President," *The Portable Frederick Douglass*, ed. John Stauffer and Henry Louis Gates Jr. (New York: Penguin Classics, 2016), 362.

Chapter Four

Lincoln's Persistent Racial Ambivalence

Colonization

> As to the method by which this difficult work is to be effected, if permitted to be done by ourselves, I have seen no proposition so expedient on the whole, as that of emancipation of those born after a given day, and of their education and expatriation at a proper age. This would give time for a gradual extinction of that species of labour.
>
> —Thomas Jefferson, "Letter to Edward Coles"

> Why should they not go? Here they are in the lowest state of social gradation—aliens—political—moral—social aliens, though natives. There, they would be in the midst of their friends and their kindred, at home, though born in a foreign land, and elevated above the natives of the country, as much as they are degraded here below the other classes of the community.
>
> —Henry Clay, "Speech before the American Colonization Society"

If Steven Spielberg's *Lincoln* is the cinematic counterpart to the Lincoln Memorial at the west end of the Mall, then Eric Foner's *The Fiery Trial: Abraham Lincoln and American Slavery* could be considered its authorized intellectual biography. While Spielberg's two-and-a-half-hour epic happily canonizes the sixteenth president, Foner's four-hundred-plus-page treatment renders Lincoln all the more admirable for his various limitations overcome. While Spielberg eschews any ambiguity when it comes to presenting Lincoln, who appears as a master retail politician with an unquestioned moral core, Foner places Lincoln squarely in historical context in order to address the vagaries of his short-lived but event-filled political career. This is not to say that Spielberg and Foner don't end up in roughly the same essentially patriotic place. It is to say that Foner's Lincoln does justice to its subject by looking at him as much as possible in the round, while Spielberg's Lincoln begins and ends in transcendence.

Foner offers a narrative history of Lincoln's relationship to slavery that charts his evolution on the subject.[1] Though clearly a man of his times and a reflection of many of the racial prejudices of his day, Lincoln's capacity for growth is what Foner finds most noteworthy and impressive. Ready to challenge any existing state of affairs, Lincoln's attitude toward and positions on slavery were mobile, always on the move, responding and adapting to contemporary social and political developments as well as to rival understandings of the issue, whether these came from abolitionists, apologists, or advocates. Lincoln's political stances were likewise on the move, susceptible to shifts and alterations. Foner places Lincoln's segues within a larger progressive framework, with Lincoln surmounting prior limitations or shortcomings in his thinking and therefore in his proposals, policies, and actions. Thus Foner's Lincoln is another version of the sixteenth president as a self-made man who labored to achieve the greatness America would come to recognize, appreciate, admire, honor, and commemorate. Foner may not romanticize Lincoln, but his treatment of him closely parallels heroization.

Indeed Lincoln's pronouncements and positions on slavery shifted during his career in public life and politics. Foner's account suggests revisions were the product of a gradual awakening and sophistication in moral terms as Lincoln came to appreciate and understand the problematic character of many of his presumptions and long-held beliefs.[2] His policies would correspondingly change—for the better, of course—which meant that a new world of possibilities more closely aligned with America's professed ideals became possible. Lincoln and America would shadow one another, amending themselves in tandem. This kind of celebratory and congratulatory narrative possesses considerable appeal and enjoys widespread acceptance (it reflects and reinforces the immortal Lincoln ensconced on the Mall in Washington, D.C.). Insofar as it constructs a Lincoln flattering to America's sense of its own exceptionalism, however, it should be subjected to strict scrutiny—for democracy's sake.

The suspicion here is that Lincoln's (alleged) metamorphosis, given its predominantly reactive character, is better described as a series of contingent shifts and maneuvers in response to larger national events convulsing the country, which means they do not necessarily entail a larger process of moral enlightenment and growth. As Lincoln proceeded from one position to the next, he often did so grudgingly, in minimalist fashion, as if necessarily bowing to the pressure of inescapable forces beyond his control—but only to a point. What's more, while publicly advocating for new positions that suggested the country was moving in a more inclusive direction, he would continue to hold—and even promote—positions, often behind the scenes, that would take the country in the opposite direction. Change was effectively thrust upon him.[3] Foner's story of evolution gives the impression that Lincoln is deeply enmeshed in a process of self-generated self-overcoming as he sheds and leaves behind racial prejudices that cannot withstand rational critique. This forms a key part of the myth of the self-made man in its later stages. Instead, Lincoln seems to relinquish this or that prejudice and affirm a more egalitarian standpoint while nevertheless clinging to a racialist perspective that he cannot abandon. It's not that Lincoln repeatedly takes two steps forward and one back, which results in positive gains overall. It's more that Lincoln routinely hedges his bets, which might insulate him from the fallout, whether real or feared, of any political miscalculations.

Moreover, Lincoln's writings on slavery evince great concern about the character of the American republic. This is not a question of making preservation of the Union his principal ambition. It is about American political identity. No political community is or can be perfect, but America understands itself to be forever obligated to more fully realize its founding ideals and bring political reality into alignment with them ("in Order to form a more perfect Union"). In this discursive context, Lincoln does not oppose slavery by delineating the everyday horror, cruelty, and sadism inflicted upon its millions of victims. First and foremost slavery is problematic because it's a stain on the image of the American polity, exposing its hypocrisy and fraudulence, and thus jeopardizing (what should be) its rightful standing in the world. There is a kind of narcissism at work in this preoccupation, which is essentially a concern about the (white) self. It is not a concern about (black) others, in this case the human beings wrongly subjected to radical evil for purposes of exploitation and self-interest, however ideologically grounded the subjection might also be. It's not that political communities are wrong to be concerned with the status and standing of their political identities. Moral reflexivity is indispensable. Rather, their moral and political concerns need to be discriminating. For example, the political subject that performs evil is not morally equivalent to the human subject that suffers it. A polity may experience injury as a result of its own actions, but self-inflicted harm does not enjoy equal moral concern to the harm inflicted on others.

Lincoln's commitment to colonization can be traced in his major addresses throughout his career. This was no mere flirtation. It was a deeply held social and political conviction that did not lend itself to straightforward shedding or abandonment, even in the face of enormous criticism and opposition that crossed racial lines. That it was a commitment he shared with his two greatest heroes, Jefferson and Clay, should not be underestimated either. This is one reason to start a review of Lincoln's writings on colonization with Henry

Clay. That said, Lincoln's commitment to colonization also reflects the political ethos discussed in chapter 1: the politics of elimination. Rather than deal with the profound complications and entanglements of a postemancipation and, later, postwar world, where questions of citizenship, rights, and power-sharing (among other things) would be difficult to sort out, Lincoln (and the United States) could obviate the need even to address them by cleansing the continent of the freed slave's troublesome presence. This presence was so troublesome that Lincoln persisted in his scheme though it never managed to encompass anything more than a tiny fraction of African Americans. For Lincoln it seemed that the removal of even a small number of blacks was considered a positive good in and of itself.[4]

HENRY CLAY'S EULOGY (JULY 1852)

Lincoln salutes Henry Clay as a lover of liberty, noting that Clay was born in 1776, the year the United States, then "a few feeble and oppressed colonies," and against all odds, declared its independence from Great Britain.[5] Lincoln recapitulates Clay's long and distinguished career of public service, where his dedication to liberty manifested itself at home and internationally. Clay, for example, supported struggles for freedom in South America and Greece.[6] But it is the eulogy's conclusion that demands attention.

"Having been led to allude to domestic slavery so frequently already," Lincoln says, "I am unwilling to close without referring more particularly to Mr. Clay's views and conduct in regard to it."[7] What does Lincoln feel compelled to communicate? Though Clay was a slave owner, he was in principle opposed to slavery. This opposition can be seen in his earliest and latest public efforts, "separated by a period of more than fifty years," to achieve gradual emancipation in Kentucky.[8] Clay was a moderate who rejected the extremism of Northern abolitionists and Southern fanatics alike. Each would see America's founding undone rather than abandon their sacred principles. The former rejected the Constitution for its complicity with slavery. The latter mocked the Declaration of Independence for its commitment to equality.

Lincoln finds the assault on equality particularly troubling. It is a recent and disturbing development in the South. To counter it, Lincoln turns to Clay and, in a curious twist, a speech Clay made in 1827 to the American Colonization Society. In it, Clay denies that the society has any intention of interfering with slavery where it currently exists. He even refers to the "obligations of obedience" of slaves. As for the property of slave owners, the society has no power or desire to affect it. Rather, if the society had its way, "the execution of its scheme would augment instead of diminishing the value of the property left behind."[9] Colonization, in other words, would benefit Southern slave owners. But those who reproach the society would rather extinguish liberty throughout the nation, including in the human soul, its logical terminus, than see slavery abolished.[10]

According to Lincoln, the society was dear to Clay, "one of the most cherished objects of his direct care and consideration." He died its president. Lincoln attributes to Clay the belief that colonization was "no demerit in the society, that it tended to relieve slave-holders from the troublesome presence of free negroes [sic]." This is not all. Clay thought it morally fitting that Africa's children should be returned to it. They were "torn from [the land] by the ruthless hand of fraud and violence." Nevertheless, slavery did them extraordinary good, for it exposed them to "the rich fruits of religion, civilization, law and liberty." This means that slaves would return to their native land better than they were when they arrived here. Clay suggests that this transformation may have been the work of an inscrutable God. Who else could convert a crime into a blessing for "that most unfortunate portion of the globe?"[11]

Lincoln enthusiastically joins Clay in his ruminations, which give new meaning to American exceptionalism. Colonization would not be the product of racial animus and distaste but the generous gift of one people to another. America can deploy its power for good. "This suggestion of the possible ultimate redemption of the African race and African continent, was made twenty-five years ago. Every succeeding year has added strength to the hope of its realization. May it indeed be realized!"[12] Rather than think through the possible ramifications, especially for blacks, of colonization, Lincoln then warns the United States that it should learn from the example of Pharaoh's Egypt. What happens to those who cling to a captive people who have served them for hundreds of years? Disease and death. "May like disasters never befall us!"[13] Lincoln can imagine no better ending to the slavery agitation than the combination of abolition and colonization. This would fulfill Henry Clay's most ardent wish. Lincoln's, too.[14]

LINCOLN AT PEORIA (OCTOBER 1854)

Following passage of the Kansas-Nebraska Act in 1854, which repealed the Missouri Compromise of 1820, Lincoln reentered the public domain. A speech he gave in Peoria, Illinois, in October of 1854 rejuvenated his political career, which at the national level had consisted of one term in the House of Representatives. With the repeal of the compromise, slavery again convulsed the nation. According to the terms of the Kansas-Nebraska Act, slavery was no longer automatically prohibited in states entering the Union north of thirty-six degrees, thirty minutes north latitude. The people living there would themselves determine whether they would join the United States as a free or a slave state. Stephen Douglas, the driving force behind the act even though he once wholeheartedly supported the compromise, christened this new approach popular sovereignty. It disrupted the precarious yet stable accommodations that had been worked out regarding slavery following the Louisiana Purchase in 1803 and the (misnamed) Mexican-American War of 1846–1848. In both of these episodes, each party to the contest over slavery's extension had achieved some of what it wanted. Neither side was content, but neither was willing to jeopardize the Union in pursuit of its ultimate ambition. Douglas's Kansas-Nebraska Act, on the other hand, needlessly threw the country into life-and-death turmoil. This does not mean that Lincoln considered slavery anything other than an intractable problem.

He did. Thus Lincoln engages in a fascinating thought experiment in the Peoria speech. After agreeing with the South that "they are no more responsible for the origin of slavery, than we," he also concedes "that it is very difficult to get rid of it, in any satisfactory way."[15] He even makes the remarkable claim that if the roles were reversed, if slavery existed in the North, they would be doing just what the South is doing. While insisting that he will not blame Southerners for "not doing what I should not know how to do myself," that is, getting rid of slavery, Lincoln nevertheless imagines a number of possible solutions.[16] What comes to mind *first*? He would free and immediately deport ("send") them to Liberia, which he describes, without comment, as "their own native land." While Lincoln thinks highly of this solution, especially "in the long run," he recognizes that it could not be put into effect now.[17] There are not enough money and ships to execute the task, however desirable the result. What's more, if they were shipped to Africa they would not survive. Deportation would constitute a death sentence. Death apparently marks the limit of Lincoln's willingness to exercise power. Violence does not. He would send them whether or not they want to go. If they resisted, they would presumably be coerced. Lincoln's favored solution, then, would effectively reenslave the people he had just liberated. Once accomplished, the expatriated Americans would live in exile from the land where they were born, raised, and lived. Lincoln would have eliminated them from the political scene. Decisionism predates his presidency.

Nevertheless, simultaneous emancipation and colonization is Lincoln's solution of choice. This is a remarkable position for Lincoln to embrace, if just in theory.[18] He has already ridiculed Douglas for his supposed neutrality on the question of slavery. "This declared indifference, but as I must think, covert real zeal for the spread of slavery, I cannot but hate."[19] Why? Because of what Lincoln calls "the monstrous injustice of slavery itself."[20] Despite this righteous characterization of slavery, Lincoln does not provide any details on the exact nature of the injustice. What's more, Lincoln insists that the status of the new territories regarding slavery is a matter of concern not just to the people of these would-be states but to the nation as a whole. Insofar as territories are a resource to be exploited to full advantage they pose a national question—in racial terms. "The whole nation is interested that the best use shall be made of these territories. We want them for the homes of free white people. This they cannot be, to any considerable extent, if slavery shall be planted within them. Slave states are places for poor white people to remove FROM; not to remove TO. New free States are the places for poor people to go to and better their condition. For this use, the nation needs these territories."[21] Lincoln's white colonization plans thus mimic his relocation plans for blacks. The extension of slavery would make it more difficult to get them out of the country. In addition, Lincoln cites the real harm that the extension of slavery into the territories would do to the fundamental liberties of white people. If Nebraskans were allowed to decide the question of slavery themselves and then voted for it, they would be able to enter the Union, thanks to the electoral college, with greater electoral power than northern whites. Lincoln finds this subversion of freedom intolerable.

Given Lincoln's preoccupation with the racial composition of the country, he quickly moves to what appears to be a greater concern about the effect that slavery has on the nation's "republican example [and] its just influence in the world."[22] In addition, America's enemies can "taunt" it for hypocrisy. This is a self-regarding luxury that only a white nation can afford. He even worries about the deleterious effect that the institution of slavery has on slave owners, the "really good men amongst ourselves" who are forced "into an open war with the very fundamental principles of civil liberty," and have their behavior reduced to nothing but the pursuit of self-interest.[23] Thus, it might have been helpful if Lincoln had taken a moment to reflect on the monstrous injustices of slavery. If he had, he might have realized that it involved more than the denial of equality and the deprivation of freedom. It involved more than a social system of domination, oppression, and exploitation enforced by private sadism, violence, and cruelty backed up by the armed might of the state. It also involved stealing a country from those who built it, which is one reason why emancipation followed by colonization would have constituted yet one more of slavery's monstrous injustices.

Lincoln would have been complicit in letting Southern slave owners reap and keep the rewards of their morally indefensible institution. It never occurs to Lincoln that many, perhaps most of the people he would not just prefer but would like to deport are also Americans, born and raised in the United

States. Africa is not their native land—America is their home. Lincoln cannot determine the identity of others by geographical ascription.

This blindness reflects Lincoln's attitudes toward Indians, Native Americans, who were repeatedly colonized, forcibly relocated from the eastern and southern United States. Lincoln shared much of the country's indifference to the ultimate fate of Indians. The important thing was to remove them so the United States could expand and remain as white as possible. Indian removal policy concerned itself very little with whether or not Indians would be able to survive in their new "homes." Likewise, if Lincoln could have managed to secure sufficient funds and acquire enough ships to send newly freed slaves to Africa, would he have done so if they did not all land in a day and survived more than ten? Lincoln is evidently thinking in terms of what minimal provisions would need to be made for colonization to be deemed possible—not successful, whatever that might mean, but possible.

Lincoln also considers emancipation accompanied by a grant of social and political equality. He has no argument to make against this solution, but asserts "my own feelings will not admit of this."[24] Even if this were not the case, the great majority of white people share Lincoln's prejudices. This affective fact makes any objection rooted in justice irrelevant. Converting a majority sentiment into a "universal feeing," which may inadvertently indicate the intensity of his own feelings, Lincoln insists that such feelings, "whether well or ill-founded, cannot be safely disregarded."[25] This renders equality out of the question. Lincoln does not specify which of his feelings disallows black equality, but they are of sufficient visceral strength that colonization is the preferred policy. This predilection should come as no surprise. Earlier in the speech, Lincoln praised Jefferson for ensuring, through the Ordinance of 1787, that the Northwest Territory would not countenance slavery, thus making it "the happy home of teeming millions of free, white, prosperous people, and no slave among them."[26] Lincoln did not write "no black among them," but blacks were scarce and often, as in Lincoln's Illinois, unwelcome.

After Lincoln demolishes the argument that self-government entails allowing each would-be state to decide for itself whether it will allow slavery in its confines, he reflects on what the Kansas-Nebraska Act means for the country. It aggravates "the only thing which ever endangers the Union."[27] He then insists that Douglas's initiative disrupted an almost idyllic period in the country's history, at least for white people. "When it came upon us, all was peace and quiet. The nation was looking to the forming of new bonds of Union; and a long course of peace and prosperity seemed to lie before us." Lincoln can imagine nothing disturbing this pleasant prospect, except the Kansas-Nebraska Act's repeal of the Missouri Compromise. The matter had already been solved in "every inch of territory we owned."[28] What Douglas and his accomplices have done is not only place the Union in jeopardy, but effectively invite a civil war in Nebraska and Kansas, as well as the rest of the country.

Lincoln's assignation of responsibility to Douglas and his accomplices was more than warranted. They needed to be called out, and Lincoln did it. His assessment of the condition of the nation at the time of Douglas's misadventure, however, borders on delusional—unless you can only consider the state of white people in the Union, of course. It's not just that slave rebellions had erupted in Lincoln's lifetime. It's that slavery is not and cannot be a condition of peace and quiet. The daily domination and violence inflicted on human beings, a form of war, is discordant and loud. This is where Lincoln's repeated failures to catalog the intimate horrors of slavery in his public addresses enables him to mischaracterize the social and political circumstances of the country in a way that facilitates his own always already limited response to slavery's evil. Lincoln reentered politics not to eradicate slavery but to oppose its extension. As far as he was concerned, the existing institution of slavery enjoyed the full protection of the law, which he "acknowledge[s] . . . not grudgingly, but fully, and fairly."[29] This is Lincoln's nation of peace and quiet, which also includes, by ignoring, American Indians, a theme developed in the next section of the chapter.

Given Lincoln's analysis of the Kansas-Nebraska Act and his assessment of slavery expressed in it, what does he propose as a response to monstrous injustice? The restoration of the Missouri Compromise. Lincoln calls on the South to join him in this endeavor, to emulate the spirit of prior generations that were able to reach compromises to keep the Union together and united. "The peace of the nation is as dear to them as to us."[30] Earlier in the speech Lincoln had made a point of claiming that he harbors "no prejudice against the Southern people."[31] Here he vindicates that claim. How wrong could any one person be as Lincoln is here? If the South had answered his call, what might have been the result? According to Lincoln, "it would be worth to the nation a hundred years' peace and prosperity."[32] That also amounts to one hundred more years of monstrous injustice. Lincoln always insists, and this is a sign of his supposed tragic pragmatism, that he "would consent to any GREAT evil, to avoid a GREATER one."[33] How his beloved Union can countenance human suffering and sacrifice on that scale as a price for its existence he does not say. If slavery still existed in 1954, surely even Lincoln would have to ask himself what it means to say that the country aspires to realize the principles of equality articulated in the Declaration of Independence.

Foner describes Lincoln's response to the Kansas-Nebraska Act as anticlimactic. It might be better characterized as schizophrenic, especially when one considers that Lincoln thinks the spread of slavery to Nebraska, however objectionable, is, taken in context, relatively trivial. The Slave Power has much grander ambitions: "With them, Nebraska alone is a small matter—to establish a principle, for FUTURE USE, is what they particularly desire. That future use is to be the planting of slavery wherever in the wide world, local and unorganized opposition cannot prevent it."[34] The existing institution of slavery cannot rest content with the status quo. It must expand to survive—hence its global ambitions. Compromise is impossible with this kind of enemy. Lincoln seems to understand this when he writes, "Let no one be deceived. The spirit of seventy-six and the spirit of Nebraska, are utter antagonisms; and the former is being rapidly replaced by the latter."[35]

Still, Lincoln appeals to the patriotism of his "fellow countrymen—Americans south, as well as north," to stop this madness. To convince them he returns to white political self-regard. "Our republican robe is soiled, and trailed in the dust. Let us repurify it. Let us turn and wash it white, in the spirit, if not the blood, of the Revolution."[36] Lincoln's metaphors betray his brutal vision for America, which reflects his commitment to colonization. This commitment, in turn, matches the commitment of another one of his heroes, Jefferson, to rid the country of blacks. Jefferson would repurify the nation and wash it white by removing all the children of slaves from the country, making it inevitable, according to Jefferson, that blacks here would die off and eventually disappear. And even Lincoln has to agree, "in point of mere fact," that the U.S. "government was made for the white people and not for the negroes."[37]

THE KANSAS-NEBRASKA ACT AND INDIANS

Lincoln's condemnation of the Kansas-Nebraska Act, as noted, revolved around his opposition to slavery's extension in American territories, which, in turn, would not only give this evil institution a new grip on life, it could lead to the nationalization of slavery. Contrary to the founders' belief, the public mind could no longer rest content that slavery was on course for ultimate extinction, even if it might take generations. Lincoln was willing to tolerate slavery's existing presence in American life if it meant saving the Union. Despite the grave moral flaws (the intolerable sacrifices imposed on blacks) of this approach, Lincoln tried to combine principle and pragmatism in his opposition to slavery.

The Kansas-Nebraska Act's racial implications, however, exceeded the question of slavery. Regardless of slavery's final disposition in either state, it presupposed and engendered the elimination of Native peoples from their homes, thus enabling whites to relocate and settle the now-emptied land.

Lincoln, however, shows no concern for principle of any kind regarding the extension of white domination over Indian land and the denationalization of Native peoples. This would not be the first time that Indians had been forcibly dispossessed. "The single biggest factor affecting American Indian life leading up to the Civil War was the constant threat of their removal from their homelands. In 1830, the United States Congress passed the Indian Removal Act which gave the President the authorization to exchange unorganized public-domain land in the Trans-Mississippi West for Indian land in the East. The Indian nations 'emigrating' would *allegedly* receive perpetual title to these new lands as well as compensation and assistance in emigrating."[38] This project, implemented through war or the threat of war, affected nearly one hundred thousand Indians up and down the Atlantic coast and in the Northeast. The violence and death toll, in the tens of thousands, did not concern the United States.[39] What's more, dispossession set its own example.

Thanks to the Kansas-Nebraska Act, Indian land suffered severe contraction. Native peoples were perpetually required to accept offers they couldn't refuse. The Delaware People, which had been forced to move from southwestern Missouri to Kansas, would now have to leave Kansas as well.[40] The nation's attention, however, was focused on what would happen to white people. In the case of the formation of the Kansas and Nebraska territories, this reorganization famously led to a dress rehearsal of the Civil War. The term "bleeding Kansas" refers to white Northern and Southern factions fighting each other for control of the future states. It also referred to "a new era of frontier violence and intimidation, especially directed at the Indians of eastern Kansas . . . aimed at forcing [them] out of the region from Kansas City to Topeka." For some even this removal was not sufficient. In the 1860 presidential campaign candidate William H. Seward, then governor of New York, called for Indian removal south of Kansas, too. He was not unique in this regard.[41] Simply put, "America's idea of progress had no place for Indians."[42] Lincoln shared this sentiment. He did not raise any questions about, let alone objections to, the violent implications of the Kansas-Nebraska Act for Indians. He objected to slavery's extension, but he did so at least in part to keep blacks out of the territories and preserve them for whites, a racial motivation impossible to deny given his silence over the ethnic cleansing of these territories. Lincoln contributed to the consensus that deemed Indian removal the condition of white expansion and advancement.[43] The nation was not removing reds to let in blacks.

Despite this kind of treatment, more than twenty thousand Indians fought in the Civil War (on both sides). The principal motivation was straightforward: not just self-interest but self-preservation. "In the deepest irony of all, many fought because they believed it was their last best hope to halt a genocide that had begun in the east in the early seventeenth century, one that continued throughout the Trail of Tears westward in the 1830s, and exploded again after the California Gold Rush of 1849. Yet the Civil War, rather than the last best hope, proved to be a final nail in the coffin in Indian efforts to stop the tide of American expansion."[44] From the moment Confederate guns were trained on Fort Sumter to the end of the Civil War, including "the years of heaviest fighting," the Union pursued military and economic policies that expropriated Indians and destroyed their ways of life.[45] In Kansas this meant that despite the loyal service of many Delaware Indians during the war, nothing "could save them or their lands."[46] They would not even be compensated for the relatively trivial (compared, say, to the overall war budget) losses they suffered from Confederate retaliation. What's more, once the North had triumphed, "Interior department officials advocated the immediate removal of the Delaware from the entire state of Kansas."[47]

Lincoln, of course, objected to slavery, and he did so in part because it amounted to a form of theft. He did not think it right that one person should live at the expense of another's hard work. He preferred to let blacks alone, which is not to say that he considered them equals, certainly not at the time of the Kansas-Nebraska Act. For Lincoln slavery was also objectionable because it was gratuitous. There was no reason for its existence. Americans often laid blame for the institution on their British forebears. If not for them, we would not be saddled with this terrible institution and the agitations accompanying it. With Indians, the relationship was not one of chattel slavery. Whites did not own reds. At the same time, Lincoln could not let Indians alone in the same way he advocated that whites let blacks be. It's not because he planned to colonize blacks later. It's that the white-Indian relation was anything but gratuitous. It operated in the realm of necessity. Whites could easily do without black property or labor, but whites could not do without Indian land, or, from the white perspective, the lands that Indians occupied. The nation's condition of possibility was Indian removal and its continued expansion also rested on Native dispossession. Leaving Indians alone would stunt America's rightful growth across the continent.

For the American nation fully to realize itself, any and all impediments had to be eliminated. Whether "western" lands claimed by states along the eastern seaboard, lands acquired from France in the Louisiana Purchase, or lands taken in the military conquest of Mexico, the United States assumed that the continent belonged to it and it alone. Lincoln, for example, applauds Jefferson for Virginia's approach to its western territory. It ceded the lands that would become Ohio, Indiana, Illinois, Michigan, and Wisconsin on the condition that slavery be barred from them. Lincoln never questions the legitimacy of Virginia's claim to these lands, let alone whether it could cede them to the national government (or dispose of them in any fashion). Lincoln simply assumes ownership. Accordingly, the Native peoples who lived there were not part of or party to the governmental transaction between Virginia and the national state, to make it "the happy home of teeming millions of free, white prosperous people, and no slave among them." The assumption was that there would be no Indian among them either. Lincoln does not need to state it since no one (no one white, anyway) would disagree.

As Lincoln narrates the history of America's acquisition of western lands, whether through money or war, he either presumes the legitimacy of territorial transactions orchestrated by white imperial power indifferent to the presence of other peoples or he sanctions the right of the country to take what it wants from another sovereign nation thanks to its superior force. Native peoples did not exist in America's calculations. Erasure wasn't even required. It was pre-given. Thus Lincoln writes of the Nebraska territory that for decades after its acquisition from France it was "substantially an uninhabited country, but now [early 1850s] emigration to, and settlement within it began to take place."[48] In the same manner, Lincoln considered Iowa and Minnesota "wilderness," which means that prior to settlement it was considered empty land ready for white arrival. Lincoln can recognize the property rights of slave owners over other human beings, but he cannot recognize the land rights of Indians over their own territory.

This approach enables Lincoln to speak of America's western additions as "new country," as if no one preceded it and already considered it their home. He can express great consternation at the Kansas-Nebraska Act because its potential consequences might include a war between the states, but he evinces no concern for actual violence done to Native peoples before the act (in California, for example) or the new violence that will be done to them as a result of it. The mere possibility of white bloodshed trumps real Indian death. While Lincoln worries that America's republican example in the world will be tainted by slavery and leave the country open to the charge of hypocrisy by its enemies, he has no such republican worry regarding Indians.

Lincoln cannot see that America's republican example was already damaged beyond repair because of its perpetual wars against and colonization of Indians. Lincoln insists that he extends the sacred principle of self-government not just to individuals but to "communities of men," but this does not and cannot include them. Lincoln considers Negroes men, but not Indians. That Lincoln does not consider them men may account for his perception of America before the Kansas-Nebraska Act as "all . . . peace and quiet." It may also account for Lincoln's silence about his feelings toward Indians. He speaks for "the great mass of white people" when he says he does not consider blacks social and political equals and would not make them such. Lincoln makes a point of saying it because it is a possibility he wants to foreclose. There is no such possibility with Indians, which is why he does not even have to bother denying it. Nor does Lincoln speak of America's first colonization project: Indians. Just as slavery cannot be allowed to take root in Nebraska and Kansas ("we want them for the homes of free white people"), Indians cannot be allowed to remain there. They were relocated once. They can be relocated again. They can always be relocated. And unlike freed slaves they do not have to be asked, merely told. Relocation also means that Lincoln does not need to conduct mass executions numbering in the hundreds. Less visually and emotionally spectacular but equally efficient mechanisms are available for Indian reduction.

DRED SCOTT (JUNE 1857)

Lincoln reiterated his commitment to colonization in the pointed speech he delivered in Springfield, Illinois, in June 1857, in response to the Dred Scott decision that had been announced the previous March. Chief Justice Roger Taney's expansive ruling further roiled the nation, still reeling from the Kansas-Nebraska Act. In this address, Lincoln declares both his disagreement with the Scott decision and his commitment to have the court overrule it, but he offers no resistance to it. In fact, he goes out of his way to reject any notion of resistance to the Supreme Court, deeming it an act of revolution.

Nevertheless, Lincoln, early on, corrects Taney for the historical record. Taney's claim about the racial character of the founding cannot stand. "Chief Justice Taney, in delivering the opinion of the majority of the Court, insists at great length that negroes were no part of the people who made, or for whom was made, the Declaration of Independence, or the Constitution of the United States."[49] Citing dissenting Justice Benjamin Curtis's opinion, Lincoln "reminds" his audience that "in five of the then thirteen states, to wit, New Hampshire, Massachusetts, New York, New Jersey, and North Carolina, free negroes were voters, and, in proportion to their numbers, had the same part in making the Constitution that the white people had."[50] Here Lincoln credits blacks with a founding role in American politics, a role that augments the nation-building slaves performed in the economic and structural realms. Yet Lincoln does not treat any blacks with the respect and even awe that he treats other founders.

Lincoln's address is a response to Stephen Douglas's speech in Springfield two weeks earlier. Lincoln's disagreement with Douglas revolves around their respective readings of the Declaration. Rather than engage the Dred Scott issue on the merits, however, Douglas changes the subject and levels what Lincoln considers a slanderous charge that he feels compelled to answer. While Douglas "finds the Republicans insisting that the Declaration of Independence includes ALL men, black as well as white; and forthwith he boldly denies that it includes negroes at all," he then proceeds with the accusation that those who read the Declaration as Lincoln does are guilty of desiring "an indiscriminate amalgamation of the white and black races."[51]

According to Lincoln, Douglas's motive for making such a scurrilous charge—trying to capitalize on the visceral feeling that "there is a natural disgust in the minds of nearly all white people" to such mixing—is purely political. Recently two of his closest political allies in Illinois, James Shields and William Richardson, were, "politically speaking, successively tried, convicted, and executed, for an offense [the Kansas-Nebraska Act] not their own, but his. And now he sees his own case, standing next on the docket for trial."[52] Shields lost his reelection bid for the U.S. Senate in 1854 and Richardson was defeated in his gubernatorial run in 1856. Douglas hopes to avoid the same electoral death with his race-baiting. Lincoln won't have any of it, but his response is anything but principled. "Now I protest against that counterfeit logic which concludes that, because I do not want a black woman for a *slave* I must necessarily want her for a *wife*. I need not have her for either, I can just leave her alone."[53]

When Lincoln writes that *nearly* all white people feel natural disgust toward interracial intimacy, he might be suggesting he is not among them. Yet Lincoln and Douglas concur on this score. "But Judge Douglas is especially horrified at the thought of the mixing blood by the white and black races: agreed for once—a thousand times agreed. There are white men enough to marry all the white women, and black men enough to marry all the black women; and so let them be married. On this point we fully agree with the Judge."[54] Lincoln actually outdoes Douglas in his natural disgust. For Lincoln "slavery is the greatest source of amalgamation."[55] Lincoln even converts the Dred Scott case into "a strong test as to which party most favors amalgamation."[56] According to Lincoln, his answer to this problem is superior to Douglas's. "A separation of the races is the only perfect preventive of amalgamation but as all immediate separation is impossible the next best thing is to *keep* them apart *where* they are not already together. If white and black people never get together in Kansas they will never mix blood in Kansas."[57]

What's more, despite his denial of carnal knowledge with the black woman, Lincoln cannot leave her alone. He has other, very definite plans for her (and the black man). Thus immediate separation may be impossible, but separation represents perfection for Lincoln, a pragmatist who supposedly eschews any such notion in politics. Separation as the "perfect preventive" reflects the natural disgust toward blacks that Lincoln cultivates. He concludes by arguing that separation can and "must be effected by colonization."[58] Unfortunately, no political party is making an effort in this direction. Lincoln does not pretend to speak for all Republicans or the Party, but he insists that his position is a popular one and that the GOP's "chief plank in their platform—opposition to the spread of slavery—is most favorable to their separation."[59] It's as if Lincoln is suggesting that many Republicans favor colonization whether they know it or not. The only thing standing in the way of this policy is lack of political will, which can be easily solved. "Will springs from the two elements of moral sense and self-interest. Let us be brought to believe it is morally right, and, at the same time, favorable to, or, at least, not against, our interest, to transfer the African to his native clime, and we shall find a way to do it, however great the task [remaining before us] may be."[60] Lincoln still refuses to consider black people Americans and the United States as their native land, for that would make the formation of the will needed to see them removed more problematic. He prefers to imagine them leaving the United States as the Israelites left Egypt and slavery—all together.

Lincoln's disavowal of a politics of resistance at the beginning of the address becomes more remarkable still by its end. He considers Douglas's Democratic Party the one "which most favors amalgamation."[61] His evidence? If the Dred Scott case had been rightly decided, Scott, his wife, and his two daughters would have been declared citizens, which would have effected its own separation. "Could we have had our way, the chances of these black girls, ever mixing their blood with that of white people, would have been diminished at least to the extent that it could not have been without their consent."[62] This is the rare instance where Lincoln alludes to the daily horror and brutality of the institution of slavery, in which masters "can exercise this particular power [rape] which they hold over their female slaves."[63] This power, in turn, leads to forced pregnancy and the birth of "mulattoes in spite of themselves—the very state of case that produces nine tenths of all the mulattoes—all the mixing of blood in the nation."[64] While Lincoln does not accuse Dred Scott's owner—or slave owners in general—with indulging this gruesome sexual will to power, he identifies it as one of slavery's defining characteristics. Yet even the practice of "forced concubinage" is not enough to get Lincoln to act in actual defiance of Dred Scott.[65] This is one example where Lincoln did not theorize, let alone recommend, the kind of creative constitutional thinking he would exercise regarding war powers when he became president.

THE HOUSE DIVIDED (JUNE 1858)

Lincoln's 1858 address to the Illinois Republican State Convention is not just a masterful piece of political theater. It borders on prophecy. Lincoln identifies two alternative futures for America, one in which slavery is extinguished and freedom reigns throughout the nation, the other in which slavery is a living institution in each and every state, "North as well as South."[66] Tracing national turmoil over slavery to the passage of the Kansas-Nebraska Act in 1854, Lincoln argues that America is headed toward a crisis that will finally resolve the slavery question: "'A House divided against itself cannot stand.' I believe that government cannot endure, permanently half slave and half free. I do not expect the Union to be dissolved—I do not expect the house to fall—but I do expect it will cease to be divided. It will become all one thing or all the other."[67] Lincoln thus combines hope and fear—hope that one day American will finally be rid of the evil of slavery; fear that efforts to halt the spread of slavery and ultimately bring about its extinction might fail, or even backfire, and witness its nationalization instead.

For those who might be disinclined to believe Lincoln's prognostication, especially regarding the South's national ambitions for slavery and their chances of success, he offers them an impressive conspiracy theory that neatly brings together major players—and thus institutions—in American government. Lincoln may (or may not) believe the story he tells, but the details are riveting and the effect is incendiary. Lincoln is worried that the country is being slowly put to sleep by Stephen Douglas's doctrine of popular sovereignty, which is accompanied by a professed indifference to the future of slavery in the territories. As long as the people themselves are able to decide whether slavery should exist in their domain, Douglas declares himself satisfied. He wants the rest of the country to join him in this alleged indifference. In this way, the country could continue to live half free, half slave, as it has done since the founding.

Lincoln fears Douglas might succeed, which means he needs to awaken the people from potential slumber and alert them to the danger that lurks behind the reassuring words of Douglas and his coconspirators. Who are the players in this treacherous subterfuge? What are its details? What evidence does Lincoln possess of its existence? Lincoln has an answer to each of these questions. Do not question whether he has the goods: "Let anyone who doubts, carefully contemplate that now almost complete legal combination—piece of *machinery* so to speak. . . . Let him consider not only *what* work the machinery is adapted to do, and *how well* adapted; but also, let him study the *history* of its construction, and trace, if he can, or rather *fail*, if he can, to trace the evidence of design and concert of action, among its chief architects, from the beginning."[68]

The Kansas-Nebraska Act was the conspirators' first move. While Douglas maintained that it would put an end to slavery agitation in the country by letting the people decide its fate in contested territories, it had precisely the opposite effect. In its aftermath, slavery again bitterly split open the nation.

What's more, while the legislation ostensibly left the people in the affected territories "perfectly free to form their domestic institutions in their own way," the authors of the act inserted a suspicious qualifier into its wording that threw doubt on the nature of this perfect freedom. The people were free to do as they chose, "subject only to the Constitution of the United States."[69] What exactly did this formulation mean? Opponents sought clarification and tried to amend the measure so that it explicitly stated that these territories might exclude slavery, should they so decide, but the act's proponents defeated it. The refusal was suspicious. It seemed inconsistent with the very legislation they were promoting and the public reasons given in its defense. There had to be a reason for rejecting it, but what was it? To answer, as they did, that this was a question for the Supreme Court to determine was no answer at all.

While this legislative maneuvering was taking place, Lincoln notes, the Dred Scott case started making its way through the federal courts in Missouri. This was no coincidence. Nor was it a coincidence that the court delayed its decision until after the 1856 election, presumably to assist James Buchanan's candidacy. Buchanan served as President Pierce's ambassador to Great Britain, thus keeping him out of the country as political warfare erupted over the Kansas-Nebraska Act. He had no need to get involved. Still, in his inaugural address, Buchanan urged the country to respect the pending court decision regardless of the outcome. Pierce, for his part, delivered his fourth annual message to Congress and effectively offered a dress rehearsal of the Dred Scott decision yet to come, pronouncing with great authority on the power (or lack thereof) of Congress to legislate regarding the territories (and states).

Admitting that "we cannot absolutely *know* that all these exact adaptations are the result of a preconcert," Lincoln nonetheless insists that "when we see a lot of framed timbers, different portions of which we know have been gotten out at different times and places and by different workmen—Stephen, Franklin, Roger, and James, for instance—and when we see timbers joined together, and see they exactly make the frame of a house or a mill, all the tenons and mortices exactly fitting, and all the lengths and proportions of the different pieces exactly adapted to their respective places, and not a piece too many or too few—not omitting even scaffolding—or, if a single piece be lacking, we can see the place in the frame exactly fitted and prepared to bring such piece in—in *such* a case, we find it impossible not to believe that Stephen and Franklin and Roger and James all understood one another from the beginning, and all worked upon a common *plan* or *draft* drawn up before the first lick was struck."[70] The single piece missing was another Supreme Court decision declaring that states, just like territories, could not keep slaves out of their jurisdictions. A case (*Lemmon v. New York*) working its way through the courts provided Taney with just the opportunity the conspiracy needed to fully nationalize slavery (a need that went unanswered only because the war rendered it moot).

While Lincoln's accusations of conspiracy have drawn great attention, less attention has been paid to his own machinations. What work was Lincoln doing as he exposes the conspiracy? Not just for the immediate Senate campaign, but for his own projects and purposes? Take his approach to Dred Scott. What happens when a slave owner brings his property with him to a free state? Is the slave thereby freed? The national courts will not decide. Rather the courts of the slave states will adjudicate the matter. Lincoln notes the implications: "what Dred Scott's master might lawfully do with Dred Scott, in the free State of Illinois, every other master may lawfully do with any other one, or one *thousand* slaves, or in any other free State."[71] Relying on the racial aversion and animus of his audiences, Lincoln deploys the specter of thousands of slaves relocated to Northern states to pinpoint the nefarious nature of the Scott decision. The thought of the possibility of a mass black presence in the North will not only stoke opposition to Douglas and the conspiracy. It could also help cultivate a sensibility favorably disposed to colonization. Whites might not have given the matter much thought, but Lincoln is doing his own molding of public opinion, something that he can shape and draw upon later. For Lincoln the nationalization of slavery amounts to the nationalization of blacks. He suggests it without declaring it.

David Zarefsky appreciates the rhetorical and political genius of Lincoln's House Divided speech.[72] He also admires Lincoln's skill in positioning himself as a moderate politician. Posing the alternatives as a choice between the nationalization of slavery, on the one hand, or its containment, on the other, Lincoln avoids the pitfalls attached to abolitionism. While Zarefsky rightly identifies Lincoln's determination to counter Douglas's efforts to tranquilize the public regarding slavery's ultimate fate, thus paving the way for a Supreme Court decision that would legalize slavery across the nation, he ignores Lincoln's own efforts to lull the public to sleep.

When Lincoln writes that the nation "will become all one thing or all the other," the second possibility is not a reference to abolition. Zarefsky writes: "The alternative to national slavery, then, was *containment:* keeping the institution within its current limits so that people would think that it *ultimately* would die out."[73] Lincoln believed that "slavery was wrong but that abolition was a drastic act with unacceptable social consequences. Not knowing what else to do, he postponed slavery's demise until the distant future, meanwhile insisting at least that the evil not be allowed to grow."[74] Zarefsky does not indicate that the unacceptable social consequences to which Lincoln alluded pertained to whites and whites alone. The social price that Lincoln could not see whites paying meant the human burden would fall to blacks. White rights and security once again come at black expense. How long would they have to go on paying for so-called unacceptable social consequences? Indefinitely. The distant future knows no exact limit. Zarefsky notes that "Lincoln did not even pose 'ultimate extinction' as one of his two alternatives. He said that the alternative to national slavery was that 'the public mind shall rest in the belief that it was in the course of ultimate extinction.' Not the future act itself, but public opinion that it was forthcoming, would resolve the crisis Lincoln thought the nation had to meet. . . . Moreover, there was a direct correlation between the strength of this public conviction and the length of time that Lincoln was willing to wait. So long as the nation was clear about its basic commitments, he was willing to condone political compromises and long delays in fulfilling them."[75]

No wonder Lincoln had an appreciation for the possibilities of conspiracy in politics. They could be productive. For Lincoln, with slavery's extinction projected into the distant future rather than looming on an approaching horizon, he opens the space he needs to pursue the project of colonization. This is what political compromise and long delays make possible. Colonization also renders, in theory, the charge of abolitionism irrelevant. Black freedom loses its sting to whites in the North if newly freed blacks are to be relocated elsewhere. Lincoln knows that colonization is a minority position within white and black communities, but this reality could be made to change with time—much time—on his side. Containment and colonization thus fit together as perfect complements. If the Slave Power conspiracy combined "public political acts" with "secret designs,"[76] Lincoln's slavery politics mimicked it. He publicly opposed slavery's extension and while specific plans for colonization may not have been deliberately withheld from public view, neither were they well advertised. It was a charged issue, and opponents to it such as Frederick Douglass made their objections known. Lincoln seemed to desire not a conversation on the idea of colonization. Rather he sought a fait accompli.

As Phillip Magness notes, Lincoln doesn't mention colonization publicly following the Emancipation Proclamation, which might (seem to) suggest that Lincoln abandoned the notion following its issuance. Lincoln's discretion, however, does not mean he did not pursue it well into 1863 and even 1864.[77] Lincoln's determination was so great that he ignored Secretary of War Edwin Stanton's vehement opposition to colonization. Stanton did not want the military to have to compete with colonization projects for bodies.[78] Given Union difficulty in maintaining an adequate force—one reason Lincoln went after Clement Vallandigham with such viciousness—Stanton's antipathy ordinarily would have prevailed. That it didn't prevail speaks to the strength and depth of Lincoln's commitment to colonization. He pursues it as Union forces are on the verge of fighting at Gettysburg, a battle that will later become the occasion for a dramatic statement of American ideals and purposes. Remarkably, Lincoln's indifference to Stanton's position undercut part of Lincoln's rationale for the proclamation. If military necessity dictated the liberation of as many slaves as possible and their enrollment in the armed forces, how is it that Lincoln could spare hundreds, even thousands, of young able-bodied men for what amounted to a social and political fantasy? It's as if only Stanton took Lincoln's argument from necessity seriously.

COOPER UNION ADDRESS (FEBRUARY 1860)

Lincoln's New York speech took place prior to his nomination as the Republican Party's presidential candidate in 1860. The speech, in fact, helped Lincoln win the nomination. In it he turned to the founding era and identified the Republican Party as the rightful heir to the founders' vision of America. Though they had to accept and tolerate slavery as the price of the new Constitution, they did not support it and took measures, both in the document itself and in later legislative acts, to place it on the road to eventual extinction. The Republican Party and Lincoln modeled themselves on the founders' approach. Lincoln took great pains, again, to make it clear to his Southern brethren that slavery would be left alone where it already existed. He and the party pursued a genuinely conservative agenda: they were opposed only to slavery's extension into the territories. They had no greater political or legislative ambition even though they believed slavery wrong. This made them the legitimate successors to the founding generation.

Though speaking in front of an eastern audience, Lincoln was largely addressing the South. To the charge that the Republican Party was a radical and insurrectionary faction whose activities would lead to slave rebellions and white deaths, Lincoln ridiculed the possibility of any kind of uprising. Slaves possessed neither the inclination nor the means to initiate a bloody revolt, the example of Nat Turner notwithstanding. Even if such a thing were attempted, it would be discovered quickly and crushed. Isolated instances of resistance will no doubt recur, but "no general insurrection of slaves, as I think, can happen in this country for a long time."[79]

Lincoln's speech then takes an unexpected turn. Having reassured Southerners that their visions of murderous slaves are preposterous, Lincoln introduces an issue that appears seemingly out of nowhere. He invokes and quotes Jefferson (from the latter's autobiography), who understood what needed to be done regarding slavery. "It is still in our power to direct the process of emancipation and deportation, peaceably, and in such slow degrees, as that the evil will wear off insensibly; and their places be, pari passu, filled up by free white laborers."[80] Jefferson speaks for the state of Virginia, not the national government, which enjoys no emancipation power. Lincoln thus uses a slave owner from a slave-owning state to address Southern slave owners. Jefferson is one of their own. When Lincoln speaks he channels Jefferson's authority and prestige in the South. Lincoln does not speak of colonization but, through Jefferson, deportation, which lacks any voluntary connotations. And while Lincoln denies the federal government has the power to emancipate, he does not deny it has the power to deport. He is silent on the matter. Jefferson, however, as Lincoln surely knew, once proposed removing all black children from the country, as we saw above. The older generations would remain in place since they would die off eventually. No blacks would then remain in the United States.

Lincoln doesn't endorse Jefferson's scheme, but he does bring national attention to the question of colonization and tries to capitalize on Jefferson's status in the American pantheon. Lincoln no doubt understands that Southern fears of widespread black vengeance were not rational (nor were they necessarily irrational) and could not be soothed through reasoned analysis about their dim prospects. Yet merely raising the issue stokes, however gently, the fear and renders the project of colonization an attractive possibility. Why risk premature violent death? Why not remove blacks from the land and thereby remove the threat, however remote? Lincoln does not overtly suggest this way of thinking, but the thought (as a possible reaction) is lodged in the bent of his formulations. The best solution to a problem is to eliminate it.

LINCOLN'S FIRST ANNUAL MESSAGE TO CONGRESS (DECEMBER 1861)

Not surprisingly, Lincoln's first annual message to Congress is preoccupied with the war. The specter of foreign intervention in the conflict between the states haunts his opening remarks, though he believes that foreign powers possess the intelligence to recognize that a united America serves their interests, especially their commercial well-being, better than a fractured union. The South has been assiduously courting foreign assistance-cum-intervention, but has failed to secure it. Nonetheless, Lincoln urges Congress to attend to the defense of the United States given the possibility that the South might ultimately succeed in its foreign recruitment. National security calls for attending not only to the country's extensive seacoast but also to its "great lakes and rivers." The United States is vulnerable and needs to fortify itself.

Despite pressing war concerns, Lincoln devotes part of the message to the question of colonization. "From the very beginning of his administration, Lincoln considered ways of laying the groundwork for colonization," Eric Foner writes. In March this meant sending his diplomatic representative to Guatemala with "secret instructions" to obtain territory for a black colony. In April, as the South moved toward war at Fort Sumter, this meant meeting in the White House with a shady entrepreneur who was peddling a colonization scheme in Chiriqui (present-day Colombia).[81] Lincoln was always thinking, conspiring. How many locations might full-blown colonization require? In a prelude to addressing black emigration, Lincoln wonders why the country has not yet recognized the sovereign, independent states of Haiti and Liberia. Though he invokes the possibility that "important advantages might be secured by favorable treaties with them," this could also apply to the project of colonization, which Lincoln initially assigned to private interests to accomplish. He sees no "good reason" why recognition should not be granted and wants Congress to join him in this diplomatic action.[82]

Toward the end of the message Lincoln finally raises colonization. As a result of the first Confiscation Act, in which "the legal claims of certain persons to the labor and service of certain other persons have become forfeited," many blacks have been liberated and become dependent on the United States, a situation calling for amelioration.[83] While Lincoln argues they "must be provided for in some way," he takes the occasion to press his plan for colonization.[84] Imagining that "some of the States will pass similar enactments for their own benefit," this would increase the number of blacks available for emigration.[85] Given that there might be two sources of bodies for export, Lincoln thus urges Congress that "steps be taken for colonizing both classes (or the first mentioned if the other shall not be brought into existence) at some place or places in a climate congenial to them."[86] Here Lincoln is not content to take advantage of the contingency surrounding the lives of only the newly freed slaves. He sees an opportunity for a wider colonization scheme. "It might be well to consider, too, whether the free colored people already in the United States could not, so far as individuals may desire, be included in such colonization."[87] Though Lincoln does not claim that free colored people have any such desire, which would seem to be a prerequisite for implementation, this does not mean that such desire cannot be induced.

Lincoln informs Congress that land (abroad) and money must be appropriated to execute any such colonization plan, but this is well within the power of Congress and the national government, as even Jefferson finally recognized. To counter possible objections to this scheme and underline its benefits, Lincoln seizes on the racial prejudices of the day to finalize his argument: "If it be said that the only legitimate object of acquiring territory is to furnish homes for white men, this measure effects that object, for the emigration of colored men leaves additional room for white men remaining or coming here."[88] In case there is any doubt about the importance of colonization, Lincoln ups the rhetorical ante as he brings the very fate of the Union into play: "On this whole proposition, including the appropriation of money with the acquisition of territory, does not the expediency amount to absolute necessity—that without which the Government itself cannot be perpetuated?"[89] Lincoln effectively places the future of the American republic on the departure of blacks from the continent. Despite the war of Southern aggression, Lincoln assigns ultimate responsibility for America's democratic experiment to the willingness of blacks to leave their homeland—not with the defeat of Southern armies by Northern guns. This extraordinary suggestion is mere prelude to Lincoln's efforts the following year to directly implicate the black community in its own expatriation.

LINCOLN AT THE WHITE HOUSE (AUGUST 1862)

In the summer of 1862 Lincoln issued an invitation to Washington, D.C.'s black community and subsequently met with five prominent free black men at the White House to convey his plan for colonization following emancipation. Colonization, Lincoln informed his visitors, was not just an idea he favored. Given that Congress had allocated monies for this purpose, he now considered it his duty to pursue it. Lincoln recognized that he would have to raise and answer one question immediately; otherwise his effort would fail instantly. Why should "people . . . of African descent" (he still cannot think of them as Americans) leave the country? Lincoln's answer is nothing short of astonishing—astonishing because it reduces people—and assigns almost magical significance—to skin color. "You and we are different races. We have between us a broader difference than exists between almost any other two races. Whether it is right or wrong I need not discuss, but this physical difference is a great disadvantage to us both."[90]

Lincoln does not stop there. He seems to hold physical differences responsible for the slavery imposed on blacks. Lincoln thus raises the undeniable fact of their suffering but insists that whites have suffered, too. "I think your race suffer very greatly, many of them by living among us, while ours suffer from your presence. In a word, we suffer on each side." Lincoln then draws what he thinks is the inevitable conclusion. "If this is admitted, it affords a reason at least why we should be separated."[91] Ignoring the fanciful claim about white suffering, one could draw many conclusions from this condition of racial coexistence other than separation. Lincoln says suffering is a reason for separation, but since he is prepared to act on it, it is not just any reason for him, not just one reason among others. It is sufficient unto itself.

Lincoln's meeting with five of Washington's free black elite not to discuss but to promote and push colonization (in rather heavy-handed fashion) took coercive advantage of his presidential position. This was not a friendly conversation between equals on a matter of mutual interest. Lincoln deployed the power of his office to deliver a message. Support for emigration in the black community had ebbed and flowed for years based on an assessment of the current political scene.[92] For example, as prospects for blacks deteriorated in the 1850s with passage of the Fugitive Slave and Kansas-Nebraska acts, and the Dred Scott decision, it's understandable why many blacks might consider departure. As fear would rise in the black community, so would interest in emigration.[93] The Civil War threw this kind of calculation into doubt. With the advent of war, possibilities for black lives opened considerably. What would happen to them if the South were defeated? What might a postwar world look like? Since the war's outcome was unknown, most prominent black leaders thought it best to "wait and see" what transpired.[94] Many others, like Frederick Douglass, remained unalterably opposed to leaving. Given these conditions, what did it mean for Lincoln to gather "representatives" of Washington's black community to "discuss" the issue?

While Lincoln rarely left Washington during the war, the invitation to local black leaders meant he could convene a meeting with an audience that would be more hospitable than one drawn nationally. Thanks to the long-term efforts of the African Civilization Society in Maryland and Virginia, Lincoln would find more support in the capital than other regions of the country. What's more, as Kate Masur writes, "the benefits of freedom within the United States remained illusory for many black Washingtonians that [1862] spring and summer. Under provisions of the Fugitive Slave Act, 'loyal' slaveholders could demand remittance of human property that had escaped into the District of Columbia, and local officials in the capital were more than willing to remand fugitives to their owners."[95] Still, prior to the meeting, members of the black community that selected the delegates to meet with Lincoln passed two substantive resolutions that let it be known they were opposed to emigration and found the role they were playing in Lincoln's colonization plans problematic since they could not claim to represent all blacks.[96]

Lincoln did appear to enjoy some success thanks to the meeting. Edward Thomas, the chair of the delegation and initially opposed to emigration, changed his mind after the encounter with Lincoln, citing "all the advantages [that] were so ably brought to our views."[97] Thomas's description of his change of mind calls attention to itself insofar as Lincoln used the gathering not to convince and persuade but to moralize and compel his audience. Given the power imbalance between the participants and the location of the meeting, what did it mean for Lincoln to deliver this communiqué? Masur writes, "As Lincoln's invitation itself implied, the war was opening new possibilities for African Americans' participation at the highest levels."[98] Lincoln of course was looking for directed participation. I mentioned that the resolution passed in the black community before the meeting advised a wait-and-see approach, especially since prospects for blacks in America might improve dramatically thanks to the war. Lincoln's initiative, if anything, tended to subvert such hope. It might even induce a new sense of fear and dread in African Americans. If Lincoln is telling us to leave now, they might wonder, when the war's outcome has not been decided and we might even be called to serve and fight, what might this augur for the future? Lincoln's call for a "meeting" on colonization represents one of the first steps in the implementation of colonization. Realization had a very long way to go, but this was a concrete beginning. Blacks were not going to be forced to leave at the point of a gun, but this does not mean they would not feel pressured to leave.

The first colonization scheme Lincoln supported gained the support of hundreds (and perhaps more) of Washington's black residents, but "support for emigration remained a minority position among African Americans."[99] Lincoln persisted nonetheless without displaying, as far as I know, any concern for how the decision of people in the black community in support of emigration might hurt those who rejected it. No doubt Lincoln assumed that if he could secure one or two colonization trips to Central America, this might set an example that others would follow and a trickle might soon turn into a torrent, which would have pleased him.[100] Nevertheless, Lincoln would never be able to free the country of every black person. There were simply too many blacks in America for his perfect colonization dream to come true, which, pragmatic politician he purported to be, he had to know. Yet his will to expatriate blacks was so strong that even small successes seemed to carry great weight, which is one reason he would pursue colonization into 1864 and perhaps never actually give up on the idea of it.[101] Lincoln had been advocating colonization in public well before he ever ran for president (as far back as his tenure in the Illinois state legislature, in fact), and "even before the first shots were fired at Ft. Sumter, Lincoln directed his newly appointed minister to Guatemala, Elisha W. Crosby, to investigate the prospects of colonization in Central America." What's more, "in his first year in office Lincoln called upon to Congress to fund a larger colonization program" and connected it to official legislative efforts such as the First Confiscation Act.[102]

Leaders in the black community understood, however, that black expressions of support—to say nothing of actual departure—could be considered unpatriotic, especially during wartime, and could thus damage the position of blacks after the war when they might otherwise find themselves well positioned to reap (at least some of) the benefits of loyal service. If many of them fought and died in the war, how could they be denied citizenship (as Lincoln himself would later come to appreciate)?[103] This recognition might also speak to Lincoln's determination to pursue colonization not just despite but because of the notable failures in Panama and Haiti. Failure adds urgency to the problem of black presence. After all, Lincoln was actively pursuing colonization as he was drafting the preliminary Emancipation Proclamation (which spoke of colonization, unlike the final version).[104] Lincoln was prepared to doubly use blacks: to fight the war and remove them after it was over as a "reward" for their service. He may have abandoned the idea, but that he was prepared to implement it, if possible, any time, speaks to the dubious power of the evolution or change of heart thesis.

LINCOLN'S SECOND ANNUAL MESSAGE TO CONGRESS (DECEMBER 1862)

In Lincoln's second annual message to Congress, he declares what is not in doubt: "I cannot make it better known than it already is, that I strongly favor colonization."[105] Unlike prior interventions into the tangled accusations and counteraccusations that constitute American public discourse on slavery, Lincoln gave his position definitive institutional life. He proposed three constitutional amendments, two of them pertaining to the abolition of slavery, compensation for slave owners, and the status of slaves freed during the war. The third amendment addressed colonization: "Congress may appropriate money, and otherwise provide, for colonizing free colored persons, with their own consent, at any place or places without the United States."[106]

The colonization amendment, which Lincoln noted "does not oblige, but merely authorizes, Congress to aid in colonizing such as may consent," was nothing if not gratuitous. Congress required no such authorization. Why, then, propose the amendment? For one thing, giving the colonization project formal constitutional support draws attention to it. In addition, if Lincoln can implicate Congress and state legislatures, the odds of success increase. For those who think it could not happen for logistical reasons, a constitutional amendment might serve as a catalyst to concrete action.

When Lincoln discusses the colonization amendment, he repeatedly deploys the language of deportation, suggesting that despite the language of consent free colored persons may have no choice in the matter.[107] Here, as I mentioned earlier, Lincoln plays a dangerous political game. Some were in favor of forcing blacks to leave the country, including Lincoln's attorney general Edward Bates. Regardless, once colonization is introduced as the policy of choice for dealing with the future of blacks in America (or of not dealing with their future in America), Lincoln cannot control the final form it might take. He might be opposed to forced emigration, but he would be the first to admit that he does not control events.

Lincoln's constitutional proposal follows up on the pledge he made in the Preliminary Emancipation Proclamation to continue to support colonization efforts. In this pronouncement, Lincoln imagined the possibility of colonization on the North American continent, a possibility he withdraws in the second annual message to Congress. Regardless, Lincoln promotes colonization not only just prior to issuing the final Emancipation Proclamation, in which he will invoke military necessity to use blacks in the war, but also in a way that means the project can continue after the proclamation takes effect and blacks are in uniform. Lincoln may no longer discuss colonization in public after January 1, 1863, but that does not mean he has given up on the project.

George Kateb describes this as follows: "The best that could be said is that he sincerely thought that whites would never accept blacks as equal citizens and that it would be good for blacks to emigrate. When it became clear that blacks had little interest in leaving, he dropped his defense of colonization in his efforts to secure abolition of slavery through constitutional amendment."[108] What Kateb ignores is that Lincoln did not drop his pursuit of colonization when it became clear that blacks had little interest in emigration (long before a constitutional amendment to abolish slavery). If Lincoln had been responsive to the will of black people, he would never have pursued colonization. Blacks started holding conventions in the 1850s, including in Illinois, to denounce it.[109] Yes, some blacks did favor emigration or were at least willing to leave, but black support, as it were, for colonization tended to rise and fall with the condition of blacks in America. Their first choice was to remain in America because they were Americans and this was their home. When circumstances looked bleak, however, as they did in the 1850s with the Fugitive Slave Law, the Kansas-Nebraska Act, and the Dred Scott decision, emigration became a more attractive idea, as I mentioned above.[110] In these kinds of fraught circumstances, however, it's not clear what it would mean for blacks to consent to colonization.

Not surprisingly, Lincoln's efforts to promote and enact colonization generated backlash. The more he advanced it, the more blacks opposed it. This is why he took his case directly to black leaders in Washington, D.C. This effort failed, too, as we just saw. What's more, the publicity attending the meeting led to an upsurge in racism and violence against blacks.[111] Nevertheless, Lincoln moved forward with his colonization scheme. As Eric Foner remarks, Lincoln, against all the evidence, "still assumed that large numbers would agree to be colonized outside the country."[112]

Lincoln concludes his second annual message with a string of stirring words and phrases, some of his finest. He insists that we "rise with the occasion," that, since "our case is new, so we must think anew, and act anew." Try as we might, "we cannot escape history," which means "we will be remembered in spite of ourselves" for a long time to come. "The fiery trial through which we pass, will light us down, in honor or dishonor, to the latest generations." Everything is at stake: "We shall nobly save, or meanly lose, the last, best, hope of Earth."[113] Despite the inspirational rhetoric, Lincoln positions himself to fail his own tests. In seeking to colonize freed slaves, who helped create and defend the country from which he would remove them, Lincoln does not rise with the occasion. Rather, he resorts to "the dogmas of the quiet past," even though they "are inadequate to the stormy present." That is, colonization is tantamount to a new monstrous injustice to be perpetrated against blacks. He's right that America cannot escape history, but colonization constitutes a form of denial that blacks are Americans, part and parcel of American history.[114] The country cannot be conceived without them and their contributions. If colonization somehow "succeeded," and blacks were removed, it would be remembered as the crowning cruelty of slavery's legacy. It would also be remembered for its futility, for the lasting imprint of blacks on American life and society cannot similarly be removed. The only way to lose the last, best hope of Earth is to "lose" the very people who maintain their patriotic devotion to their homeland despite the brutal crimes whites repeatedly inflict on them, especially under the cover of fundamental constitutional law. Ironically, the more Lincoln demeans and disrespects them, the more they rise to the occasion and prove themselves greater citizens than Lincoln could ever imagine or hope to be himself.

Kateb both does and does not seem to recognize the problem colonization poses for Lincoln. On the one hand, Kateb stresses that Lincoln "rarely wavered in his commitment to human equality." He did nullify two emancipation proclamations issued by the military, but he thought them to be either legally dubious or politically rash. Colonization, however, presents a more intractable difficulty. Kateb writes, "But suppose it were said that his long-lasting espousal of the policy of urging without compelling black people to settle outside the United States was a major deviation from his commitment?"[115] The hypothetical formulation suggests that Kateb may not take the question posed seriously. What's more, even though Kateb effectively admits that there is no good answer to this question, it suggests its own answer, one that lets Lincoln off the hook. To say that Lincoln's long-standing espousal of colonization constitutes a major deviation from his commitment to equality leaves that commitment intact, if not unchallenged. Deviations are departures, exceptions even, but they are temporary (which is what Kateb ultimately concludes) and leave the norm or standard unscathed.

Commitments to equality and colonization compromise each other. Lincoln presumes that he knows what is best for blacks; he "consults" them only to tell them what they ought to do; and he persists in a half-baked scheme they do not support until it becomes a practical and political impossibility he cannot overcome. Lincoln's pursuit of colonization, in short, denied political principle and defied political logic. Not even military necessity, the demand for black bodies in uniform, weakened his commitment to it. Lincoln professed equality, but colonization enacted white primacy. It failed, but for him it was never wrong or a mistake. If Lincoln had grown morally on racial issues as Foner argues, surely Lincoln would have publicly retracted or renounced his commitment to colonization. For one thing, equality and justice entail more than the cessation of gross wrongdoing. They require making amends, at least in some fashion, whether material, symbolic, or both. Lincoln's public silence on colonization after the final Emancipation Proclamation ultimately signaled nothing more than the project's "official" demise. Here it is worth recalling that colonization experienced a political rebirth owing to the collapse of efforts to promote gradual emancipation in the Border States early in 1862, Delaware in particular.[116] For the elimination of slavery to remain a possibility, then, colonization had to be added to the equation (it was "part of a broader antislavery strategy").[117] This means that a new kind of black service, emigration or deportation, would be needed to entice slave owners who were reluctant to give up their property, even with compensation, and concerned about the status of blacks in the postwar world. "Colonization could refute the charge that abolition meant racial equality."[118] Blacks, in short, would be sacrificed again for the good of the nation, this time through removal. For Lincoln political necessity could justify anything.

PACE FONER

Eric Foner admits in *The Fiery Trial* that he "admire[s] Lincoln very much."[119] In particular, Foner emphasizes what he refers to as Lincoln's "capacity for growth." It's the "hallmark of [his] greatness."[120] This is not to say that Foner does not also have an appreciation for Lincoln's shortcoming and failings. If anything, the evolution that Foner highlights in Lincoln would not be possible without them. Thus Foner will "take Lincoln whole" because he wants to "show [him] in motion."[121] Foner, it seems, gestures toward an account of Lincoln that affirms his ambiguity, but is it anything more than a gesture?

In the preface, while Foner seems to appreciate Lincoln's deficits, his characterization of one of them, colonization, tends to downplay and dilute it. For example, Lincoln had more than a "long association" with the idea of colonization. He was one of its leading proponents. He tried to make it happen. He clung to the idea well after it became clear that it was pointless to pursue it since it was not what blacks wanted. This means that for Lincoln colonization was more than a "hope that many of them [blacks] would agree to emigrate to some other country."[122]

It's not just that Foner's narrative frame of evolution and growth tends to undercut any notion of Lincoln's essential ambiguity. It's that this particular narrative entails that Lincoln (his record, his views, his policies, etc.) be presented in a way that allows for the evolutionary Lincoln to emerge in the first place. For example, Foner characterizes "Lincoln's career [as] a process of moral and political education and deepening antislavery conviction."[123] While no doubt true, deepening antislavery conviction looks different when juxtaposed with Lincoln's almost obsessive but certainly imperial commitment to colonization. What if the latter enabled the former? What kind of evolution are we then talking about? Are we talking about evolution, at least in a positive sense, at all?

In the main body of the text, Foner catalogs Lincoln's career as a proponent of colonization. While Lincoln advocated a civic nationalism or patriotism rooted in equality that welcomed immigrants to this country who could swear allegiance to America's founding political principles, which means that blacks should have been included, he also effectively embraced "a racial nationalism that saw blacks as in some ways not truly American."[124]

Foner recognizes that "for decades, colonization had faced the seemingly insuperable difficulty that most free blacks repudiated the idea."[125] This situation changed somewhat in the 1850s with the Fugitive Slave Act, Kansas-Nebraska Act, and the Dred Scott decision, which means that Lincoln did his part to contribute to the existential anxiety that led some Northern blacks to reconsider the idea of colonization. Lincoln thus does his best to take advantage of the dire straits of a subordinate and subordinated people. Still, the vast majority of blacks remained opposed to colonization and even started to hold conventions, in Illinois no less, denouncing it.[126] Foner asserts that "it was likely that Lincoln was aware of these gatherings, which were reported in the republican press, but there is no record of a comment from him about them. They did not alter his public commitment to colonization."[127] Lincoln, in short, ignored the dominant will of the black community. He refused to listen to them. Foner attributes Lincoln's position, in part, to his lack of involvement or even exposure to blacks, which the war would eventually change—and thus "his outlook regarding the place of blacks in American society would finally begin to change."[128]

In the meantime, Lincoln continued to push colonization. "Numerous colonization schemes surfaced in 1862."[129] Given the federal money available for colonization, the project attracted its fair share of opportunists. Lincoln was interested in a number of projects put forward by private interests, which could be counted on to betray the subjects of their schemes in order to turn a profit. More importantly, "as talk of colonization increased, so did black opposition."[130] What was Lincoln's response? Did he finally listen? Or was he listening all along? Either way, "to counteract this *reluctance* to emigrate, Lincoln, for the *first and only* time, took the idea of colonization directly to black Americans."[131] These sentences are extraordinary. Blacks were expressing more than reluctance, a word that suggests something less than rejection and outrage, and might even suggest an openness to persuasion. That Lincoln approached the black community directly for the first and only time does not make it any less objectionable. What's more, Lincoln did not invite them to the White House to engage them in political contest on an issue of great public moment. He invited them to a lecture—and a moralizing one to boot. Again, rather than respect the general will of the black community, which would have been the decent thing to do vis-à-vis an exploited, brutalized people, Lincoln doubles down on his always already doomed colonization scheme. And he did so despite the increase in racism and violence that attended its public promotion.[132]

Ultimately, Lincoln does abandon the colonization project, but only in the face of insurmountable obstacles, whether continued opposition from the black community or logistical problems that should have made the idea unthinkable—and thus unmentionable—in the first place. The money and material required to realize Lincoln's large-scale vision of emigration dwarfed the resources the United States could (or would) devote to it. Foner considers colonization dead when Lincoln orders the navy to rescue desperate colonists off the coast of Haiti in early 1864, but he does not comment on why it took Lincoln so long to act. It was known that colonists were diseased and dying from the get-go in Haiti in the early spring of 1863, but it took Lincoln nearly a year to respond.[133] Lincoln, then, does not abandon colonization because he has come to recognize the error (and injustice) of his ways. Rather than coming to an understanding that colonization was wrong, Lincoln is forced to give up on the idea because it cannot be made to work.

Ironically, when Foner writes that "by 1864, although Lincoln still saw voluntary emigration as a kind of safety valve for individual blacks dissatisfied with their condition in the United States, he no longer envisioned large-scale colonization," he actually damns him.[134] Lincoln was committed to colonization to the point that he would continue to support it in any form in which it might be considered available. The image of solitary blacks so desperate that they would leave their home and homeland, by themselves, to travel hundreds, even thousands of miles to a foreign land where they are strangers should have prompted Lincoln to scorn it. He would never have affirmed such a possibility for dissatisfied whites.

Foner's evolutionary Lincoln runs into another difficulty. As we saw in chapter 1, Lincoln was willing to sacrifice the Constitution and citizens of the United States if it served American war aims—this despite his profound commitment to the founders, the Constitution, and rule of law. If circumstances suggested or dictated that Lincoln turn course, he would do it. Given Lincoln's treatment of Clement Vallandigham, it would not be unfair to argue that Lincoln's position did not so much evolve as devolve. His commitment to the holy trinity I just mentioned proved to be less than advertised. There is no reason to believe that a political actor capable of this kind of maneuver on fundamental rights involving white citizens would not do something similar regarding blacks, whether free or slave. Foner's growth thesis presumes and posits a kind of irreversibility. Once Lincoln's views (on race) move in a more capacious direction, their course is set. They will not reverse themselves. There is no reason to think this given Lincoln's constitutional machinations. If circumstances changed and it required that he sacrifice the gains blacks had made in order to "save" the Union, could it be doubted that he would hesitate to do so? If not, what does this say about his growth?

Pace Foner, then, Lincoln's peculiar iconic status does not stem from an effectively romanticized rags-to-riches account of his life and legacy. Lincoln's obsessive, bordering on fanatical, commitment to colonization, for example, forms a critical part of a political complex that reflects rather than subverts his exemplarity insofar as it allows (white) America to simultaneously affirm and call into question certain aspects of white supremacy and privilege and thus profess faith in its founding ideals while failing to ever fully deliver on them—the best of both worlds, a beautiful ambiguity.

NOTES

1. Eric Foner, *The Fiery Trial: Abraham Lincoln and American Slavery* (New York: W.W. Norton, 2010).

2. David Brion Davis notes Lincoln's vehement opposition to slavery and simultaneous rejection of abolitionism. He attributes Lincoln's position on slavery to the influence of Henry Clay, namely, "the ideas of gradual emancipation and an eventual colonization of blacks outside the United States as the only effective way of undoing the evils of slavery." Davis recognizes that Lincoln's support of colonization is problematic and does his best to downplay it, especially its consequences. "Lincoln's

interest in the possibilities of voluntary colonization led to a number of ill-conceived blunders, including the government's sponsorship in 1863 of a colony of a few hundred African Americans on a small island near Haiti. After many of the settlers died of smallpox or starvation, a naval ship brought the survivors back to the United States." Advocacy is reduced to mere interest and death to a blunder. Davis, *Inhuman Bondage: The Rise and Fall of Slavery in the New World* (Oxford: Oxford University Press, 2006), 307; 406, note 38.

3. Echoing Foner, John Burt writes that "Lincoln was not proud of his racism, only realistic about its power and intractability. Racism seemed irrational to Lincoln, but he knew the pull of that irrationality because he felt it. To concede that an irrational feeling is intractable is not to argue that it is rational or right. Lincoln did not use the depths of these feelings as an excuse for leaving them totally untouched but cautiously suggested ways to modify those feelings gradually. This is far different from the use other people made of the assumption that widespread racism made it impossible to imagine how white people could outgrow it." Colonization, however, seemed exempt from Lincoln's project of self-overcoming. He would ultimately drop his pursuit of colonization, but not because he had realized its appalling character no matter how one looked at it. He dropped it because it had exhausted itself and died a political death beyond Lincoln's powers to keep it alive, let alone resurrect it. John Burt, *Lincoln's Tragic Pragmatism: Lincoln, Douglas, and Moral Conflict* (Cambridge, MA: Harvard University Press, 2013), 66.

4. Burt claims that "Lincoln's thinking about colonization could not have been entirely merely a strategic misdirection, because he continued to entertain what seem to be harebrained schemes about colonization well after he had issued the Emancipation Proclamation. But there was also something halfhearted and unthought through about all these schemes, which suggests that Lincoln's commitment to them was shallow." As we will see below, there's no reason to believe Lincoln's thinking was to any extent "merely a strategic misdirection." What's more, not all of the colonization schemes he considered were harebrained. Some may have been long shots, but many were serious, and his continued commitment to them suggests anything but shallow support. Burt's generosity here strikes me as unwarranted. Burt, *Lincoln's Tragic Pragmatism*, 360.

5. Abraham Lincoln, "Eulogy on Henry Clay at Springfield, Illinois," *The Writings of Abraham Lincoln*, edited and with an introduction by Steven B. Smith (New Haven, CT: Yale University Press, 2012), 43.

6. Ibid., 51.

7. Ibid.

8. Ibid.

9. Ibid., 53.

10. Ibid.

11. Ibid., 53, 53–54. Burt argues that "what was behind colonization for Clay was not fear of black people but fear of white people. Lincoln's point in the eulogy for Clay is . . . that in Clay's mind, as (in some moods) in Lincoln's, colonization was a firmly anti-slavery and anti-racist doctrine, not *merely* a form of ethnic cleansing." Burt, *Lincoln's Tragic Pragmatism*, 358, 359, emphasis added. It's not clear to me

how antiracism and ethnic cleansing go together, unless recognizing one's racism and trying to resist it instead of indulging perhaps its worst manifestation is antiracism.

12. Ibid., 54.

13. Ibid.

14. On Henry Clay's eulogy, Burt stresses Lincoln's long quotation of a passage from Jefferson regarding emancipation and colonization. Burt argues that for Jefferson emancipation was nothing more than a "bagatelle." Expatriation was the "crux" of the slavery question. Jefferson "assumed that it would be impossible for former slaves and former masters to share a republic with each other, and he was daunted by the difficulties of separating them from each other." Burt does not simply take Jefferson at his word regarding the unproblematic cost of emancipation. He recognizes that Jefferson might have taken this position "only to emphasize the gravity of the problem of how master and slave might live together after emancipation." What, though, would (supposedly) make peaceful coexistence impossible? "It is extremely hard to imagine giving power to those whom you have given reason to hate you. That those whom one has subjected and repressed really do have reason for this hate does not make the act of handing power over to them any easier, and indeed the thought of the anger and desire for revenge that would seem to be the natural concomitant of repression would provoke nightmares enough to make a common life difficult even without paranoid fantasies and a demonic vision of the otherness [of] the other."

Burt seems unduly sympathetic to white fear. For one thing, the South would not be defenseless in the aftermath of the war. Following surrender, they took their guns home with them. They did not lay down their arms. For another, the South would not be "giving power" or "handing power over" to the newly freed. They would be sharing power with them, as long as they could swear their allegiance to the United States. The South, in short, was far from disempowered and vulnerable. Looking at it from the other direction, African Americans would indeed have reason for hate and might harbor a desire for revenge, but to act on either of them would not only be pointless but self-defeating. The last thing they would need after emancipation, whenever it came, was a race war. Whatever "racial panic" Jefferson might have been trying to "ward off" with his colonization scheme, the assumption about coexistence was a matter of Southern projection. Besides, from a moral point of view, it is problematic to refuse to right a wrong because you fear the consequences that might result, consequences for which you would also be responsible for having committed the wrong in the first place. This stance doubles down on the immorality and criminality in question. There should be no sympathy for such self-imposed dilemmas. Burt, *Lincoln's Tragic Pragmatism*, 351, 66, 352.

15. Lincoln, "Speech on the Kansas-Nebraska Act at Peoria, Illinois," *The Writings of Abraham Lincoln*, 66.

16. Ibid.

17. Ibid. Burt at one point describes Lincoln's affirmation of colonization at Peoria as a "very qualified endorsement," but "his frank recognition of its likely impossibility in the same speech" does not qualify the endorsement. One can fully favor an idea and appreciate the unlikeliness of its realization. The latter does not qualify the former, it seems to me. Burt, *Lincoln's Tragic Pragmatism*, 362.

18. Burt insists that "Lincoln mentioned colonization in the Peoria speech . . . mostly to claim that it was an unworkable notion." He considered "three possible courses" of action following emancipation and found "all three solutions . . . to have fatal problems." Burt then repeats his assertion that "Lincoln's thinking about colonization in the Peoria speech was meant simply as a demonstration of how intractable the problem of ending slavery was." Perhaps, but in publicly proposing colonization, Lincoln was disseminating a horrific idea that might have seized hold of the American imagination and become a reality, whether it was actually workable or not. What then? Lincoln could have set in motion a mass slaughter. Either way, Burt admits that the colonization "fantasy died hard; as late as the Grant administration, serious efforts were undertaken to purchase the Dominican Republic as a homeland for freed American slaves." Much of the responsibility for this undue determination surely must rest with Lincoln.

Regarding the question of hate, Burt would have done well to consider the reconciliation experience America gained when it resisted, rebelled, and fought a long war of liberation against the hated British and their loyalist allies and restored normal relations with (most of) them soon thereafter. How is it, then, that the third option Lincoln considered, social and political equality, can be rejected out of hand because of prejudices (hard feelings)? Burt, *Lincoln's Tragic Pragmatism*, 352–53, 362.

19. Lincoln, "Speech on the Kansas-Nebraska Act at Peoria, Illinois," 66.
20. Ibid.
21. Ibid., 78.
22. Ibid., 66.
23. Ibid.
24. Ibid., 67.
25. Ibid.
26. Ibid., 61.
27. Ibid., 80.
28. Ibid.
29. Ibid., 67.
30. Ibid., 82.
31. Ibid., 66.
32. Ibid., 82.
33. Ibid., 80.
34. Ibid., 83.
35. Ibid., 85.
36. Ibid.
37. Ibid., 90.
38. Laurence M. Hauptman, *Between Two Fires: American Indians in the Civil War* (New York: The Free Press, 1995), 4–5, emphasis mine.
39. Ibid., 6.
40. Ibid., 20–21.
41. Ibid., 11.
42. Ibid.
43. Ibid., 12.
44. Ibid., ix–x.

45. Ibid., x–xi.
46. Ibid., 28.
47. Ibid., 37.
48. Lincoln, "Speech on the Kansas-Nebraska Act at Peoria, Illinois," 65.
49. Abraham Lincoln, "Speech on the Dred Scott Decision at Springfield, Illinois," *The Writings of Abraham Lincoln*, 112.
50. Ibid., 112–13.
51. Ibid., 114–15. Douglas insists that the equality posited in the Declaration of Independence referred to British subjects alone, whether of Great Britain or those on the North American continent. Lincoln finds this incredible, even appalling, for it excludes not only Negroes (obviously) but also a great many white people. It encompasses the English, Irish, and Scots, but it leaves out "the French, Germans, and other white people of the world." They are "all gone to pot along with the Judge's [Douglas's] inferior races." Lincoln's Indians would be included among Douglas's inferior races.
52. Ibid., 114.
53. Ibid., 115.
54. Ibid., 117.
55. Ibid., 118.
56. Ibid.
57. Ibid.
58. Ibid.
59. Ibid.
60. Ibid., 118–19.
61. Ibid., 118.
62. Ibid.
63. Ibid.
64. Ibid.
65. Ibid.
66. Abraham Lincoln, "'House Divided' Speech at Springfield, Illinois," *The Writings of Abraham Lincoln*, 126.
67. Ibid.
68. Ibid., 126–27.
69. Ibid., 127.
70. Ibid., 130.
71. Ibid., 129.
72. David Zarefsky, "Abraham Lincoln, 'A House Divided': Speech at Springfield, Illinois (16 June 1858)," *Voices of Democracy* 6, 2011, 28–29.
73. Ibid., 29. Emphasis original.
74. Ibid.
75. Ibid. Zarefsky cites this stance as evidence of Lincoln's moderation, at least in the eyes of Whigs, but Lincoln's pragmatism here also reveals its cruel and sacrificial character. While slavery's extinction is postponed to the distant future, the people subjected to its daily horrors die in the immediate present.
76. Ibid., 34.

77. Phillip W. Magness, "James Mitchell and the Mystery of the Emigration Office Papers," *Journal of the Abraham Lincoln Association* 32, no. 2, 2011, 53.
78. Ibid., 52.
79. Abraham Lincoln, "Cooper Union Address," in *Lincoln: Political Writings and Speeches*, ed. Terence Ball (Cambridge: Cambridge University Press, 2013), 105.
80. Abraham Lincoln, "Address at Cooper Institute, New York City," *The Writings of Abraham Lincoln*, 294.
81. Foner, *The Fiery Trial*, 184–85.
82. Abraham Lincoln, "First Annual Message," http://www.presidency.ucsb.edu/ws/?pid=29502.
83. Ibid.
84. Ibid.
85. Ibid.
86. Ibid.
87. Ibid.
88. Ibid.
89. Ibid.
90. Abraham Lincoln, "Address on Colonization to a Committee of Colored Men," 142.
91. Ibid., 142–43.
92. Kate Masur, "The African American Delegation to Abraham Lincoln: A Reappraisal," *Civil War History* 56, no. 2, June 2010, 120.
93. Ibid.
94. Ibid., 130.
95. Ibid., 123.
96. Ibid., 130.
97. Ibid., 135. Quoted in Masur. George Kateb greatly exaggerates when he writes that "the delegation . . . went away apparently persuaded." Kateb, *Lincoln's Political Thought* (Cambridge, MA: Harvard University Press, 2015), 91.
98. Ibid.
99. Ibid., 144.
100. Burt argues that, in the end, "colonization . . . was mostly, but not entirely, strategic cover for Lincoln, not policy, although strategic cover can become policy under the right kind of pressure, and if Lincoln's remarks to the Committee of Colored Men are any indication, he might have been willing to press even more strongly for voluntary colonization had any remotely plausible plan for doing so presented itself and had the would-be colonists had the slightest enthusiasm for it." Given Burt's own recitation of Lincoln's long relationship to colonization and colonization schemes, it's not clear why Burt concludes that Lincoln only "might" have pursued colonization with more vigor given different, that is, more receptive circumstances. Burt, *Lincoln's Tragic Pragmatism*, 362.
101. There are (other) Lincoln readers who claim that Lincoln did not believe in colonization at all, but deployed it as a ruse to reassure Northerners that their war efforts would not result in their own harm with blacks migrating northward and taking their jobs and undoing their way of life. This is known as the lullaby thesis, and while

it seems designed to exonerate Lincoln and (even) make him look like a master politician, it strikes me as incredible. First of all, Lincoln did more than pretend to believe in colonization. He did his best to put it into practice, and his efforts resulted in grave harm to many African Americans. Those who had decamped to Haiti actually had to be rescued by the U.S. Navy. Second, if Lincoln did turn Machiavellian, he would have been gambling with the lives of other human beings in a way that perhaps only slave owners could appreciate. Besides, this wasn't just the strategy of a wily politician facing terrible decisions in the White House. This was a position Lincoln held his entire political career, including when he had no real reason to reassure white Northern citizens. See Phillip W. Magness and Sebastian N. Page's splendid *Colonization after Emancipation: Lincoln and the Movement for Black Resettlement* (Columbia: University of Missouri Press, 2011), 8–10.

102. Magness and Page, *Colonization after Emancipation*, 3.

103. Masur, "The African American Delegation to Abraham Lincoln: A Reappraisal," 143.

104. Magness and Page note that Lincoln's sustained efforts on behalf of colonization well into 1863, some two years after the standard narrative of Lincoln on slavery assumes they had ceased, "were detached from any sweeping sense of philosophical significance" and challenge the nation's official memory of Lincoln. "Colonization defies the conclusiveness granted to the slavery narrative by the final act of emancipation, seen as a fitting cap to centuries of struggle." *Colonization after Emancipation*, 5. On the other hand, colonization fits perfectly well with Lincoln's politics of elimination. When faced with a "problem" that defies resolution, he seeks to remove it altogether from the political scene so that it no longer needs to be addressed.

105. Abraham Lincoln, "Second Annual Message to Congress," in Ball, 163.

106. Ibid., 159.

107. Ibid., 164.

108. Kateb, *Lincoln's Political Thought*, 61.

109. Foner, *The Fiery Trial*, 130.

110. Ibid., 129.

111. Ibid., 225–26.

112. Ibid., 233.

113. Lincoln, "Second Annual Message," 166.

114. Foner notes of Lincoln: "He found it impossible to imagine a biracial society. . . . In fact, by the 1850s, the vast majority of black Americans—a far higher percentage, indeed, than of the white population—had been born in the United States." Foner, *The Fiery Trial*, 128.

115. Kateb, *Lincoln's Political Thought*, 61.

116. Foner, *The Fiery Trial*, 183–84.

117. Ibid., 128.

118. Ibid., 125.

119. Ibid., xx.

120. Ibid., xix.

121. Ibid., 21.

122. Ibid., xx–xxi.

123. Ibid., xx.
124. Ibid., 127–28. See also John Schaar, "The Case for Patriotism," *Legitimacy in the Modern State* (New Brunswick, NJ: Transaction Books, 1981).
125. Foner, *The Fiery Trial*, 129.
126. Ibid., 130.
127. Ibid.
128. Ibid., 131.
129. Ibid., 222.
130. Ibid., 223.
131. Ibid, emphases added.
132. Ibid., 225–26.
133. Ibid., 258–59.
134. Ibid., 260.

Chapter Five

What to the Indian Is the Gettysburg Address?

No wonder Lincoln journeyed to Pennsylvania in November 1863: Gettysburg fulfilled what had been promised in Philadelphia.

—Harold Holzer, *The Gettysburg Address: Perspectives on Lincoln's Greatest Speech*

But nothing in the Address hit home quite so effectively as the single aspect of the Address that we are least likely to recognize at once, and that was the survival of democracy.

—Allen C. Guelzo, "Little Note, Long Remember: Lincoln and the Murk of Myth at Gettysburg"

We are all doctrinal monotheists and our only patriotic god is the god of battles. We took the land from others whom we regarded as of no account.

—John Schaar, "The Case for Patriotism"

If, at Lincoln's inauguration following decisive reelection in 1864, the nation expected a celebration of (impending) military victory, or an extensive, wide-ranging encomium on the first four years of his administration, or an inspirational vision of Reconstruction, it received a largely self-lacerating sermon on the justness of divine punishment for the sins of slavery instead.

If, at the dedication of a new national cemetery commemorating Union dead following one of the Civil War's decisive, most gruesome battles, the nation expected a rousing tribute to the generals who planned and the soldiers who executed it, it received an abstract discourse on the larger meaning and significance of the conflict instead.[1]

If the Second Inaugural is widely considered Lincoln's greatest speech insofar as it effectively commended God for taking so many of the nation's young men for its profound moral transgressions, the Gettysburg Address must be rated his most moving public oration insofar as it effectively demanded of the nation that more and more of its young men die on its behalf.[2]

Either way, each address was stunning in its brevity, seemingly finished before it started, thereby giving their respective audiences little chance to absorb or react to them.

Nietzsche once mischievously insisted that it was his "ambition to say in ten sentences what everyone else says in a book—what everyone else *does not* say in a book."[3]

Lincoln, in the bloody aftermath of Lee's repulsion from Northern territory, managed to say in ten sentences what no one else ever quite managed to say in any number of books.[4]

The Gettysburg Address deserves the praise accorded it, a response that has only grown and intensified with time. It is a masterpiece of historical vision, patriotic politics, and rhetorical punch. Even Lincoln's most vehement contemporary critics appreciated its significance (they showed their appreciation through denunciation), perhaps more so than friends and allies.[5]

The Gettysburg Address, however, is essentially Janus-faced. It relies on a carefully crafted combination of racial presumption, willful blindness, and criminal concealment to work its problematic emotional magic. According to some, Lincoln transformed the United States when he delivered his dedicatory remarks—for the better, of course. Neither judgment is likely to survive close scrutiny unscathed.

At its core, the Gettysburg Address is tantamount to a celebration of national political violence, conducted through affirmation and thus erasure. It reflects the exceptionally troubled character of American democracy since its storied founding in 1776. The Gettysburg Address, that is, cannot shake its essential whiteness—not despite but actually because of its finest political ambitions.

While Lincoln is lauded for placing the Declaration of Independence at the center of American political life and redeeming the Constitution in the process, the Gettysburg Address is effectively a declaration of war against Indians, whose nations pose the only remaining threat to Jefferson's continental empire of liberty.

It's time to hear anew these 272 fraught words.

BLOODLETTING

By the summer of 1863, the Civil War had been dragging on for two inconclusive years. Stalemate haunted both sides. No end was in sight. The Confederate States of America believed Northern public opinion would be critical to winning secession. Thinking as much politically as militarily, the South wagered that a successful invasion of the North could prove decisive in the struggle for separation—even if any territory taken could not ultimately be retained. Lee's 1863 incursion into Pennsylvania would not be the first such foray, but the timing seemed propitious for scoring a knockout political blow.

The carnage of the Battle of Gettysburg shocked an already nonplussed nation. Total casualties topped fifty thousand, with nearly eight thousand killed. The numbers and visuals were gruesome, and the strategic outcome of the battle, no decision, augmented their horror.

Lee's invasion was repulsed. And prior to it, the South provided the country with a timely reminder about the nature of Confederate identity and principles. Lee's forces engaged in a campaign of terror in southern Pennsylvania in the days leading up to the battle—to gather information, steal whatever supplies were handy, and enslave and reenslave any blacks encountered. Their actual legal status meant nothing to Confederate forces. The very idea of a free black was not just an absurdity but an obscenity to them. Lee very nearly prevailed, but questionable generalship cost him in the end, and the North forced his retreat back to Southern territory.

Yet Union forces (now) under the command of George Meade, rather than seize the moment, failed to pursue Lee and deliver a fatal blow to his retreating army and thus the Confederate war effort. Lee was ultimately able to cross the Potomac to safety. A chance to end the already interminable conflict had been lost, infuriating Lincoln. He had replaced Hooker and other generals because of their failure (or refusal, given Southern sympathies) to be sufficiently aggressive, and Meade had made the same intolerable mistake at perhaps the most inopportune moment. The South might have been stunned and reeling, but the North was hardly celebrating after the battle. Each side suffered terrible losses in the bloodiest engagement of the war.

The conflagration at Gettysburg hardly seemed to present an occasion for great civic oratory. Garry Wills astutely observes, "It would have been hard to predict that Gettysburg, out of all this muddle, these missed chances, all the senseless deaths, would become a symbol of national purpose, pride, and ideals. Abraham Lincoln transformed the ugly reality into something rich and strange—and he did it with 272 words. The power of words has rarely been given a more compelling demonstration."[6]

For the North, each state was represented at the Battle of Gettysburg, including Minnesota, which guaranteed Lincoln a complete Union audience, as it were, at the cemetery's opening. The war between the sections, however, was not the only armed conflict conducted during Lincoln's first term in office. War was also waged against American Indians, in particular the Dakota Sioux in Minnesota, as we saw in chapter 1. The two conflicts were linked. Minnesota would have trouble meeting its troop quotas because of Indian resistance, potentially affecting the war's outcome, especially if the state set a negative example for the draft quota. Nevertheless, Minnesota was effectively granted an extension when Lincoln advised them to "attend to the Indians." Though formally denied more time, Lincoln conceded to Minnesota's governor that "If the draft cannot proceed of course it will not proceed. Necessity knows no law."[7] This meant American military endeavors during Lincoln's tenure in office exceeded the hostilities ordinarily captured by the term Civil War. It also encompassed what could rightly be considered a foreign or international war between sovereign powers that constituted an immediate and unwelcome distraction, on the one hand, and pointed to the inescapability of new, additional wars once the South was defeated, on the other hand. Each conflict posed its own distinct threat to the (so-called) territorial integrity of the Union, initially Lincoln's greatest (and only) concern vis-à-vis the South. But as far as the North was concerned, only the intraracial war could lay claim to legitimacy.

Not surprisingly, Northern elements insisted (without any foundation) that the Confederate States were responsible for the Indian uprising in Minnesota. Nothing else could explain the "sudden" insurrection—certainly not American history or policy. The presumption of Southern involvement exacerbated the outrage Minnesotans (and others) felt about the violence and deflected their own culpability. A conspiracy wasn't needed, of course, to justify a war of extermination against Indians. Either way, the military could acquire invaluable experience in the search-and-destroy ethos Union forces deployed against them, which in certain respects prefigured the total war they would eventually wage against their Southern enemy—with one notable exception. The North did not (nor would it) eradicate the people of the South as such, despite their responsibility for death and destruction on a scale Indians could not match.

Lincoln's Gettysburg Address, then, illuminates American national identity in unexpected ways. Lincoln not only uses the cemetery's opening to wage ideological civil war and disseminate propaganda against the Confederacy, as Wills argues.[8] The address unthinkingly presumes the reality of conflicts larger—and other—than those raised by the Southern war of aggression.[9] That is, it subsumes the inter-national wars of conquest and expansion that preceded, accompanied, and followed the Civil War.

LINCOLN'S LEGERDEMAIN

Lincoln's conclusory opening to the Gettysburg oration invites critical examination. It may operate in the realm of political mythology, but this doesn't necessarily make it a myth to transmit unremarked. Lincoln locates the founding principles of the United States in 1776 and the Declaration of Independence, not 1787 and the new Constitution ratified by "we the people." In American political life, this means the Declaration is central and the Constitution secondary, the best approximation of the Declaration at any given moment. On Lincoln's reading, the founders created a system that made it possible, though not inevitable, that the nation would come progressively closer (and closer) to realizing the values expressed in the Declaration. The Declaration's sweeping equality claim means that even though the nation's fathers were white and founded the nation with and for other white people, those of color were also normatively included. Presumably this logic entails people with black *or* red skin. Nevertheless, while Lincoln (ultimately) envisaged including the former in some fashion, he remained forever indifferent, at best, to the latter.[10]

At first glance, Lincoln's initial words appear bold and daring: "Four score and seven years ago our fathers brought forth on this continent, a new nation, conceived in Liberty, and dedicated to the proposition that all men are created equal."[11] The magical, miraculous verbs of creation and birth, however, are not as benign as they (might) sound. American colonists forged a new nation out of the old one they were divorcing. The separation they effected was born in and of violence and war—and not only against their British brethren. The new nation was also brought forth thanks to slavery. The enormous wealth it generated was critical in financing and thus winning the Revolutionary War. Without slavery, there would have been no liberty.[12] The new nation was also fashioned out of aggression against Native peoples, for whom the "new nation" meant dispossession, displacement, destruction, and death.[13] Absent Indian killing and removal, there would have been no territorial grounding for the new nation, which does not look so new after all. This aggression, moreover, started long before 1776. It started from day one.[14]

Lincoln's invocation of the Declaration of Independence, which presupposes and establishes the democratic credentials of the United States, thus betrays a willful ignorance of American history. The Declaration delivered to a distant monarch was a comprehensive document of indignation and discontent that could have been employed by Native peoples to catalog the list of offenses committed against them by the would-be American nation. They suffered (and were suffering) from "a long train of abuses and usurpations . . . design[ed] to reduce them under absolute Despotism," which made it "their right . . . their duty, to throw off such" despotism. After all, "the history of [the United States] is a history of repeated injuries and usurpations, all having in direct object the establishment of an absolute Tyranny over [Native peoples]" that British ambitions in America cannot rival. Indian nations could take the "Facts . . . submitted" by the thirteen colonies to "a candid world" and present them to the United States itself. It has "kept among" them "standing Armies without the[ir] Consent." It is guilty of "waging war against" them. It has "burnt their" villages "and destroyed the lives of [their] people." It is intending "to compleat the works of death, desolation, and tyranny, already begun with circumstances of Cruelty & perfidy scarcely paralleled in the most barbarous ages, and totally unworthy of . . . a civilized nation." Moreover, protests by Indians were "answered only by repeated injury." And Indian nations already enjoyed the "separate and equal station" to which the American colonists aspired. The authors of the Declaration, however, claim sovereign Native peoples to be nothing more than "Savages, whose known rule of warfare, is an undistinguished destruction of all ages, sexes, and conditions." They are mentioned only as the tools of the tyrannical king who incites them. Thus they are part of the bill of indictment. Indians stand in the way of American independence. They always obstruct the rightful extension of "*our frontiers.*"[15]

When Lincoln writes in the second paragraph, "*Now* we are engaged in a great civil war, testing whether that nation or any nation so conceived and so dedicated, can long endure," his nineteenth-century temporality is deceptively insufficient, if not exactly mistaken.[16] The so-called new nation, carved out along the eastern seaboard, harbored imperial ambitions even prior to its birth. It thought of itself as a continental enterprise, not a regional endeavor. And this new nation was certainly not born dedicated to the proposition that all men are created equal. The founders' assumption of racial superiority informed and enabled the original conception. If the idea of equality had substance, they would have looked elsewhere to establish a permanent home for themselves. Rather, once they stepped foot on the continent, the land was theirs and (to be) theirs alone. The liberty that ultimately followed was thus predicated upon a negation of the liberty (and equality) of others. For them, self-determination was incorrigibly singular.

The problem, then, with Lincoln's treatment of the past is not just that it erases, again, founding crimes. It's that it erases them through affirmation. Lincoln does not raise the question of founding political crimes because no such question needs to be raised—no crimes took place. 1776 is an occasion for *national* pride, not shame or embarrassment. No other nation(s), in Lincoln's awestruck Gettysburg narration, paid a price for American success. It was an accomplishment without consequences. This is an exceptional version of American exceptionalism.[17] It also erases, because it ignores, the racial violence that proceeded from the founding. Founding crimes cannot be restricted to the era of conception and birth. They continue in perpetuity, each transgression leading to the need for subsequent offenses. Each exercise of creative-destructive nation-building, that is, engenders resistance to it. It may aspire to completeness, but it cannot attain it—hence the need for subsequent offenses. The exercise of violence on another people, then, means perpetual removal, perhaps elimination.[18]

The Gettysburg Address affirms this history of violence in one fell swoop. When it comes to the question of America's original commitment to equality, Wills deems Lincoln's singular assertion of it a remarkable sleight of hand. He insist the thousands assembled had their constitutional pockets picked, as Lincoln substituted his account for theirs without their knowledge or consent.[19] Sean Wilentz effectively challenges Wills's assessment, noting that Lincoln was hardly the first to identify the Declaration of Independence as the foundational document of American democracy. This position "had been a staple of antislavery politics at least since the Missouri crisis in 1819." Nor was there any subterfuge involved. Lincoln had been making the claim "for nearly a decade."[20] This minor scholarly disagreement, however, may obscure a more important issue.

What led Lincoln (and others) to make this claim? What work do Lincoln's words perform? Wills writes of the address, "Lincoln is here not only to sweeten the air of Gettysburg, but to clear the infected atmosphere of American history itself, tainted with official sins and inherited guilt. He would cleanse the Constitution." Unlike William Lloyd Garrison, who burned the document "that countenanced slavery," Lincoln "altered [it] from within, by appeal from its letter to the spirit, subtly changing the recalcitrant stuff of that legal compromise, bringing it to its own indictment."[21] Insofar as Wills restricts himself to atmospherics and acknowledges one instance of founding racial tyranny, vis-à-vis African Americans but not Indians, he reveals Lincoln's limited aspiration. Wills rejects the essential whiteness of the Declaration of Independence and, like Lincoln, he assumes America's dialectical capacity to transcend itself and become *bi*colored. Wills thus reiterates Lincoln's understanding of the founding fathers, who might appear to be fatally compromised by their accommodations with slavery, but Lincoln documents the efforts they made to contain and then constrict the institution so that it would suffer ultimate extinction. Wills does the same for Lincoln, claiming that he mimicked the framers and did what he could, often behind the scenes, to contain and gradually eliminate slavery.[22] Whether or not this argument is compelling, it is worth nothing that Wills does not even try to make a similar claim for progressive justice regarding Native peoples. It pertains to Lincoln and blacks alone. In this respect Wills is faithful to Lincoln's complicated legacy. He applauds Lincoln for not wasting time trying to make abolitionist arguments in a context where such arguments were bound to fail. Rather, he made known his opposition to slavery, for which he could make a compelling case without embracing the broader abolitionist ideology regarding full equality. Again, whether or not this provides suitable grounds for veneration, Lincoln does not even gesture toward the same kinds of (minimal) arguments in favor of equality and freedom for Indians. This is more than a question of an omission that can be corrected later. Rather, Lincoln effectively implicates newly freed blacks in the national project of settler colonialism. What this means, then, is that Wills's contribution to Lincoln as a democratic icon worthy of admiration calls for its own subversion.[23]

Lincoln's (newly free) America might become increasingly bicolored, but not tri- or multicolored: Indians were not to be included, not ever.[24] Their removal and exclusion, even elimination, are the conditions of possibility of the American nation as it invents and reinvents itself. Reinvention refers not just to the realization of ideals but also to the realization of its extended continental ambitions, which Lincoln affirmed and advanced. Thus, when Wills writes, "Both North and South strove to win the battle for *interpreting* Gettysburg as soon as the physical battle had ended. Lincoln is after even larger game—he means to 'win' the whole Civil War in ideological terms as well as military ones. And he will succeed: the Civil War *is*, to most Americans, what Lincoln wanted it to *mean*. Words had to complete the work of the guns," the South never had a chance.[25] Ironically, however, the South would lose one race war, at least on the battlefield, and then become partners in another, one it had also long been fighting and could win, especially in league with the Union. What Wills doesn't say here is that Lincoln's rhetoric converts words into weapons, capitalizing on a kind of linguistic violence. Words can lead to more work, that is, more violence, to be completed by guns. Thus, when Wills writes, "When [Lincoln] refers to the fathers, it is usually to call them the authors of the Declaration of Independence. . . . The act of bringing forth a new nation conceived in liberty is always an *intellectual* act for Lincoln," he actually damns Lincoln, for founding is also necessarily a material act whose violence is signaled in the words reflecting it.[26] Lincoln does not wish self-government to perish from the Earth, but neither does he respect its establishment everywhere on it. Rather than exercise his powers to progressively realize it wherever possible, he actually works to prevent it on the North American continent where success might mean another people—in life-and-death competition with America—would enjoy self-government.

Perhaps Lincoln can accommodate blacks because whites have lived side by side with them in America from the beginning, though in a master-slave relationship. The same is not true of Native Americans, who have largely lived apart as sovereign nations and peoples. If blacks represent difference, Indians represent otherness. Difference can be accommodated. Otherness must be excreted. Blacks might read the Declaration and wonder how and why it does not already include them as equal citizens in a country they themselves built. Native Americans might read the Declaration and recognize themselves as already possessing the status that white colonists now claim for themselves, which means they don't need a Declaration to proclaim themselves free. They were already free when "we the people" emerged to introduce, realize, and perfect their (white) principles. The only way for the ideals embodied in the Declaration to apply to Native peoples on Lincoln's progressive model would be for whites to deny and take those ideals from them. Later, they would then be granting what they had no right to usurp in the first place. Native Americans flourished before whites arrived to show them what they did not enjoy because they had taken it from them.

RECRUITMENT SPEECH FOR PERPETUAL WAR

Insofar as the fighting at Gettysburg did not definitively clarify the Civil War's final resolution, the country faced at least another year of conflict. The volunteer system had collapsed and conscription was confronted with its own challenges, including violent resistance, as the New York City draft riots attested. Lincoln thus used the dedicatory occasion for traditional patriotic purposes, much as Pericles did in his famous Funeral Oration in ancient Athens during the Peloponnesian War with Sparta.[27] Lincoln needed to inspire and induce young men to fight the war, in part because of the many incentives to shirk their duties, including those folded into the Conscription Act itself, as mentioned in chapter 1, where a man could avoid service if he could find a substitute or buy his way out of it by paying a fee.

As Mark Schantz argues, Lincoln redefined the meaning of death in America.[28] It's not that human mortality did not already enjoy a prominent place in American cultural life. The rural cemetery movement demonstrated otherwise. It was common practice for people to reflect on the meaning of loss for their family or for themselves. Lincoln, however, moved them in another direction. Remembrance would now take on a more nationalistic quality: "The dead at Gettysburg belonged fully to the American nation, not to their families, not to their friends, and not even, in the end, to themselves."[29] This also meant that the cemetery, while belonging to the people of Gettysburg and to Pennsylvania, would principally belong to the United States. The cemetery represented a national project.[30]

Not surprisingly, then, Lincoln invokes the founding fathers in the opening paragraph to identify them, to quote Wills, as the "begetters of the national idea."[31] It is this idea that will inspire the nation at war. We will fight now on behalf of that idea just as the founders did in the first generation of the country's life. This makes the founders an inspiring presence. "The fathers are always relevant because the idea is never old. It is life-giving every time new Americans are begotten out of it. Americans are *intellectually* autochthonous, having no pedigree except that of the idea."[32]

The force attached to this idea can be seen in Lincoln's 1858 Fourth of July Address, cited by Wills. While there are blood descendants of the founding generation among us, they have no special claim to their fathers' legacy. Lincoln estimates that half of the American population stems from Europe, and he cites German, Irish, French, and Scandinavian immigrants who became citizens as our equals. They may not be able to look to America's glorious past and identify with those remarkable figures that brought the country into being, but they can read the words these men placed in the Declaration of Independence and identify with them and make them their own. They are entitled to them as much as anyone else. Lincoln's examples, however, are European, white. He did not look to or even gesture toward those "outsiders" already within the United States for similar inclusion. "The 'great task remaining' at the end of the Address is not something inferior to the great deeds of the fathers. It is the *same* work, always being done, and making all its champions the heroes of the nation's permanent ideal."[33] If it is always being done, it is not always being done for all people, especially those who are geographically autochthonous.

Wills nevertheless champions Lincoln's faith in the permanent possibility of a new birth of freedom that is "always available to people begotten of a proposition in the first place," and turns to Lincoln's Peoria address for support: "Our republican robe is soiled, and trailed in the dust. Let us repurify it. Let us turn and wash it white, in the spirit, if not the blood, of the Revolution."[34] Contra Lincoln, the blood imagery is apt. America's republican robe was never pure. As previously mentioned, in the early days of the Revolution, when the war looked lost in late 1776, George Washington, as he retreated from Long Island, took time to eradicate Indians along the way, looking to a postwar world in which the colonists have managed, somehow, to prevail. They did not plan, if possible, to share a land they considered theirs alone, land for which they fought and died. The very idea of the founding thus inspired Washington and his men to acts of racial cleansing (or purity).[35] Wills notes that "we assume, today, that self-government includes self-rule by blacks as well as whites; but at the time of his appearance at Gettysburg Lincoln was not advocating, even eventually the suffrage for African Americans." Why? The great task Lincoln mentions "is not emancipation but the preservation of self-government."[36] Wills's omission of Indians here is telling, insofar as the United States, since its founding, effectively governed Indian self-rule. That is, Native peoples were anything but self-governing, particularly over land, which Lincoln, in his fight to save the Union, a territorial entity, held sacred.

To repeat, Lincoln writes in the second paragraph: "*Now* we are engaged in a great civil war, *testing* whether that nation or any nation so conceived and so dedicated, can long endure."[37] The suggestion of Lincoln's contemporary temporal focus notwithstanding, this is not America's first endurance test. Since the Declaration, the possibility of a nation so conceived and dedicated has been perpetually tested. Indians always constituted the first test and the new nation never passed it. In fact, it never had a chance of passing it.[38]

Nevertheless, Lincoln must attend to the Civil War's successful prosecution. Thus he turns to perhaps the most powerful weapon he enjoys for leverage: the dead. "We are met on a great battlefield of that war. We have come to dedicate a portion of that field, as a *final resting place* for those who here *gave* their lives that that nation might live. It is altogether fitting and proper that we should do this." Lincoln provides no specifics about the Battle of Gettysburg. He does not single out officers for exceptional performances, nor does he mention individual soldiers by name. He speaks of the "brave men, living and dead, who struggled" on the fields of Gettysburg and what the living must do in their name to honor them. Above all, Lincoln does not want them to die for nothing. This means that the living must be dedicated to continuing the work that the "honored dead" did so much to further. They "nobly advanced" this work but did not finish it. While Lincoln downplays the significance of the words anyone in his position may utter, if the living are to complete the "task remaining before" them, his words must be able to inspire and motivate. Lincoln tries to put the focus on those who "gave" their lives, but the focus must, despite denials, come back to him, especially in a war that has (often) lacked popularity. Lincoln must convince young men to keep fighting, volunteer, or alternatively, to obey conscription orders. The North desperately needs bodies, and Lincoln uses the Gettysburg dead to secure them. He is arguing that the living owe a debt to the dead and that that the only way to repay the debt is to risk and possibly sacrifice their lives in return.[39] Ironically, this means they must make themselves available to be similarly honored in the future.[40]

There is no end to this logic. The war (*this* war) may end, but there will always be more wars, and the need to honor the accomplishments of the dead always remains. How will the last of the Civil War dead be honored by those who follow them in uniform? They won't have long to learn the answer. Sacrifice need not mean death in every instance, but the willingness to serve-cum-sacrifice always entails the possibility of death. It is patriotism's death logic, and Lincoln's version of it is picture perfect: economical, riveting, inspirational, rousing, and poetic. Lincoln insists that it is "from these honored dead [that] we take increased devotion."[41] Yet who is this "we," exactly? Without comment, Lincoln doesn't honor both the living and the dead who fought nobly at Gettysburg—only the latter. What separates them other than the fortunes of war, that is, chance? The living, then, find themselves effectively erased. Those who fought and survived do not merit equal tribute. Only by dying does one receive the highest accolades from the nation. When Lincoln speaks directly to the living and informs them of their duty, then, he is also, by definition, speaking to the living that fought at Gettysburg. Apparently they have not yet done enough. They, too, must (re)dedicate themselves to the task remaining before them, as if they were not sufficiently dedicated already—because they did not die. They must fight again and die if they want to receive the highest praise from the state. This degree of dedication is necessary since the unfinished work of which Lincoln speaks has another enemy awaiting it that will receive full attention once the South is suppressed. Gettysburg is the occasion for Lincoln's oration, but it could have been given at any Union victory—or defeat. It is inherently mobile. What's more, not all those who have died in the Civil War have been killed fighting Southern insurgents. Some have been fighting Indians. They, too, are covered by Lincoln's words. He is using the idea of a (sacred) final resting place to inspire young men to volunteer for war so this nation might live, now *and in the future*. He does not mention that the conduct of this war must entail disrespecting and destroying the sacred final resting place of others, more specifically, of those who preceded them on the continent: First Peoples, old nations.

The Gettysburg Address, the unlimited temporal flexibility of which may not initially sink in or be apparent, prophecies a reunified nation, North and South, ready to move into the future against a common enemy.[42] It thus implicitly points to the upcoming tests the nation will face with Indian Tribes (how Native Americans are referenced in the Constitution). As already demonstrated by the 1862 war with the Dakota Sioux, the presence of Native peoples blocked westward expansion. Following the Civil War, when gold was discovered on Native American lands, the United States would not hesitate to break treaties and force Indians to relocate to smaller and smaller reservations—or make war on them if they refused. The persistent refoundings enacted through perpetual inter-national wars also tested the nation's dedication to its founding principles, but whites did not need much incentive to rush west for the possibility of untold riches. Lincoln's Gettysburg Address could be considered one of the documents undergirding this migration and conquest. It's not hard to imagine, for example, President Grant delivering it on the grave site of the Battle of Little Bighorn in June of 1876 to pay final respects to the honored dead and to guarantee that they, too, do not die in vain.

For Steven Spielberg, Lincoln's call to—and for—permanent arms and sacrifice may be his greatest legacy. As we saw in chapter 2, Lincoln is first encountered as he watches his troops depart for the Battle of Wilmington.

Two young (white) soldiers approach him with nervous awe, thrilled to be in his presence. Before reciting to him his most famous speech, they inform Lincoln that they were present at the Gettysburg ceremonies and enlisted only after hearing him speak his inspirational words. For them, the war was not worth fighting until then—though it did take them over a year to sign up. But they are determined to carry on the work of the founders and their fellow soldiers, as he implored them. Life is considered the ultimate sacrifice, and they are prepared to make it. What, though, is the unfinished work, the cause, for which these post-Gettysburg soldiers are willing to fight and die? For what did their predecessors at Gettysburg fight and die? As Garry Wills argues, it is not emancipation but self-government.[43] This means that the new birth of freedom Lincoln anticipates for the nation is not really a new birth but a first birth. Self-government without emancipation is a contradiction in terms. At the same time, it involves an underside.

Lincoln may be determined to ensure "that government of the people, by the people, for the people, shall not perish from the Earth,"[44] but he cannot see the United States as the principal suppressor of self-government on the continent America calls its own—regardless of the Civil War's outcome. Again, this is not incidental to the Declaration of Independence but constitutive of it. White dominion was predicated on black and especially red subordination. When Jefferson asserted that declaring independence makes it necessary for the United States, as it assumes its separate and equal station among the powers of the earth, to show a decent respect for the opinion of mankind and state the reasons for divorce, he did not imagine the Indian nations as addressees. They were not considered separate and equal powers of the earth, and their opinions were irrelevant.

Following the founders' example after the Revolutionary War, once the Civil War concludes Lincoln and America can turn their attention westward, toward continental expansion through, among other things, the railroad. Indians stand in the way. While Schantz notes that no Southerners were buried at Gettysburg, the earthly exclusion did not prevent a wider reconciliation with this mortal enemy, "Unlike the oration delivered by Edward Everett, Lincoln spent no time in the Gettysburg address parsing out Union or confederate troops or assigning blame to the South for the carnage of the war. . . . [H]e stayed away from recrimination with respect to the secessionists. In its capacious reach . . . the Gettysburg address adumbrates the posture Lincoln would strike in the Second Inaugural address in which he laid out the phrase 'with malice toward none; with charity for all' as a guiding principle for the postwar nation. At Gettysburg, Lincoln opened the possibility for any American—in the North or in the South—to be dedicated to the broader mission of American democracy."[45]

162   *Chapter Five*

   Not surprisingly, Schantz's articulation of the details of Lincoln's Gettysburg ethos reveals the exclusiveness and betrayal at work in it. Not every American can be dedicated to the broader mission of American democracy. Native Americans cannot be dedicated to it because it means their eradication. Lincoln and America did bear them malice. Schantz signals this limitation when he confines what it means to be an American to those (whites, the former Civil War combatants) living "in the North and in the South," a racially informed geopolitical designation that in this context omits Native peoples. While Schantz concedes, "The burial of the Civil War dead thus communicated in no uncertain terms that some Americans lived, and died, outside the scope of Abraham Lincoln's elastic remarks at Gettysburg," what he does not say is that Southerners could fold themselves into the nation and easily find themselves buried in another national soldier's cemetery in the future should they choose to join the national mission.[46] Nothing, except their reversible commitments to slavery, secession, and war, prevents it in advance. They could affirm and embrace a way of life that would, in time, become their own. There was no necessary incommensurability between North and South. The latter would not be displaced or destroyed and could do without—would be better off without—the institution of slavery. No such dynamic applied to American Indians. In their confrontation with white sovereignty, they stood to lose everything, permanently. To join the American mission would be tantamount to declaring and waging war against themselves. What's more, Lincoln could not insist on the idea that they leave America because they hailed from elsewhere. They were the indigenous peoples, which Lincoln seemed to forget when insisting that blacks, not the nation of immigrants Lincoln represented, deport themselves. Schantz incidentally signals this reality when he writes, "the 'new birth of freedom' to which Abraham Lincoln referred was not a goal to be pursued in the next world, but a political program to be realized in contemporary America."[47] Yes, *America*, all of America, not just the South, named the scope and target of Lincoln and the country's ambition.

   Chandra Manning goes Mark Schantz one better. In "Shared Suffering and the Way to Gettysburg," she argues that Lincoln's new vision for America rooted in the centrality of the Declaration of Independence was "achieved and achievable specifically through shared suffering and loss."[48] Lincoln and the soldiers who fought and bled for the Union became united in understanding that the war, given its extraordinary carnage, would not mean very much if the Union were simply restored to the status quo ante.[49] Slavery needed to be abolished. This gave the Union "a worldwide significance." Manning thus quotes Lincoln's first message to Congress in which he claimed that the Civil War "embraces more than the fate of these United States. It presents to the whole family of man, the question, whether a constitutional republic, or a democracy—a government of the people, by the same people—can, or cannot, maintain its territorial integrity, against its own domestic foes."[50] Manning's narrative canonizes Northern forces that saw through to the end "a journey characterized chiefly by suffering and loss, but suffering and loss that neither [Lincoln] nor they were willing to allow to descend into meaningless nihilism."[51]

Manning ignores, presumably because Lincoln also ignores, the suffering inflicted on Indians on the way to Gettysburg and the suffering that would be inflicted on them after Gettysburg. The territorial integrity of the United States consisted of a fluid, shifting, expanding set of borders and boundaries. Maintenance may have been the goal vis-à-vis the South, but aggrandizement names the national mission, as Lincoln well knew. He presided over a country and military that, not long before he assumed office, invaded and conquered Mexico and seized half of its territory. Native Americans were subjected to the same treatment—not once, but repeatedly, despite treaty commitments. The domestic foes to which Lincoln refers are the seceding Southern states, but these are not the only domestic foes the United States boasts. The difference is that the Southern states were making war against their own country without legitimate cause or reason, and trying to take part of it. They were attacking what was also theirs, something to which they still belonged, according to Lincoln. Again, none of this holds true for Native peoples, who were trying to hang on to what little was left of something larger that was wrongfully taken from them, something that they initially possessed by themselves.

Manning praises Lincoln's conclusion to the Gettysburg Address insofar as "he emphasized that securing the declaration's legacy required the descendants of the founders not simply to continue residing on the North American land mass but specifically to uphold the form of government 'of the people, by the people, and for the people' that the founders had established."[52] It's as if the founders had actually established such government, that none had been excluded, and that it had come at no cost—especially to others. Yet the North American land mass to which she refers was not the founders' to reside on as they pleased, though Manning writes as if they had made it their own through the war that the Declaration formalized in writing. She thereby erases Native Americans from the land mass where they do in fact reside. Thus when she writes admiringly that the Civil War, exemplified by Gettysburg, was a combination of "triumph and tragedy" and that "the Gettysburg Address and the new birth of freedom heralded at its climax were products of loss as much as victory, of being plunged into death and ugliness with no luxury of skipping over them or easy remedy of sinking into them, but only the necessity of trudging through them," she privileges the self-inflicted wounds of warring white people who cannot see that what they do involves more sovereign peoples than themselves.[53] Whites are not the world.

In *The Fiery Trial*, discussed in the last chapter, Eric Foner seems to appreciate Lincoln's terrible shortcomings regarding Indians. While he argues that Lincoln's political career, perhaps especially his presidency, was characterized by evolution and that his capacity for growth was impressive, Foner also notes that "Lincoln's attitudes regarding blacks stand in stark contrast to the lack of change when it came to Native Americans."[54] Still, he insists that Lincoln "was never an Indian hater" and compares his attitude and conduct to General John Pope and Minnesota Governor Alexander Ramsey.[55] Pope was responsible for crushing the Dakota Sioux rebellion in Minnesota and would have exterminated the entire tribe if possible. Ramsey urged Lincoln to approve the execution of every one of the three-hundred-plus Sioux put on trial in bogus military courts and condemned to death. Foner cites Lincoln's mandatory review of capital sentences to make his case. "Lincoln carefully reviewed the trial records and commuted the sentences of all but thirty-eight. (Nevertheless, this still constituted the largest official execution in American history.)"[56] Though implying, given the sheer number of them, that Lincoln was generous and merciful in his commutations, Foner ignores the irremediably problematic nature of each and every trial, as well as their political character (this was racially motivated punishment for a war of resistance, after all). Nor does Foner comment on the meaning of the mass execution. The defendants were not executed as individuals.

"Overall, not surprisingly, Lincoln devoted little attention to Indian policy during his presidency. He gave army commanders free rein when it came to campaigns against Indians in the West." Foner admits the results were "predictable": massacres of hundreds of Indians on numerous occasions.[57] Lincoln furthered what today is called ethnic cleansing. For Lincoln, Indians "lacked civilization and constituted an obstacle to the economic development of the West," not to mention to "the unified nation-state that emerged from the war."[58] Lincoln and America wanted Indian land, and thanks to legislation such as the Pacific Railroad and Homestead Acts, they got it—though Foner considers this nothing more than "encroachment," despite noting that "in his message to Congress, Lincoln spoke of the need to extinguish the 'possessory rights of the Indians to large and valuable tracts of land.'"[59] Lincoln supposedly tried to combine white expansion with "the welfare of the Indian," but as Foner notes, "he did not acknowledge that these aims were mutually contradictory."[60] Still, Foner's claim that Lincoln probably did "not have any special animus toward Indians" and that his "policies were depressingly similar to those of virtually every nineteenth-century president" becomes telling.[61] Lincoln did not consider them at all, which enabled his mass killing and dispossession of Indians. Animus can be addressed, but not indifference.

How does Foner account for the difference in Lincoln's treatment of blacks and Indians? "The influences that operated to change his views regarding blacks had no counterpart when it came to Native Americans."[62] This difference remains despite the fact (as Foner notes) that thousands of Indians served in the Union Army during the war. Lacking the support of "a large social movement," this patriotic sacrifice amounted to nothing for possible inclusion and citizenship in the postwar American polity.[63] Nor, of course, did it suggest to Lincoln that Indians could—and were entitled to—govern themselves on their own land. What Foner does not mention is that Lincoln did have one influence that might have led to the change that is so admired in him: his experience with blacks themselves. When one set of prejudices begins to erode, it often calls into question other prejudices simultaneously exercised or indulged. Apparently, however, Lincoln's racism toward Indians was so entrenched that the gradual awakening he (supposedly) experienced with blacks made no larger impression on him. The pronounced lack of capaciousness throws doubt on the evolution narrative Foner presents, especially given Lincoln's unduly long and strong commitment to colonization.

LINCOLN BEYOND GETTYSBURG

This is not to deny that the Gettysburg Address can function as a source of inspiration in ways that Lincoln did not imagine or intend, but might still be considered within the spirit of his remarks and thus his political vision. Jean Baker neatly summarizes the political character of the speech and argues that "in time these 272 words would become a much-heralded delineation of American values, and, as such, they would provide a vision for women."[64] Apparently not satisfied with this result, Baker expands her reach. "To the extent that the Gettysburg Address has been hailed as an American classic, it must be so for all the people."[65] Baker does not explain what she means by "all the people," but given its comprehensiveness, why should she? Her statement would seem to deny any and all exclusions.

In the next paragraph, however, Baker notes the limited ambitions of the American Revolution, which was designed to terminate British rule, not change the face of America. She notes that while the new nation may have been conceived in liberty, "it certainly had not changed the legal position of women or slaves." Would the inclusion of these two groups have sufficed if they had been named? Here Baker turns to the meeting of women at Seneca Falls, New York, "to organize a woman's movement." They issued a "Declaration of Rights and Sentiments," a document that looked not to the U.S. Constitution but the Declaration of Independence for inspiration. "Like Lincoln, these women believed that the American Revolution promised but had not delivered liberties to all. Like Lincoln, who had the abolition of slavery on his mind, they believed that the nation had been conceived to install these freedoms. In their belief half the population had been denied them not because of their race, but because of their sex."[66]

Baker's assessment broadens the Revolution's failing to include women, but she seems to assume that once white and black men and women are covered, the Revolution's promise can be considered fulfilled. Yet Baker's bicolor scheme, however admirable, is limited. It speaks to white and black women but not, apparently, to white, black, and red women (or men). The blindness to Indians would resurface in 1876 on the one-hundredth anniversary of the Declaration of Independence when "the suffrage women of America issued a woman's Declaration of Independence" in which they noted "the unfinished nature of America's experiment in self-government." They assumed, "while *all men of every race, and clime and condition have been invested with the full rights of citizenship* . . . all women still suffer the degradation of disenfranchisement."[67] While such a sweeping assessment might make for pleasing, rousing rhetoric, it runs afoul of enthusiastic overstatement. While the suffrage women are issuing their declaration, American Indians continue to fight for their existential lives in, among other places, the western United States. The Battle of Little Bighorn had been fought just two weeks before. The point is not to make a comparative claim about suffering. The point is that the blindness inherent in Lincoln's Gettysburg Address, which reiterated the blindness of the founders' Declaration of Independence, also strikes the women's movement.

Louis Masur suffers from a similar blindness.[68] Theorizing the Gettysburg Address as a continuation of Lincoln's commitment to emancipation and a new role for blacks in the war, Masur explores Lincoln's public writings from the Emancipation Proclamation on January 1, 1863, to the address in November. In this context the proclamation constitutes not an end for Lincoln but a beginning on the question of emancipation.[69] While I think Masur is right to link the address to emancipation, he arguably falls prey to Lincoln's soaring rhetoric in the process. Referencing Lincoln's correspondence with workingmen's groups in Manchester, England, he quotes Lincoln approvingly for insisting that the United States "was built upon the foundations of human rights," and that the conclusion of the war would result in "the universal triumph of justice, humanity, and freedom."[70] It is the claim to universality that is deeply troubling. It's not just that universal justice would not be achieved; it could not be realized—not in the United States as it was then constituted. Masur highlights Lincoln's letter to James C. Conkling in August in which Lincoln, among other things, condemns the South for its resort to violence. Once the South has been defeated and peace comes, "it will then have been proved that, among free men, there can be no successful appeal from the ballot to the bullet; and that they who take such appeal are sure to lose their case, and pay the cost."[71] It is one thing to denounce those who support a political order as long as it delivers results to their liking but then turn on it when they suffer electoral defeat. It's another thing to condemn those who never had access to a ballot (and never wanted it) who turn to violence when they can no longer stomach their violent oppression. American Indians do not mimic Southern rebels.

At the same time, Lincoln's intellectual indebtedness to Daniel Webster made it inevitable that he would approach Southern secession and Native American insurrection in similarly violent fashion. Craig Symonds delineates the influence that the Webster-Hayne exchange in the U.S. Senate had on Lincoln. Robert Hayne, senator from South Carolina, followed in the ideological footsteps of John C. Calhoun when he argued for a dual system of sovereignty to govern the United States. Claims to the contrary, Hayne did not fear the exercise of undue national power per se. Rather, he feared for the future of slavery and saw future national power as a possible threat to its continuation. When national power was used on behalf of slavery (in such legislation as the Fugitive Slave Act), he had no issue with its exercise. Webster, to say the least, had the better of the constitutional arguments. Hayne may well have longed for a return of the Articles of Confederation, but the 1787 Constitution offered him no support for his states' rights claims. With arguments for dual sovereignties theoretically and politically bankrupt, the Confederacy would seek a single version for itself through secession. Lincoln would crush this in the name of territorial integrity. Indian nations posed an even greater threat, for they represented not so much dual sovereignty but a prior contending sovereignty the legitimacy of which Lincoln was helpless to discredit. The so-called Confederate States were bitter losers in a system they could no longer dominate to their liking. Native peoples, vis-à-vis whites anyway, were nothing of the kind. Given a history of military setbacks at the hands of white settler colonialism, they suffered one loss after another, but they remained in the right.[72] The South was the aggressor in an illegitimate war. Native peoples were the casualties of illegitimate white aggression.

Lincoln remarks: "The world will little note, nor long remember what we say here," but this humble effort to concentrate attention on the Union dead merits close attention—and not because Lincoln was so famously wrong. For one thing, he was not altogether wrong. The Indian world, for one, did not note or remember what Lincoln said at Gettysburg. Why would it? What did a ceremonial occasion designed to salve the (white) nation following perhaps the ghastliest battle of a fratricidal war have to do with it? What's more, the Indian world was no doubt familiar with the United States' august self-conception, its sense of its own exceptionalism and entitlement. Lincoln had nothing new to offer it. It had all been heard before.

Nevertheless, when Lincoln argues that the world "can never forget what they did here," the Indian world might well have taken notice. It would serve as a frightening reminder of the apocalyptic violence of which white people were capable. If they were ready, willing, and enthusiastically able to inflict this level of slaughter and carnage on each other for this many years, what more could they be prepared to do to them? To challenge sovereign prerogatives is to harbor a death wish. Whites believed themselves justified in inflicting any measure of suffering, including violence and death, to defend the Union. Lincoln added a divine sanction to this sense of mission: "that this nation, under God, shall have a new birth of freedom." Whose God is this, exactly? (The Second Inaugural would provide a definitive answer, if one were needed: "both parties to the conflict read the same Bible and pray to the same God.") It does not include American Indians. It functions to exclude them (and others as well). This passage can be taken to mean that God is on our side, that the violence deployed to deliver a reinvented America need not trouble us.

Native peoples, of course, could find inspiration in Lincoln's hyperpatriotic oration. Insofar as it is the duty of the living to be dedicated to continuing the fine and noble work of the dead, this kind of appeal succeeds across cultures.[73] The Indians have their own honored dead to remember and respect and the best way, perhaps the only way, to do so is to be willing to make the same kind of sacrifice, of life, that the dead have already made. Lincoln's inspirational words at the Gettysburg dedication ceremony can be turned against the very people to whom they were addressed. In this sense, Lincoln can be said to be giving aid and comfort to one of America's mortal enemies. As Don Doyle notes, "what gave Lincoln's speech at Gettysburg such sweeping power among the foreign public was his framing of the war within a much greater historic contest over the fate of democracy." While Lincoln's much-celebrated call for a new birth of freedom "is always interpreted as a veiled reference to the emancipation of American slaves," his "global audience" could take it to mean that there was hope for them.[74] Thus the Gettysburg Address was appropriated by Irish freedom fighters in their struggle against British colonial rule. When Doyle surveys the global reaction to the Gettysburg Address and notes its use by those suffering from various kinds of (violent) oppression, however, he does not include Native Americans.[75] They are perpetually denied a new birth of freedom precisely because they reside, invisibly, where these words of global inspiration originated.

Lincoln's speech, then, can aspire to greatness now only if it performs a necessary and radical self-subversion. For Lincoln's words to achieve the greatness they have already been accorded in so many quarters, they have to be brought fully to bear at home. If they could inspire foreigners to (try to) liberate themselves, perhaps they could return home and lead to the liberation of the "foreigners" still among us. Lincoln's great oration would then become multidirectional, first deployed by the North against the South, then by Indian nations against the United States as a whole, both North and South. The Gettysburg Address then might constitute a legitimate democratic artifact. It's one thing for a society to hold its own ideals against itself, especially when they're being violated not just indefensibly but also gratuitously. This is a standard conservative element of patriotic (and nonpatriotic) discourse. It's another thing to enable, even invite, another people to use your ideals against you when that people has been the object of a cruelty and sadism you can barely, if at all, admit. Unless and until the Gettysburg Address is read and understood as a reflection of a constitutive warlike disposition, through which freedom and domination have been linked, it cannot aspire to the greatness so many (already) ascribe to it. Forget the Gettysburg Address as a manifestation of myth and legend. It was a weapon of war deployed against a doppelgänger on behalf of a conception of justice that was always blind to its constitutive injustices. Lincoln didn't understand that the enemy it targeted also rightly included the very nation it celebrated.

THE DECLARATION OF INDEPENDENCE

Lincoln's Gettysburg Address was delivered in November of 1863, but the battle it commemorated took place four months earlier in July, just before the Fourth and its eighty-seventh anniversary. The Gettysburg oration thus brings to mind Lincoln's July 10, 1858, speech in Chicago, a response to an address Senator Stephen Douglas made the night before as part of his reelection campaign. While Lincoln spent much of his speech dissecting Douglas's position on popular sovereignty and slavery, he also took the occasion to think about Fourth of July commemorations and the Declaration of Independence.

According to Lincoln, the debt owed to the founders of the country cannot be overestimated. The prosperity we enjoy can be directly traced to their world-making activities, however flawed they might also have been. In 1776 the United States might have been a small country with a small population, but "we are now a mighty nation, we are thirty—or about thirty millions of people, and we own and inhabit about one-fifteenth of the dry land of the whole earth."[76] Lincoln's pride in reciting these statistics points to a future in which they continue to grow, which names the duty of each succeeding generation. Lincoln, of course, does not specify the character of this mighty nation, but one aspect of it soon becomes apparent.

While we can trace our lineage back to fathers and grandfathers responsible for creating the nation, the same cannot be said for everyone. "We have besides these men—descended by blood from our ancestors—among us perhaps half our people who are not descendants at all of these men."[77] As seen above, Lincoln is referring to European immigrants from Germany, Ireland, and France, as well as the Scandinavian countries. They enjoy an equality with us "in all things" even though they cannot trace their ancestry to our blood relatives. No matter. The Declaration of Independence proclaims principles with which they can identify, an identification that provides all the connection they need to the founding generation.

Stephen Douglas offers an alternative account of the Declaration, insisting that it established an equality between "the people of America" and "the people of England" alone. It thus excluded later European arrivals. Lincoln, despite his disagreement, takes Douglas seriously enough to recognize the threat he poses to liberty. Douglas's construal of the Declaration would allow one people to dominate another, "the arguments that kings have made for enslaving people in all ages of the world." Lincoln not only objects to the argument "that says you work and I eat, you toil and I will enjoy the fruits of it."[78] He also wonders where this line of reasoning stops, or even if it can stop. Today it might mean the Negro, Lincoln says, it will mean someone else tomorrow.[79] Once the (so-called) principle is established, it can be expanded at will.

If Lincoln wonders where making exceptions to the Declaration of Independence stops, he need look no further than the American Indians on the country's frontiers. He articulates a vision of civic nationalism and (apparently) rejects its racial counterpart, but even the civic version presupposes a racial limit enabling it. The principles Lincoln affirms seem to be open to all people, but insofar as equality was extended to Indians it would mark the end of American territorial sovereignty across the continent. For the United States, this marking would be tantamount to a scar or series of scars on its precious territorial integrity. Sovereign power cannot tolerate such limitations. Indeed Lincoln ridicules arguments made for kingly rule: "they always bestrode the necks of the people, not that they wanted to do it, but because the people were better off for being ridden."[80] But while this kind of claim is crumbling regarding slaves, it retains its full force regarding Indians. (Lincoln himself ordered the death by hanging of thirty-eight Indians four and one-half years after he delivered his Chicago speech, as we saw in chapter 1.) Remarkably, Lincoln feels little or no embarrassment over the founders' incorporation of slavery into its Constitution. For them it was a matter of necessity. The founders accepted a serious evil to attain a serious good. One could not be secured without the other. Once the ideal standard is established it could be subsequently realized, so the story goes, with greater precision because the founders also made sure that slavery was put on course for its ultimate extinction. No such provisions applied to Native peoples, however, which means they were irrelevant when Lincoln implored America to "unite as one people throughout this land."[81] For one thing America cannot be united as one people throughout this land. The land contains many other united peoples and they have no desire to be united on another people's terms. This is a white man's colonial dream. It is the Indian's worst nightmare.

Ironically, Lincoln readily affirms the membership of Europeans through the Declaration of Independence, "the father of all moral principle in them," which means "they have a right to claim it as though they were blood of the blood, and flesh of the flesh of the men who write [it]."[82] I say ironically because American Indians are extended no such generosity, even though they are connected to the founding (and every subsequent) generation through literal bonds of blood—perpetual violence and warfare. Not only did their sacrifice make America possible. They embodied the Declaration's ideal of self-determination, legitimate government by consent, and paid the ultimate price for it. Lincoln, of course, cannot see it. It's possible to imagine the foundation of the county without slavery, but its condition of possibility was Indian removal—by any means necessary. Both crimes were horrific, but one was contingent and the other essential. Thus Lincoln can spin noble lies about the founders having no choice but to submit to the temporary necessity of slavery, but he has no such narrative option regarding Indians. After all, with Indians the founders were not putting an institution on course to ultimate extinction but peoples themselves, a destructive creation to which Lincoln himself has contributed. The American founding was intrinsically, constitutively violent and so were its successive (re)foundings.

Likewise Gabor Boritt praises the Gettysburg Address while wearing certain racial blinders. "But quoting the Declaration of Independence in November 1863 cut much deeper: it defended the Emancipation Proclamation that had drastically changed the character of the war. It presented a strong message about liberty, without speaking of slavery outright and so alienating many."[83] Lincoln's strong message about liberty was not directed to everyone in the United States. It did not apply to Indians. The point is not that Lincoln should have included other subject peoples in his oration. It's that Indians function here as Lincoln's constitutive unthought. That is, Lincoln's vision of America can barely contain what are to him displaced Africans in its line of sight. Incorporating free blacks and newly freed slaves into the American nation in a way that more fully realizes Jefferson's principle of equality poses problems of the highest order. Under such pressured circumstances, it would be effectively inconceivable for Lincoln and the country to (re)consider its treatment of Native peoples and how they related to the American ideal—not that either had any intention of doing so.

As Boritt proceeds through the speech, he notes the significance of the war for America's conception of self-government. "In his July 4, 1861, war message to Congress, [Lincoln] explained that 'our popular government has often been called an experiment,' and it remained to be seen whether it would succeed over the long run. The Civil war was *the* test . . . the rebel bullets aimed at the equality of all."[84] Boritt speaks more truth than he knows. The Civil War posed *a* test, but it was not and could not be *the* test of American democracy. The Civil War was an internal conflict, one that took place between fellow citizens of the same nation. Rebel bullets, moreover, were aimed not at the equality of all but at the equality of whites and blacks. *The* test of democracy would be a war between rival peoples with contending sovereignty claims to the same territory that do not allow for reconciliation to a status quo ante. Indian and white claims were always already irreconcilable, one reason the wars between these peoples were so fevered.

The Civil War, on the other hand, included moments of civility—from prisoner exchanges to the manner of Lee's surrender to Grant and Grant's magnanimous acceptance—that inadvertently pointed to the possibility of postwar reunification. Not so for the Indians. They were trapped between contending colonialisms and (often) forced to choose sides. If they sided with the Union, Confederate bullets would be aimed at them, especially when the Union failed, as it did, to protect them. If they allied with the South, as some did, they faced Northern wrath, especially if the war went wrong. Boritt gives no thought to the bullets aimed at Native peoples during the war. What's more, the last best hope of Indians might have been an indefinite continuation of the white man's war of mutual annihilation, one of Lincoln's redemptive fantasies, as we will see in the next chapter. To the extent that attention and resources were devoted to the Civil War, to that extent would westward expansion and usurpation perhaps be impeded or at least delayed. The war could not go on forever, of course, but some peoples on earth did not have a stake in its speedy resolution either.

Boritt recognizes Lincoln's extraordinary ambition: "[his] thoughts encompassed the world. The United States was, as he said in 1862, 'the last best, hope of earth.' Would the vision of progress that most Americans shared fail? The United States had a universal mission, but the focus now had to be at home."[85] Boritt fails to inquire, the last best hope for whom? American progress was exemplified by, among other things, its westward expansion—a project to which Lincoln attended while he was orchestrating the war. Indians stood in the way of that so-called progress, which means that they stood in the way of hope. The last best hope had more than one force threatening it. As for the universal mission, it would not mean, if brought to the Indians, their liberation but their death and possible extinction. They were not looking for the white race to extend to them what it had previously been denied. This did not matter to Lincoln's America, not in the end, because, as Boritt points out, "he was a nationalist and could speak of Americans as an 'almost chosen people.'"[86] There can be but one chosen people on "shared" land, and this title is guarded jealously.

This jealously did allow for (some) generosity. Boritt notes, "God helped Lincoln 'to see the right' of abolishing slavery and leading the country toward black citizenship." Once again, what Lincoln sees is partial, limited. Perhaps Lincoln's ability to see, however partially, the humanity of one race made it impossible for him to see the humanity of another subject race, especially one that constituted itself as separate peoples. Whites and blacks were on intimate terms with each other, even in relationships of domination and segregation. For Lincoln blacks represented difference, but not otherness—unlike Native peoples, which must also not die in vain. They must die—but for us.

NOTES

1. David Herbert Donald, *Lincoln* (New York: Simon & Schuster, 1995), 460.

2. Its appeal crosses national boundaries. Harry Jaffa, in his appreciation of the greatness of the speech, writes in a kind of awe: "As Soviet tanks were crushing the Hungarian revolution of 1956, the final message of the Hungarian freedom fighters, broadcast on the Free Hungarian Radio, was a reading of the Gettysburg Address." Harry V. Jaffa, *A New Birth of Freedom: Abraham Lincoln and the Coming of the Civil War* (Lanham, MD: Rowman &Littlefield, 2004), 78.

3. Friedrich Nietzsche, *Twilight of the Idols* and *The Anti-Christ*, tr. R. J. Hollingdale (New York: Penguin Classics, 1968), 104.

4. Garry Wills writes: "The compactness is not merely a matter of length. There is a suppression of particulars in the idealizing art of Lincoln, as in the Greek [funeral] orations. This restraint produces the aesthetic paradox that makes these works oddly moving despite their impersonal air." Garry Wills, *Lincoln at Gettysburg: The Words That Remade America* (New York: Simon & Schuster, 1992), 53.

5. Donald, *Lincoln*, 465–66; Wills, *Lincoln at Gettysburg*, 38–39.

6. Wills, *Lincoln at Gettysburg*, 20.

7. Scott W. Berg, *38 Nooses: Lincoln, Little Crow, and the Beginning of the Frontier's End* (New York: Pantheon, 2012), 97.

8. Ibid., 25. Gettysburg could be considered an accidental cemetery. The number of dead from the battle overwhelmed the local graveyard, and bodies were buried in rudimentary fashion where they fell. This temporary solution would require reburial as quickly as possible in a permanent location. Andrew Curtin, Pennsylvania's governor, appointed a young Gettysburg banker named David Wills to take charge of the situation, and Wills is responsible for making the cemetery happen.

9. Ibid., 25, 37–38.

10. Harry Jaffa argues, pace Carl Becker, that Lincoln (like Jefferson) believed in the principles of the Declaration of Independence as objective facts, "open to observation by anyone at any time," grounded in reason and nature. They were not "illusions created by the time and place in which they lived." Insofar as Jaffa is right, Lincoln's constitutive violation of these principles becomes even more problematic, which, of course, Jaffa cannot see. Jaffa, *A New Birth of Freedom*, 80.

11. Abraham Lincoln, "Address at Gettysburg, Pennsylvania," in *The Writings of Abraham Lincoln*, edited and with an introduction by Steven B. Smith (New Haven, CT: Yale University Press, 2012), 417.

12. Edmund S. Morgan, *American Slavery, American Freedom* (New York: W. W. Norton, 2003).

13. In the Declaration, the colonists charged King George with scheming to keep the population of the colonies low. As Danielle Allen astutely observes, this alarmed the colonists because it would retard economic growth and prosperity, and because it would lead to a scarce and scattered population, even in the largest colonies. Low population affected the military balance of power with the various Indian nations. In short, the colonists would need an increasing supply of bodies to fight wars and thereby expand. Danielle Allen, *Our Declaration: A Reading of the Declaration of Independence in Defense of Equality* (New York: Liveright, 2014), 223.

14. William Apess writes: "December 1620, the Pilgrims landed at Plymouth, and without asking liberty from anyone they possessed themselves of a portion of the country, and built themselves houses, and then made a treaty, and commanded them to accede to it. This, if now done, it would be called an insult, and every white man would be called to go out and act the part of patriot, to defend their country's rights; and if every intruder were butchered, it would be sung upon every hilltop in the Union that victory and patriotism was the order of the day." This is why, for Apess, "the 22nd of December and the 4th of July are days of mourning and not of joy." William Apess, "Eulogy on King Philip," *On Our Own Ground: The Complete Writings of William Apess, a Pequot*, edited and with an introduction by Barry O'Connell (Amherst: The University of Massachusetts Press, 1992), 280, 286.

15. All quotes are from the Declaration of Independence. Emphasis mine. Lincoln claimed in a speech in Philadelphia on his way to Washington that all his political sentiments flow from the Declaration of Independence, the principles of which gave hope (for liberty, for an equal chance) not just to Americans but the entire world. Well, not quite the entire world. The blood of Gettysburg is a debt paid to the founding generation. The blood of those who heed Lincoln's call in the future will pay a debt to both. The blood, of course, will not be theirs alone.

16. Lincoln, "Address at Gettysburg, Pennsylvania," 417.

17. Interestingly, it mimics Lincoln's family history. Lincoln's father moved his family from Kentucky to Indiana because land there was unencumbered (free from competing and tangled property claims). This was true because Indians had been purged from it. Lincoln family success, however modest or temporary, also resulted from a founding crime.

18. As John Schaar notes, "When Europeans first came to this land they saw nothing but savages in a howling wilderness, both of which had to be conquered. Seeking neither welcome nor permission from those already here, they imposed their alien god and ways in the 'new land.' That original act of conquest and sacrilege was repeated innumerable times as the wave rolled west, until now the very land accuses the intruders." John Schaar, "The Case for Patriotism," *Legitimacy in the Modern State* (New Brunswick, NJ: Transaction Publishers, 1989), 288–89.

19. Wills, *Lincoln at Gettysburg*, 38.

20. Sean Wilentz, "Democracy at Gettysburg," in *The Gettysburg Address: Perspectives on Lincoln's Greatest Speech*, ed. Sean Conant (Oxford: Oxford University Press, 2015), 51.

21. Wills, *Lincoln at Gettysburg*, 38.

22. Ibid., 101, 287.

23. The same is true of Wilentz, who writes, "The Address describes democracy not simply as the American form of government but as a universal ideal—an ideal in great danger of being extinguished." What Wilentz misses is that Lincoln was also an agent of democracy's extinction in America. "Democracy was in retreat" in more than just "the Old World." Wilentz, "Democracy at Gettysburg," 55.

24. Steven Smith inadvertently reveals the racially problematic implications of the Gettysburg Address. Arguing that "Lincoln set out to provide the American republic with a new foundation," he links the founding to the Declaration of Independence. Smith observes that the Address's opening ("Four score and seven years ago") is "an allusion to Psalm 90. . . . The Declaration had come in his mind to represent America's Scripture. Lincoln's reference to the framers as 'our fathers' who 'brought forth' and 'conceived' a new nation was clearly intended to remind readers of the biblical patriarchs who led the chosen people out of Egypt into the Promised Land." The analogy is more apt than Smith apparently recognizes. Just as the Israelites would travel to a land, Canaan, that was already occupied and thus require the destruction of another people with prior title to the land, so the American arrival on the North American continent, its promised land, would require the annihilation (through disease, war, perpetual colonization, and more war) of Native inhabitants. Having (reputedly) God or Providence on your side renders unalloyed crimes untainted accomplishments. Steven B. Smith, "Lincoln's Second Inaugural Address," in *The Writings of Abraham Lincoln*, 479.

25. Wills, *Lincoln at Gettysburg*, 37–38, emphases original.

26. Ibid., 84–85, emphasis original.

27. Thucydides, *History of the Peloponnesian War*, tr. Rex Warner (New York: Penguin Classics, 1972).

28. Mark S. Schantz, "Death and the Gettysburg Address," in *The Gettysburg Address: Perspectives on Lincoln's Greatest Speech*, 107.

29. Ibid.

30. Ibid., 111. The nation's possession of the dead was also reflected in the federal government's assumption of much of the cost of reburial at Gettysburg. Ibid., 112.

31. Wills, *Lincoln at Gettysburg*, 86.

32. Ibid.

33. Ibid., 88.

34. Ibid.

35. Fred Anderson, Andrew Clayton, *The Dominion of War: Empire and Liberty in North America, 1500–2000* (New York: Penguin Books, 2005).

36. Wills, *Lincoln at Gettysburg*, 90.

37. Lincoln, "Address at Gettysburg, Pennsylvania," *The Writings of Abraham Lincoln*, 417.

38. Wilentz also insists that "testing had begun with Southern secession." Wilentz, "Democracy at Gettysburg," 56.

39. Here Lincoln follows Pericles, his great ancient Athenian predecessor. In the Funeral Oration, Pericles imagines sacrificing young Athenian lives in perpetuity, which is why he refused to commiserate with the parents of the war dead but instead urged them to have more children who could also enjoy the privilege of having the city, a city like no other, sacrifice their lives for it.

40. Mark Schantz notes, like Garry Wills, "What Abraham Lincoln called forth from his audience was a plea for dedication to the nation. . . . Lincoln wanted to move them to action, to renewed dedication 'to the great task remaining before us.' In deploying the language of dedication, Abraham Lincoln called forth from his audience far more than simple remembrance or recollection. He wanted action; action to bring forth the 'new birth of freedom' he had envisioned and a salvific role for the state. Action on behalf of the nation in the future would answer the heroic actions of the soldiers who had fallen, conferring upon them proper honor for 'what they did here.' Exactly what 'they' did here—that is, the Union troops at Gettysburg—Abraham Lincoln did not say. As scholars have observed, the Gettysburg Address is abstract and aphoristic." Lincoln did not have to say exactly what the Union soldiers did because everybody already knew: they killed and, more importantly, they died—for the nation. And not just to preserve the existing territorial integrity of the United States, but to enhance it, which is also part of the nation's founding legacy. Schantz, "Death and the Gettysburg Address," 116.

41. Lincoln, "Address at Gettysburg, Pennsylvania," 417.

42. Jaffa makes the following claim: "The Gettysburg Address, it should be understood, was more than an exercise in ceremonial propriety: It was a political speech intended to gain support for the Thirteenth Amendment." Yet Lincoln did not publicly advocate for the amendment when it was first introduced and subsequently defeated in the House of Representatives in the spring of 1864. He only threw his support behind it after reelection. Jaffa, *A New Birth of Freedom*, 79.

43. Harry Jaffa, similarly, connects the first and last sentences of the Gettysburg Address, positing an "intrinsic and (in Lincoln's mind) necessary relationship between the liberty and equality that are said to have attended the birth of the nation

and that form of government that, it is said, shall not perish from the earth." Jaffa, *A New Birth of Freedom*, 78.

44. Lincoln, "Address at Gettysburg, Pennsylvania," 417.
45. Schantz, "Death and the Gettysburg Address," 118.
46. Ibid., 118, 120.
47. Ibid., 119.
48. Chandra Manning, "Shared Suffering and the Way to Gettysburg," in *The Gettysburg Address: Perspectives on Lincoln's Greatest Speech*, 126.
49. Ibid., 129–30.
50. Ibid., 129. Likewise, Allen C. Guelzo writes that "Lincoln also saw the fundamental issue of the Civil War as the question of democracy's death. . . . This nation, Lincoln said, had been dedicated to the democratic proposition that all men are created equal; the Civil War was the test of whether democratic regimes . . . can long endure. It had survived two severe tests of such a government—'the successful establishing, and the successful administering of it.' But there remained one final test, 'its successful maintenance against a formidable [internal] attempt to overthrow it,' and that test was now upon them." The idea that the first two tests were successful ignores the founding's implication in ethnic cleansing and slavery, which also means that it faces more than one final test. This is also why "the genius of the Gettysburg Address" cannot be located in "its triumphant repudiation of the criticisms of democracy," for the wars Lincoln was waging in his first term enacted and proved those very criticisms, as we have seen above. Guelzo, "Lincoln and the Murk and Myth at Gettysburg," in *The Gettysburg Address: Perspectives on Lincoln's Greatest Speech*, 162, 164.
51. Ibid., 136.
52. Ibid., 137.
53. Ibid., 140.
54. Eric Foner, *The Fiery Trial: Abraham Lincoln and American Slavery* (New York: W.W. Norton, 2010), 261.
55. Ibid.
56. Ibid.
57. Ibid., 261–62.
58. Ibid., 262.
59. Ibid.
60. Ibid.
61. Ibid., 262–63.
62. Ibid., 262.
63. Ibid.
64. Jean H. Baker, "Engendering the Gettysburg Address: Its Meaning for Women," in *The Gettysburg Address: Perspectives on Lincoln's Greatest Speech*, 237.
65. Ibid.
66. Ibid., 240.
67. Ibid., 249.
68. Louis P. Masur, "'A New Birth of Freedom': Emancipation and the Gettysburg Address," in *The Gettysburg Address: Perspectives on Lincoln's Greatest Speech*.

69. Ibid., 175.
70. Ibid., 182.
71. Ibid., 184.
72. Craig L. Symonds, "Daniel Webster, Abraham Lincoln, and the Gettysburg Address," in *The Gettysburg Address: Perspectives on Lincoln's Greatest Speech*.
73. This does not mean that his death would be mourned, if it would be mourned at all, in the Indian world the way that it was received in Europe and Latin America. See Don H. Doyle, "Widely Noted and Long Remembered: The Gettysburg Address Around the World," in *The Gettysburg Address: Perspectives on Lincoln's Greatest Speech*, 278.
74. Ibid., 276.
75. Ibid., 280–81.
76. Lincoln, "Speech at Chicago, Illinois," *The Writings of Abraham Lincoln*, 147.
77. Ibid., 148.
78. Ibid., 149.
79. Ibid.
80. Ibid.
81. Ibid., 150.
82. Ibid., 148.
83. Gabor Boritt, *The Gettysburg Gospel: The Lincoln Speech That Nobody Knows* (New York: Simon & Schuster, 2006), 115.
84. Ibid., 117 (emphasis mine).
85. Ibid., 117–18.
86. Ibid., 119.

Chapter Six

American Exceptionalism or American Narcissism?

The Second Inaugural

>Those memorable words—words which will live immortal in history, and be read with increasing admiration from age to age.
>
>—Frederick Douglass, "Our Martyred President"

Lincoln's Second Inaugural address commands widespread respect as his greatest speech.[1] Delivered with the Civil War still raging, victory was more or less assured even if its exact termination date remained uncertain. Before once again taking the oath of office, Lincoln paused to reflect on the cause of the war: slavery. But he had no intention of gloating about the inevitability of victory, answering the critics of his administration, basking in the accomplishments of his first term, or pointing fingers or laying blame for the past four years of internecine struggle, however understandable that would have been. The Second Inaugural is revered for its generosity of spirit (it is free of ressentiment and a desire for revenge), including its extraordinary affirmation of slavery as a truly national institution. It may have been concentrated in one region of the country, but America—not just the South—bore responsibility for its maintenance and protection and benefited from its operations.

In Lincoln's estimation, how great was the sin of slavery? He remarks that while everyone hopes the Civil War moves to a speedy conclusion, if it should nevertheless continue until all the wealth accumulated by this evil institution is lost and every drop of blood suffered by blacks is matched by the blood of whites in fratricidal war, such a denouement would be a just resolution: God's choice of well-deserved punishment for America's offenses. In making this claim the Second Inaugural seems to be a follow-up to the Gettysburg Address. The new birth of freedom prophesied by Lincoln will not come cheaply. Given the death and destruction the Civil War has already exacted, Lincoln's notional scenario in the Second Inaugural forces the country to think of what the slaves have contributed to its prosperity. It also informs America that the Civil War to date is inadequate penance for an institution as horrific as slavery. This is not the kind of inspirational and aspirational speech that people suffering through four long years of war want to hear, perhaps especially on what is supposed to be a celebratory occasion. Nor do they want to be told that the pain the war has inflicted on the country provides no real cause for complaint. There are no white victims in these 703 words. Lincoln seems determined to puncture any arrogance or pride that might linger in America's divided soul, whether from the winning side (self-righteousness) or the losing side (bitterness).

   Nevertheless, Lincoln's racial self-obsession here is breathtaking. The perspective from which he speaks and then delivers his final judgment has been described as impersonal or distant, but it is perhaps best described as white, a white man's perspective. For 250 years slaves made and remade a country and had it perpetually stolen from them. What would it mean for slaves if Lincoln's strange, near-apocalyptic fantasy of self-flagellation came true and the war continued for years on end? For one thing, the slaves would lose more and more of the country in which they live and which they built. First white slave owners take it from them and then, rather than rightly return it after the war, the country destroys it in a mutual self-destruction pact that masquerades as just comeuppance. If Lincoln's dream materialized it would mean, for blacks, that one monstrous injustice would follow another. Whites might have their consciences soothed by this level of ruination, but what kind of atonement is this, exactly? Apparently, it's all about white people.

   Lincoln's narrow racial focus may also account for his leniency toward the South. When Lincoln refers to his First Inaugural and claims that all dreaded the prospect of war and sought to avert it—and even deprecated it—he has fabricated a history convenient to one of his nascent ambitions: reconciliation.[2] The South had threatened secession and been preparing for war for years when they finally implemented it. Lincoln dreaded war and did what he could to preempt it, but the South did not match his feeling or effort. When Lincoln writes of North and South that "one of them would make war rather than let the Union survive, and the other would accept war rather than let it perish, and the war came," the South has been assigned responsibility for the war without belaboring it.[3] At the same time, the passive formulation of the four concluding words weakens Lincoln's judgment about the South's responsibility. The war came, yes, but it did not just somehow happen, as if it were beyond either party's control. It came because the South was hell-bent on defending its "peculiar and powerful interest."[4] Race, racial hierarchy, racial supremacy, and domination constituted the foundations of its way of life, which it did not conceal but proudly proclaimed. Lincoln nevertheless flinches when he locates the war's cause in slavery, saying that it was "somehow" responsible.[5]

While Lincoln is correct that slavery represented an American problem, the South not only bears a much greater share of the responsibility for it, it is to blame for the war waged on its behalf. Lincoln bent over backward to appease the South before and after he was elected and continued to appease it in his First Inaugural speech, much to the disgust of Frederick Douglass, but Southern states were determined to rend the Union regardless of the violence and death their political project entailed.[6] Lincoln's failure to judge, the biblical injunction notwithstanding, is problematic. The South not only seceded to create a slave-based racial order of its own. It was determined to build a slave empire that would engulf the nation and then cross the border and travel south. Slavery was a global enterprise.[7] Lincoln was focused on reconciliation between North and South, but who was going to pay the price for this focus? Lincoln does not raise or consider the question.

LINCOLN AND HIS ACOLYTES

Lincoln scholars of all stripes agree that the Second Inaugural is sublime. Whatever else might divide them, especially the nature of Lincoln's race problem, they can unite on the genius of this short address. It's a brief speech, so critics are naturally going to work over the very same material. Nevertheless, the uniform response they tend to share, whether it relates to analysis or tone, betrays their commitment—and contributes—to Lincoln's iconic status as *the* figure of American exceptionalism. For America, for them, there is nothing else quite like the Second Inaugural. The Gettysburg Address offers it some competition, but it is recognizably patriotic and its indebtedness to the ancient Greeks has been argued (by Garry Wills, among others), rendering it less original, less Lincoln's own. That said, no American president or politician has delivered an address with anything resembling the dark content of the Second Inaugural to a people that have just elected him to office for a second term toward the end of a uniquely devastating war with no timeline for recovery in sight. What was he thinking?

Ronald White applauds Lincoln's Second Inaugural for its steadfast refusal to refight the Civil War and potentially compromise the peace (about) to come. While restraint in politics can be an admirable trait and a productive approach, it can also come at serious expense. In this context, Lincoln's generosity also amounts to a refusal, before the fact, to engage the South in a postwar political contest. It could be considered Lincoln's conquest or elimination of politics through poetic eloquence and providential rumination. Insisting, against not just common sense but all the evidence, that "there is less occasion for an extended address than there was at the first" swearing-in, Lincoln deserts the political realm for an ostensibly loftier plane.[8] As White argues, Lincoln rejected the human pretension involved in the notion of a tribal God, that is, a God who would be aligned with one side (or another) in a political conflict.[9] Lincoln nevertheless engages in his own pretension when he imagines that God has given "both North and South, this terrible war, as the woe due to" them for the offense of slavery.[10] As if speaking in God's name, Lincoln thereby privileges his own voice and silences others who might understand the war differently on the question of responsibility. Strangely, though, while Lincoln has God deliver punishment to whites, what does He deliver to blacks? Or what will He deliver to them? It is in this sense that Lincoln's God's justice seems truncated and makes a turn to politics necessary. Politically speaking, what could be more important after prevailing in a war over fundamental values than to resume this struggle in the political domain, for that is precisely what the South abandoned when it started the Civil War? It abandoned the political arena in favor of the battlefield. The South had enjoyed remarkable success in politics for decades—most recently through the Kansas-Nebraska Act, the Fugitive Slave Act, the Dred Scott decision, and more—but when Lincoln was elected president, it decided to make what amounted to an extra- or antipolitical move: secession. This amounted to a concession that it could not prevail in fair democratic contest, in part because the advantages that were built into America's constitutional system to enhance and protect the Slave Power no longer worked reliably.

The South was ultimately defeated militarily—but barely so, and it was unrepentant ideologically. It had not seen any democratic light—certainly not any racial light. It had to be forced to remain in (or return to) the Union. Lincoln did not need to celebrate imminent military triumph in his Second Inaugural address, but why not celebrate democratic norms, practices, and traditions? The terms and conditions of democratic life were about to change, especially along racial lines, and an elaboration of fundamental values rooted in Jefferson's Declaration of Independence, Lincoln's urtext, would have constituted a much-welcomed follow-up to the Gettysburg Address. What would the new birth of freedom Lincoln effectively demanded look like? He had nearly a year and a half to imagine it (and to imagine something other than colonization). The failure to engage the South in political contest meant that the South's reactionary ideology could remain safely concealed just beneath the surface of public life and all parties could avert formal or open conflict. Lincoln's conditions for reentry into the Union were sufficiently minimal that they could be effectively observed in the breach. What's more, constitutional amendments do not change political cultures, where real politics unfolds every day.[11]

Garry Wills considers the Second Inaugural Lincoln's greatest speech.[12] Like the Gettysburg Address, it is noteworthy for its brevity, 703 words. While Lincoln's Gettysburg oration was shorter still, 272 words, the occasions were dramatically different. As Wills notes, Lincoln's purpose at Gettysburg was, in part, to honor fallen soldiers—and he wasn't even the featured speaker. Thus, no one was expecting a lengthy conversation about national issues. What were people expecting? Lincoln's First Inaugural, on the eve of the Civil War, was a legal excursus on the question of the Union and slavery, and something similar was anticipated Lincoln's second time around—what with the war coming to an end and the nature of Reconstruction an open question.

Lincoln's brief oration, then, borders on stunning.[13] When Lincoln claims, as we saw above, that "there is less occasion for an extended address than there was at the first" inaugural, people must have thought they misheard him. What could be further from the truth?[14] Yes, Lincoln declines to say much about the status of the war, but this comes across as an appropriate form of modesty. Sherman's army had ripped through Georgia, South Carolina, and North Carolina. Grant's army had inflicted great damage on Lee, who, a month or so later, could no longer delay the inevitable. But Lincoln refused to gloat. People can read the papers themselves for accounts on "the progress of our arms." Lincoln does confess to "high hope for the future," but refuses to offer a prediction for it.[15] Lincoln, that is, refuses to give what no one has asked for. Vision, not prediction, is what people wanted. Why wouldn't he share one?

Wills applauds the Second Inaugural for its pragmatism.[16] He might have indulged in understandable self-congratulation. "With the end in sight, Lincoln did not voice the expectable, even forgivable emotion that most leaders would in such a situation—a declaration that the rightful cause had triumphed, as it must."[17] This would have provided a prelude to a grand theoretical statement about the design of Reconstruction, an abstract approach to justice that would have treated its subject broadly, in general terms, rather than with specificity. Wills concludes that taking such a "doctrinaire approach" would have been a disaster, rendering "the problems of living together again irresolvable."[18] Lincoln was worried about a "potentially more divisive peace."[19] Reconstruction required a wait-and-see, one-step-at-a-time approach that could make necessary accommodations as it proceeded. "The Second Inaugural was meant, with great daring, to spell out a principle of not acting on principle. . . . [It] was deliberately shortsighted."[20] According to Wills, this flexible, experimental approach is best exemplified in Lincoln's

Proclamation of Amnesty and Reconstruction. "Lincoln had learned to have a modest view of his ability to know what ultimate justice was, and to hesitate before bringing down the whole nation in its pursuit."[21] Lincoln would only admit that the idea behind Reconstruction was to restore proper practical relations between the states.[22]

Wills nevertheless insists that Lincoln's pragmatism is not tantamount to moral neutrality, even if "men could not pretend to have God's adjudicating powers."[23] If he had learned this in war, it would be even more important in peace, as his famous 1864 letter to Albert G. Hodges indicated.[24] If anything, "pragmatism was, in this situation, not only moral but pious."[25] Wills is convinced that many readers of the Second Inaugural focus unduly on the closing theme of charity, which is the only way they can conclude that "Lincoln was calling for a fairly indiscriminate forgiveness toward the South."[26] But the third and largest paragraph of the address features an Old Testament form of judgment that, Wills believes, makes any such assessment mistaken. In Lincoln's conjectural narration, God's providence plays some kind of role regarding the introduction of slavery. It had to come, apparently. Humans created it, but God seems to have somehow made its introduction possible or even inevitable. Either way, American slavery is the great national sin, including in the founding of the Constitution. Slavery is not to be allocated to either North or South. The country as a whole is implicated.[27] As Wills would have it, in the Second Inaugural Lincoln "said that his audience must not judge but *be* judged."[28] And the judgment is monumental. Not even the death and destruction self-inflicted through four years of war suffice. Either way, "He gives to both North and South this terrible war, as the woe due to those by whom [slavery] came." The crime committed is awesome and so punishment must match it. Wills writes: "The war was winding down; but Lincoln summoned no giddy feelings of victory. A chastened sense of man's limits was the only proper attitude to bring to the rebuilding of the nation, looking to God for guidance but not aspiring to replace him as the arbiter of national fate."[29] Lincoln, of course, would not live to steer the nation through Reconstruction. Booth's assassination and Andrew Johnson's succession thus render "the Second Inaugural . . . the towering measure of our loss."[30]

Wills's account of the Second Inaugural is impassioned and inspired, but it mimics Lincoln's oration in one key and perhaps fatal respect: its whiteness, as Frederick Douglass could have argued.[31] When Lincoln judges slavery to be American in character, this might seem like a just allocation of responsibility.[32] Yet the audience to whom Lincoln made this assessment was biracial.[33] Blacks composed a sizable portion of the inaugural audience.[34] Were they also supposed to share in the responsibility for the institution that imprisoned and exploited them?[35] They, too, are Americans. Were slaves to be included in this moral equation? Or did Lincoln not consider slaves to be Americans? Lincoln would have been well advised to use the term "white American slavery." But this he would not do because the Second Inaugural was a white address written by a white president for a white citizenry in a white country. It was concerned with the moral condition of white America's soul.[36]

Wills, as we have seen, compliments Lincoln for recognizing that he had no reason to believe he had knowledge of "ultimate justice."[37] Yet modesty here amounts to a form of moral abdication.[38] That Lincoln cannot judge as God would judge does not mean that earthly justice is impossible or undesirable. If anything, God insists on it. It is a serious human undertaking with serious consequences. This humble approach supposedly meant Lincoln would not destroy the nation in pursuit of some kind of unattainable justice. For Wills, Lincoln would have conducted Reconstruction "in light of the Second Inaugural's recognition that slavery was the great national sin. . . . Paying the cost of slavery was not something that would end with the war. It would be paid in the agony of defeated men deprived of the slave labor on which their prosperity depended. It would be paid in the effort to defend freed blacks from white hostility and persecution. Lincoln asked for charity, but he knew that the healing of the nation's wounds would be a complex and demanding process, and no one could be smug about it."[39] These are extraordinary sentences.

While it's appropriate for Lincoln not to want to exacerbate the country's burdens in the postwar world, yet given that he was (more than) familiar with the unintended consequences of many of his wartime actions, how could he do anything other than assume that his postwar actions were inevitably going to lead to the kind of entanglements that Wills compliments him for trying to avoid?[40] Why wouldn't Lincoln start with the presumption that payment would have to be great *and* it would be resented by the South, the war's bitter loser, that this would be an unavoidable consequence of the nature of the war and of a reluctant peace? Resistance was inevitable and the cost would rise accordingly. Even if "the perfectly calibrated punishment or reward for each leader, each soldier, [and] each state" would be impossible, how did perfection get installed as the criterion of political judgment for the postwar world?[41] The Confederate States of America seceded together, and collective punishment (massive land redistribution, for example) could secure a measure of justice for the freed slaves. In Wills's recitation of the costs, note that the agony of defeated white men "deprived" of their human property and their once and future prosperity, even assuming this to be a legitimate concern, comes before the protection of blacks from "white hostility and persecution," which greatly understates the threat posed to them.[42]

On the other hand, Wills argues that Lincoln embraces an Old Testament ethos, lex talionis, an eye for an eye, and that the Second Inaugural may represent its perfection. But it was not the first instance of it.[43] Lincoln enacted a version of it in July of 1863 though his Order of Retaliation, an edict he issued as commander-in-chief to protect Northern, especially black, soldiers from Confederate retaliation.[44] In the Second Inaugural Lincoln (supposedly) perfects the practice. "Yet, if God wills that [the war] continue, until all the wealth piled by the bond-man's two hundred and fifty years of unrequited toil shall be sunk, and until every drop of blood drawn with the lash, shall be paid by another drawn with the sword, as was said three thousand years ago, so still it must be said 'the judgments of the Lord, are true and righteous altogether.'"[45] Wills insists that "the symmetries of retributive justice could not be better imagined than in this sentence's careful balancing of payments due."[46]

Where, though, is the symmetry? Is it real or merely apparent?[47] The greatest wealth the slave owners possessed consisted of the slaves themselves, the most valuable assets in the nation. Lincoln's horror fantasy, by definition, thus entailed their mass death. By this time, Lincoln's long-standing colonization dream has been defeated. He now imagines the disappearance of blacks from American soil in a more directly violent form under the guise of white atonement. From the bond-man's perspective, however, all the wealth produced by slavery cannot possibly be sunk. The South could lose almost everything if it continues to fight a war it cannot win as Grant and Sherman turn to total war, but Lincoln's catastrophic economic scenario seems to exempt the nation as a whole. It is directed largely toward those responsible for the war (intent notwithstanding). The North was not at risk of losing everything, even though the wealth slavery generated exceeded regional boundaries to a considerable degree. In his Proclamation of Amnesty and Reconstruction of December 8, 1863, Lincoln had promised Southerners they could keep the property they had accumulated through slavery. Now he imaginatively breaks the promise, but not to share it with blacks. If the South were to suffer, in selective fashion, much more than the North, it might be asked, shouldn't they?[48]

If Southern slave owners (and their fellow citizens) lose the wealth they acquired illegitimately from slaves, no injustice has been inflicted, but what of the slaves themselves? The slave owners may be back where they started, as it were, but they lost what they should not have possessed in the first place. Slaves, however, helped build a nation. They should have shared in it from the get-go and never have had it taken from them. This equation, then, does not even speak to the suffering slaves endured while building a nation, something that Southern whites cannot claim. Lincoln's is a color-driven sense of symmetry, one that people of color are unlikely to share.[49] Would you rather see what you built destroyed because it is possessed by another or would you rather see what you built rightly "returned" to you? Slaves often freed themselves and took their rights in the course of the war. They also claimed their property. Lincoln could have made it official, but he didn't. As for the blood drawn by the lash and the sword, the former is the product of an illegitimate relationship of domination, the latter is a self-inflicted wound characterized by gratuity. Blacks have whites to blame; whites can only blame themselves.[50] Again, where is the symmetry here? One cannot compensate for or match the other. Still, Lincoln insists that if God should will such an outcome to the war, it "must be said" that his judgments "are true and righteous altogether." It must be said? It cannot be said.

LINCOLN'S GOD

True and righteous altogether? Who is this God? What is the quality of His judgments? And who is Lincoln, a racially compromised white man, to so insist and thus effectively speak for blacks? Is he assuming that vengeance is what a people on the verge of freedom would want, especially on such a horrifically violent scale? People who suffer terrible affliction at the hands of others do not necessarily want to see it repaid in kind. They do not want to become like their oppressors. Lincoln's horrific scenario may soothe the guilty white conscience, but under the circumstances this becomes an act of narcissism.[51] What does it do for blacks? It seems that God is now white, too. What's more, Lincoln's judgments pertain to the duration of the conflict alone. Divine wrath begins and ends with war and its cessation. Wills thus overlooks the significance of Lincoln's "Torah judgment" *preceding* his "gospel forgiveness." The first can precede the second because divine wrath and punishment effectively begins and ends with the war. Lincoln imagines God exacting retribution from North and South, but its temporality is limited. Why? Why wouldn't God continue his intervention, especially in another form, after the war? This is where Lincoln (and Wills's Lincoln) abandons moral responsibility in the name of modesty and ignorance. Wills claims that while Lincoln expressed "agnosticism about God's purposes in advance," he could also see "some, at least, of God's plan," at least, "in retrospect—such as the train of necessities leading to the abolition of slavery (the Thirteenth Amendment was in process as he delivered the Second Inaugural)." What other necessities might he have imagined for the future? It is one thing to adopt an Old Testament tone, but what does apocalyptic-sounding rhetoric do besides make for great theater? What was Lincoln prepared to enact in its wake? In other words, if Lincoln's (and God's) biblical wrath emerged here and unleashed itself on both North and South, what was he prepared to have America do to become worthy of its great national sin? You don't necessarily become worthy of sin by destroying what it produced. That would be tantamount to saying that the centuries of slave labor amounted to nothing, in the end, all to assuage white guilt.

This amounts to a self-defeating conception of justice. In particular, it cannot constitute a starting point for additional measures. Apparently Lincoln's imagination suffers from a failure of nerve. As noted above, he points to nothing concrete about the postwar world that might embody the new birth of freedom he invoked at Gettysburg.[52] Wills notes, but then ignores, the dedication Lincoln demanded at Gettysburg for "the great task remaining" and the comparative resignation of the Second Inaugural ("let us strive on to finish the work we are in"). More was called for as Lincoln took the oath of office, and he did not deliver it. Perhaps this should come as no surprise since the Gettysburg Address, while it might aspire to Periclean eloquence, works principally as a brilliant recruitment speech (as Spielberg's *Lincoln* demonstrated). After all, the fate of the Union was still at stake and the North was always in need of more bodies to put in uniform. What better way to inspire young men to enlist than to invoke the memory of the honored dead. To guarantee that they did not die for nothing, more must agree to die now. In a war as savage as the Civil War, this was no easy sell, and Lincoln rose to the occasion. With the war no longer in doubt, however, Lincoln would have to find new affective appeals for the postwar remaking of the country. For this, Lincoln did not rise to the occasion. What's more, he did not even reiterate the new birth of freedom that made the Gettysburg Address memorable. No new great task was outlined or even intimated.

Lincoln, then, is unduly focused on the white nation's relationship to God. "If we shall suppose that American slavery is one of those offences which, in the providence of God, must needs come, but which, having continued through His appointed time, He now wills to remove, and that he gives to both North and South, this terrible war, as the woe due to those whom the offence came, shall we discern therein any departure from these divine attributes which the believers in a Living God always ascribe to Him?"[53] This is a white narrative, as both North and South denote warring white factions in a Civil War about whether, initially, slavery will continue to exist where it is or whether it will expand. God's providence, God's will, God's wrath, and God's retribution all pertain to whites. Is God color-blind or is Lincoln's God a God of the white race, as Frederick Douglass might ask? On Lincoln's account God seems to be concerned first and foremost with white people, testing them to see what they would do in His world and then responding to what they did. Whites receive woes due to them. Where do blacks figure in Lincoln's God's concerns, if they figure at all? Ronald White in particular stresses that Lincoln would do everything possible to avoid refighting the war during peace, but he does not raise the possibility that this very approach might result in losing it. The first concern, refighting the war, betrays a white focus. The second concern, losing the peace, relates to blacks. Lincoln thought of the former.

On White's reading Lincoln's search for a new understanding of the war anchors the speech. The conflict's duration and intensity surprised everyone, including Lincoln. It should have ended long ago. Why didn't it? This led Lincoln to look to God as an explanation. While North and South shared responsibility for American slavery, God has "purposes" all his own above and beyond mere human activity. Here responsibility shifts from human hands to God's providence. He is active in this world of His. In this frame Lincoln invokes a retributive justice that would bring the war full circle and slavery to a close: all the wealth slavery produced would be lost and the blood slavery exacted would be matched by blood spilled on the battlefield. By leaving judgment and punishment in God's capable hands, "Lincoln could turn in his final paragraph to the more limited responsibilities of mortals."[54]

Yet what White and Wills and Donald do not ask is why Lincoln felt the need to turn to God in the first place. If an "explanation of why the war was so protracted" was needed, no turn to the heavens was required.[55] The South itself provides a thorough explanation, especially if one looks to the Confederate Constitution. Racial hierarchy and domination were the heart and soul of the Confederate regime. Slavery provided its foundations. Southern society was committed to its way of life—it was considered natural, just, right, and, perhaps most important of all, superior. Southern white identity politics would defend itself by any violence necessary. A world born in and based on violence, it tolerated no challenge to the racial order it embodied—not even the slightest criticism, especially if it came from the North. Thus Lincoln did not need to turn to God to explain the war or its length. He could have turned to his beloved Jefferson instead, who was well aware of the many corruptions, including abject dependency, the institution of slavery produced in slave owners who would have no trouble justifying it to themselves and the world. The war was so protracted for the same reason it commenced: Southern fanaticism. Even as Lincoln delivered the Second Inaugural, he recognized that "the progress of our arms" alone governed events. It finally took Lee, a beaten and exhausted military leader, to effectively end the war by surrendering on his own authority (he notified Davis in a letter dated three days later). Southern politicians did not bring it to a close. They would see Grant and Sherman continue to wage total war on their so-called Confederacy rather than quit the contest.

THE SPECTER OF COLONIZATION

Lincoln's Second Inaugural awkwardly embodies the commitment to colonization to which Lincoln adhered for most of his presidency. That is, blacks have no explicit presence in the Second Inaugural, despite the reference to the unexpected twist of events relating to slavery ("Neither anticipated that the *cause* of the conflict might cease with, or even before, the conflict itself should cease") and the commitment to care for soldiers who have suffered the burdens of war. Just as the Civil War was not originally intended to end slavery, the postwar world was not initially intended to witness the realization of social and political equality for blacks. For the sake of the Union, emancipation alone sufficed. Lincoln, that is, did not hesitate to use his considerable rhetorical skills to creatively interpret the Constitution to increase his war powers to save the Union, but he never displayed this kind of virtuosity regarding the condition of blacks, let alone their future.[56] At the Second Inaugural Lincoln may no longer have been seeking their departure or removal, but his silence about their future suggests that any movement toward full citizenship would at best be grudging.

Recall that the Emancipation Proclamation freed many slaves (in theory), but it was posited as a necessary war measure in which blacks were the chosen instrument of policy at a key moment in the conflict. Lincoln argued that no one imagined what would eventually happen to slavery when the war started, and it is precisely in the face of the vast uncertainties that accompany war that pragmatic experimentation becomes indispensable. Why, then, is there no hint of it in the Second Inaugural when it comes to the future of blacks in the equally uncertain peace? Why doesn't Lincoln at least indicate that it is now incumbent on the nation, in order to give meaningful content to the new birth of freedom promised at Gettysburg, to take the country in novel, but not altogether unprecedented directions; that the war has opened up extraordinary political possibilities and resulted in unexpected, but already widely acknowledged, debts of gratitude that must be honored? Lincoln assumes the public will find that the war effort is "reasonably satisfactory and encouraging to all," but declines to mention the nearly two hundred thousand black soldiers who made it possible.

Why, then, isn't the Second Inaugural the sequel to the Gettysburg Address, to say nothing of the Emancipation Proclamation? The Southern way of life had been defeated and discredited, but this would not stop unrepentant Confederates from denying both outcomes. They were nursing the notion of the lost cause before the war ended. When Wills concludes that "a chastened sense of man's limits was the *only* proper attitude to bring to the rebuilding of the nation," what justifies it? Such a sensibility, especially for such a great enterprise, borders on defeatist without actually admitting it. Where was this chastened sense of limits during the war? There were many instances where a chastened sensibility would have been fitting and proper, especially regarding the suppression of political freedoms in the North, as we saw in chapter 1 with Clement Vallandigham, but Lincoln eschewed it. Now, suddenly, he deems it timely for chastening—when rebuilding will require more creativity than ever before, especially since Lincoln's so-called war powers will no longer be available, or at least no longer available on the same scale, as Wills recognizes. Lincoln's "nonassertiveness" could not be more inapt. One can be bold, daring, and assertive without resorting to triumphalism, let alone submitting "to inscrutable providence."[57]

Wills argues that this apparently "resigned mood" was actually setting the stage for Lincoln's "pragmatic accommodation" that would prevent "fighting the war over again in peacetime."[58] If this approach to politics sounds familiar, it should. This is the stance that Lincoln adopted prior to the war to avoid it. Lincoln can be applauded for refusing bitterness and vindictiveness, but this does not excuse a refusal to exercise the power at the nation's disposal for various goods because it might also result in certain harms. Pragmatism seems like a wise—because cautious—approach since the "nation [was] bloodily wrenched from all normal politics and facing problems without precedent,"[59] but pragmatism also evinces an unrealizable desire to control events by taking things slowly, as they come. Yes, the war had wrenched the nation, but this did not stop Lincoln from taking a bold, decisive approach to it. If wartime was an emergency, then peace was no less of an emergency. Lincoln and the country would face the very same enemy whose race-driven viciousness had made the Order of Retaliation necessary during the war.[60]

Defeat would not soften but harden Southern resolve. If Lincoln had tried to adopt a black perspective he might have glimpsed the kind of awful postwar truths awaiting him. The North may have won the war, but that did not necessarily mean it would be able to fight and win the peace in what was obviously going to amount to a civil cold war—at the very least. The South was not disarmed, after all. Lincoln may not have wanted to fight the war again in peacetime, but only the South could deliver such an outcome. Rather than the country submitting to God's judgment, the South needed to submit to the judgment of the Declaration of Independence that exceeded even Lincoln's limited rereading of it. In other words, the South needed to understand that it was not only a conquered people but a defeated people. Its way of life was gone for good. Nothing would restore it and no thinly veiled version of its prior existence would be tolerated. The South was always already a recidivist waiting for the slightest opening. Lincoln knew the war had not changed it. He did not act—he did not even speak—accordingly.

A SHOCKING SENTENCE

George Kateb offers a compelling, disconcerting reading of the Second Inaugural, noting its difficult, unpredictable, even "wayward" character.[61] Perhaps the key to understanding this elusive speech is that Lincoln "attempted a perspective that was neither Northern nor Southern, but that of a god or ghost."[62] While Lincoln made it clear that slavery was the cause of the war, the intent of the speech was not to blame or demonize the South. Lincoln might have legitimately indulged a self-righteous anger on behalf of the North, but he declined to do so.[63] If anything, as Kateb notes, "in an almost unprecedented political act he mourned his enemies."[64]

It's the penultimate paragraph of the address that captures Kateb's attention and imagination. In it "Lincoln compressed his metaphysical outlook. The idea of a strange God, not quite Greek and only eccentrically biblical if at all, was quickly introduced. No sooner introduced, it gave way to the principle of retaliatory justice."[65] Lincoln draws from Matthew 18:7 and declares: "Woe unto the world because of offences! For it must needs be that offences come; but woe to that man by whom the offence cometh!"[66] Lincoln does not single out any one agent responsible for great wrongdoing and soon reveals the national character of sin at work in the country. "American slavery was one of those offences which, in the providence of God, must needs come, but which having continued through His appointed time, He now wills to remove, and that He gives to both North and South, this terrible war, as woe due to those by whom the offence came."[67] The South may bear distinctive responsibility for the evil institution of slavery, but the North is no innocent party. In fact, the North is the South's junior partner in crime. The South owned the slaves, but the enforced labor made them all rich, and the North was happy to share in the bounty.

According to Kateb, these sentences do more than acknowledge that where human beings are concerned sin and punishment (in this life or the one to come) are inevitable. As he notes, a traditional reading of Lincoln's turn to Matthew entails a rather passive understanding of God's providence. For Lincoln, however, as "history unfolds," God is active in his governance, "which means that providence does not merely allow things to happen; or that it brings nothing about; or that things happen solely because of human intention, and then providence sees that they are of some use." Rather, things happen "in the providence of God, that is, by the providence of God."[68]

Kateb's reading of the Second Inaugural now takes an ominous turn. God might have ended this evil conduct sooner than He did. He might also have prevented it altogether.[69] If so, what does this do to the status of human beings? "We are—many of us or most of us—the indispensable instrumentalities of necessary offences. . . . Without us, offences could not happen, and without God's will, offences would not have to happen. To offend is to play a role in God's scheme." For Lincoln, according to Kateb, this scheme absolves North and South for the sin of slavery while still punishing them for it.[70]

This is where Kateb's disconcerting analysis starts to escape his narrative control. "To be punished for offences is to endure a necessary role in God's scheme. God causes what he then punishes. This sounds Greek."[71] It also sounds abjectly white. When Lincoln writes of North and South as the critical players in God's scheme, where does this leave blacks? Do they have a place in God's providential plotting and intrigue? Or are they mere instrumentalities, too, and secondary ones at that? Kateb does not say. "Lincoln then gave a new possible reason to explain why the war lasted so long: it did not last too long and perhaps should have lasted even longer. This thought is in his single greatest sentence."[72] What is this sentence? It's the sentence—as we have seen in this chapter—that anyone who interprets the Second Inaugural must confront, which means it functions as a kind of litmus test (or inkblot). To repeat it once more: "Yet if God wills that it [the war] continue, until all the wealth piled by the bond-man's two hundred and fifty years of unrequited toil shall be sunk, and until every drop of blood drawn with the lash, shall be paid by another drawn with the sword, as was said three thousand years ago, so still it must be said 'the judgments of the Lord, are true and righteous altogether.'"[73]

As Kateb writes, "the sentence is shocking."[74] What would have to be true for Lincoln's musing to become reality, for accounts to be settled? Nothing that actually happened in the war, not "even when Sherman's march was added to the account." The "hell of deserved suffering" that Lincoln conjures actually suggests that the war was coming to an end "too soon."[75] What, if anything, would suffice "short of destroying all the living white population in an apocalypse of extermination; but perhaps an apocalypse, and nothing less, is what whites really deserved for the evil accumulated from the beginning of the slave trade to the end of slavery"?[76] This assessment effectively turns Lincoln into not just "the avenger president" but also, possibly, in the "very long run," "the redeemer president."[77] As Kateb argues, this is shocking. But not for its imaginative violence. It is shocking in its narcissistic focus on whites. What is happening to the newly freed blacks (to all blacks) while this apocalypse is raining down on the white nation? Are they mere passive spectators to the main drama unfolding all around them? Do they get a say in any of this? Aren't they part of the wealth accumulated, as I argued above? Contrary to Kateb's account, Lincoln's apocalypse would include them.

For Kateb, the punishment fits the crime, if not perfectly. Nevertheless, this scenario could have been avoided if "the American people had [taken] seriously the principle of equality that they professed."[78] If they also took seriously their religious professions of faith, they would see that they deserved whatever this murderous, even genocidal God might unleash on them, certainly something "even worse than what they endured."[79] Kateb recognizes that Lincoln's conditional speculations do not mean that he wished to see whites exterminated. "I only mean that his outrage at the white race's prolonged and remorseless violation of human equality, which the white race defended tenaciously, was so great that he contemplated the possibility that God's mercy or grace alone could be an adequate basis for a pardon."[80] Kateb also seems to appreciate the drift of his thinking, if for a moment. "Unlike God, Lincoln did not want the South or North to suffer more than victory for the North necessitated, and he certainly did not want a prolonged war: it would prolong all its horror along with the horror of black slavery. Slavery would keep on winning as long as the South did not lose."[81] Nevertheless, this God is Lincoln's God, according to Kateb, and Lincoln is more concerned with the terms of a pardon for the sins of the whites, because they are God's disappointing children who must be made whole again. Frederick Douglass was right that Lincoln was the white man's president, and here Kateb proves it, however inadvertently, as whites are the exclusive focus of his moral concern.

Kateb concludes his analysis by insisting that "the coming abolition of slavery . . . still would not settle the moral account." Why not? For one thing slavery had too much blood on its hands. For another, the wealth that slavery produced and stole "could never be paid back."[82] Perhaps, but Lincoln does not consider what would make whites worthy of the crimes they committed. Yes, "all the consumed wealth that derived from exploitation and was therefore robbed from its rightful owners" was gone, but not all the wealth produced was consumed, especially in the North—but also in the South where the land retained enormous, even unfathomable, value.[83] What about it? What's more, the American nation prospered for close to a century before the war and would prosper again. What about the wealth that accompanies the new birth of freedom? Wouldn't the distribution of that wealth be intimately involved in the moral accounting of slavery and its aftermath? Why does Lincoln not address this wealth as the war has been effectively won? Why doesn't Kateb? Each is trapped by his own whiteness. In their social and political imaginaries, their version of God would rather focus His angry energies on fixing the appropriate world-historical punishment of whites, which ironically reveals the privileged place they enjoy in God's order of things, and prepares them for the leading role they must and will continue to play in that order, than demand and guarantee justice for those of His children who have been wrongly enslaved for generations. Rather than make whites the instrumentality of his justice for those they have victimized, they remain the recipients of it.

TOLD OFTEN ENOUGH BECOMES THE TRUTH

Steven B. Smith, like Kateb, also greatly admires Lincoln's Second Inaugural, especially its generosity of spirit. "[Lincoln] attributes the cause of the war not to human intention but to the logic of events." While this does not prevent him from assigning "blame for the war squarely on those states or in that part of the country where the slave interest was 'localized,' he does not use this as an occasion to moralize or demonize the South."[84] Lincoln assumes that if we had been in their situation, we would have acted in like fashion. Later in the address, of course, Lincoln shifts the assignation of responsibility for the war to both North and South alike, "as the justice due to . . . the South for its endorsement of and the North for its acquiescence to the sin of slavery."[85]

Smith's account of the conclusion to the address is color-blind. Citing Lincoln's "shocking" assertion that there could be no grounds for complaint if God should will it that "all the wealth piled by the bondsman's two hundred and fifty years of unrequited toil" were lost and that "every drop of blood drawn with the lash, shall be paid by another drawn with the sword," he quickly turns to Lincoln's gesture of reconciliation. Reunification would be trying, and both sides needed to be warned—one about "the hubris of victory," the other about "the bitterness of defeat." For Lincoln, "the sufferings of the North as well as those of the South are both fully deserved. The speech is an attempt to express why an all-powerful God allows the existence of suffering and evil."[86] What Smith (like Kateb and so many others) does not say is that Lincoln's God is a white man's God, concerned with making sure that North and South are brought to justice for their complicity in great wrong. This being so, we "will find therein new cause to attest and revere the justice and goodness of God."[87] Will freed slaves likewise have new cause to esteem God's goodness as the world they built is decimated for the moral good of white people? Smith does not say.

Smith does turn to Shakespeare (*Hamlet* specifically) to explain Lincoln's thinking about moral responsibility. Lincoln's favorite passage from the play involves Claudius's inability to enjoy the success of his crime. According to Smith, Lincoln also could not enjoy his success, Northern victory in the war, insofar as it entailed dirty hands.[88] What Lincoln and Smith apparently can't see is that the atonement-cum-punishment the one imaginatively entertains and the other, in abundant company, affirms as a sign of his greatness would make white American hands even dirtier, as white atonement comes at the price of even greater black suffering in the postwar world.

SPEAKING TRUTH TO HISTORY

Give Lincoln his due. No president has spoken to the American people like he did in the Second Inaugural. Instead of celebrating the Union's costly victory in the Civil War, he rebuked America for (what he took to be) its greatest mortal sin. Though Lincoln's words are noticeably unapologetic, the oration comes close to effectively constituting an official apology for national wrongdoing. It would never be advisable for an elected officeholder ever to deliver such an address, especially to a people in no mood to hear it. Yet deliver it Lincoln did. Nevertheless, it is perhaps best considered an exceptional moment of ostensible antiexceptionalism. It might not be the usual way to express the nation's unquestioned greatness, but Lincoln's linguistic gifts defied normal. Garry Wills argues Lincoln picked the nation's constitutional pocket at Gettysburg. I think Lincoln, thanks to a stunning piece of chicanery, preyed on the country's vanity on the steps of the Capitol and, however indirectly, confirmed its world-historical significance by bringing a vengeful God's wrath into their social and political affairs. Of course America is going to revere and immortalize him for his generosity. The memorial in Washington, D.C., bearing his name is a (belated) thank you to Lincoln for recognizing it first.

Not surprisingly, then, the text of the Second Inaugural, accompanied by the Gettysburg Address, its predecessor in unbounded sacrificial violence, flanks the Lincoln Memorial on the Mall in Washington, D.C. These religious and political sermons define his presidency and legacy. They make for an awe-inspiring memorial adorned with inspirational words: America's homage to Lincoln. It also constitutes white America's tribute, in white marble, to its greatest white president. It is a tribute, however, to death. Not life. The Lincoln Memorial, as is, cannot be redeemed for democracy because Lincoln cannot be vindicated for it. The outsized temple and statue, attended by the solemn words inscribed there, deify not just Lincoln as a figure of white sovereign power, but also unbounded human sacrifice, especially death on behalf of an ideal nation that never was meant to be one. John Wilkes Booth had no idea what kind of damage he inflicted on the United States with his accidental gift of martyrdom to Lincoln and thus to the nation. It is a great irony of the civil rights movement that it successfully remade the Lincoln Memorial, converting it from a place of problematic worship of white sovereign power and killing to a site of multiracial democratic contestation in the pursuit of justice and equality for all—despite Lincoln and his legacy, not because of them. America, of course, adheres to its "memory" of its sixteenth president insofar as that memory enables the country to think the best of itself under any given circumstances precisely because it can also affirm the worst, including, as we saw earlier in this chapter, making the apocalyptic worst look like an act of justice. With the one-hundredth anniversary of the Lincoln Memorial fast approaching, what more fitting tribute to the promise of a never-before-seen democracy in America than to de-deify the nation's most sacred symbolic ground, reject the racial, religious, and state violence (in word and deed) Lincoln brought to unprecedented heights, and give it a democratic face-lift? Memorials are often made of stone, but that should not grant them eternality. It's time to overcome Lincoln and our obsession with him.

NOTES

1. See, for example, Garry Wills, "Lincoln's Greatest Speech," *The Atlantic*, September 1999, http://www.theatlantic.com/magazine/archive/1999/09/lincolns-greatest-speech/306551/; and Ronald C. White Jr., *Lincoln's Greatest Speech: The Second Inaugural* (New York: Simon & Schuster, 2002).

2. Abraham Lincoln, "Second Inaugural Address," *The Writings of Abraham Lincoln*, edited and with an introduction by Steven B. Smith (New Haven, CT: Yale University Press, 2012), 428. John Burt has it right, I think: "Both parties 'deprecated' war, but each was committed to a course that would make war inevitable, the one refusing to allow the Union to be destroyed without war, the other insisting upon war if it could not have peaceful secession. Lincoln's word 'deprecated' was pointedly formal, and it implied either illusion or bad faith in both parties." Burt goes on to say that for the South this meant: "Well, I don't want war. But don't try me. And don't demand anything of me. And don't hesitate to give me what I demand. And you'd better smile as you give that stuff to me too." John Burt, *Lincoln's Tragic Pragmatism: Lincoln, Douglas, and Moral Conflict* (Cambridge, MA: Harvard University Press, 2013), 686, 687.

3. Lincoln, "Second Inaugural Address," 429.

4. Ronald White's account of Lincoln's second paragraph emphasizes that war has a life if its own and that people cannot control events. He thus says of Lincoln that the war came "in spite of the best intentions of the political leaders of the land." Note that White does not say all the political leaders of the land, which would have been difficult to defend given the actions of Jefferson Davis and other Confederate leaders. They did not have "the best intentions." He does note the divisions or partisan moments in Lincoln's speech, but also characterizes them as "remarkably tame." White, *Lincoln's Greatest Speech*, 78, 79, 61, 62.

5. Lincoln, "Second Inaugural Address," 429. Burt writes, too generously, that "When Lincoln went on to elaborate that all—everyone, North and South, Democrat

and Republican—knew that slavery was 'somehow' the cause of the war, that 'somehow' captures the moral and political myopia of the generation it indicts." Burt, *Lincoln's Tragic Pragmatism*, 689. The South, however, was anything but myopic about slavery as the cause of the war. See, for example, Charles B. Dew, *Apostles of Disunion: Southern Secession Commissioners and the Causes of the Civil War* (Charlottesville: University Press of Virginia, 2001).

6. Burt remarks that "Lincoln in 1861 conceded everything he could have conceded without making a fatal sacrifice of interest and principle. Perhaps . . . he conceded rather more than he should have. And clearly not just in the First Inaugural." Burt, *Lincoln's Tragic Pragmatism*, 686.

7. See, for example, Matthew Karp, *This Vast Southern Empire: Slaveholders at the Helm of American Foreign Policy* (Cambridge: Cambridge University Press, 2016).

8. Lincoln, "Second Inaugural Address," 428.

9. White, *Lincoln's Greatest Speech*, 113.

10. Lincoln, "Second Inaugural Address," 429.

11. White, *Lincoln's Greatest Speech*, 164–65.

12. Wills, "Lincoln's Greatest Speech."

13. Ibid.

14. White does not take issue with Lincoln's claims. Rather, he argues that once Lincoln has stated what he will not say in his address, he has thereby opened up space for himself to say something new or unusual. White, *Lincoln's Greatest Speech*, 59, 51.

15. Lincoln, "Second Inaugural Address," *The Writings of Abraham Lincoln*, 428.

16. Wills, "Lincoln's Greatest Speech."

17. Ibid.

18. Ibid.

19. Ibid.

20. Ibid.

21. Ibid. One does not need a grasp of ultimate justice (whatever this term might mean) to be able to identify treason and war crimes, among other offenses, committed by the South. Lincoln considered Lee, for one, a traitor. When a citizen makes war against his own country, ultimate justice need not come into play. Earthly justice more than suffices.

22. Ibid.

23. Ibid.

24. Ibid.

25. Ibid.

26. Ibid.

27. Ibid.

28. Ibid.

29. Ibid.

30. Ibid.

31. Frederick Douglass, "The Meaning of July Fourth for the Negro," *Selected Speeches and Writings*, ed. Philip S. Foner (Chicago: Lawrence Hill Books, 1999).

Douglass, as is well known, actually complimented Lincoln on the speech at the White House reception afterward.

32. White insists that while Lincoln believed in American exceptionalism he did not reduce it to self-congratulation but folded an appreciation of ambiguity into it, as in the Second Inaugural Address where God issues his judgment. But this might (also) be just one more version of self-congratulation, as God focuses his extraordinary wrath and punishment on his chosen people. White, *Lincoln's Greatest Speech*, 159.

33. Wills does not mention the racial composition of Lincoln's audience. According to police estimates thirty thousand to forty thousand people descended on Washington for the inauguration. There were already a substantial number of black war veterans in the capital and four companies of them marched in the inauguration parade. See White, *Lincoln's Greatest Speech*, 29, 32, 33.

34. White likewise does not consider the racial composition of Lincoln's audience (who attended the inaugural or who might subsequently read or hear about it). What's more, White compliments Lincoln for using muted, subdued coloring in his language "to reduce the intensity of his words in discussing a volatile subject." Thus slaves are not spoken of as people but as an interest or cause. It is clear that for White, Lincoln "was president of all the people," which is why he spoke in less emotional tones than, say abolitionists, but this does not include slaves. White, *Lincoln's Greatest Speech*, 85, 90, 94. David Herbert Donald's *Lincoln* (New York: Simon & Schuster, 1995, 565–68) also gives no thought to the race of the crowd.

35. White notes: "It was hard for many in the North to hear Lincoln arguing that the war was divine retribution aimed at both sides." Where, though, does this leave blacks? Which side, if any, were they on? Or have they been left out of God's providence here? White, *Lincoln's Greatest Speech*, 157.

36. Wills, "Lincoln's Greatest Speech." White writes, in highly complimentary fashion, "Lincoln did not say 'Southern slavery.' By saying 'American slavery,' Lincoln asserted that North and South must together own the offense. He was not simply trying to set the historical record straight. He was thinking of the future. Lincoln understood, as many in his own party did not, that the Southern people would never be able to take their full place in the Union if they felt that they alone were saddled with the guilt for what was the national offense of slavery." It's not just that White refuses any precision with regard to responsibility (Lincoln does not set the historical record straight), and thus lets the South off the hook. He ignores Lincoln's concentration on Southern feelings at the expense of black lives in the postwar world. White, *Lincoln's Greatest Speech*, 145.

37. Wills, "Lincoln's Greatest Speech."

38. White writes of Lincoln developing a new understanding of the Civil War given its length and destructiveness. What White does not do is justify Lincoln's turn to God to accomplish it. Yet he knows this generates a problem, namely, Lincoln's "fobbing off upon God the responsibility for the incredible death and destruction of four years of war." White, *Lincoln's Greatest Speech*, 123, 149.

39. Wills, "Lincoln's Greatest Speech."

40. Ibid. Lincoln's apocalyptic fantasy arguably represents the pinnacle of a politics of elimination. In its aftermath, life would be virtually impossible, which

means the conditions of democratic politics would be altogether absent. None of the conflicts, compromises, sacrifices, hard bargains, devil's deals, and the like would have to be negotiated among contending parties. The severity of the punishment Lincoln imagines would effectively let America off the hook for the wrenching work of postwar politics. His musing might sound like a radical form of self-reflective critical justice, but from even a minor distance it feels more like abdication, as if he is saying, "We can't begin to think what we need to do, what we should do to try to make things right in the postwar world, so let's not think at all. Let's create a situation where thought isn't required." This kind of self-flagellation puts a new twist on narcissism in that it would force victims to embrace punishment along with the perpetrators responsible for gross injustices. Lincoln adopts a "let us judge not, that we be not judged" stance as he looks forward. Burt treats Lincoln in complimentary fashion for this (apparent) modesty: "What Lincoln restrained here was not his sense that slavery is wrong, but his sense of moral privilege over slaveholders, his sense that he was different in kind from them." In large part this is a result of a certain awareness: "No moral act of any consequence is available in Lincoln's world that is not rooted in a recognition of complicity: the good and the evil agent share the same fallenness and the same human nature, and the ethos of responsibility begins with the rejection of the idea that one can purify one's self by refusal of recognition of the evildoer, or, even more, by a cathartic act of violence against him." Since, on Burt's account, the institution of slavery shapes the identity of persons ("it is not merely that as a master one learns the habits of brutality and repression that make one incapable of democracy. It is also that the master, because slavery is perpetually under threat, must perpetually defend it by threats, must perpetually demonstrate who is master, both to the slaves and to the nonslaveholders, so that the master is a kind of slave to his mastery"), Lincoln is different in kind and he did enjoy a moral privilege over slaveholders to the extent that he never owned slaves and opposed slavery. The mere "fact" of fallenness is irrelevant given its minimalism. If we allow our entanglement in the world to silence the moral voice and judgment, we have compounded whatever complicity we also share. The point in a democratic context is not to purify oneself, which is impossible. The point is that a democracy demands accountability (of institutions, of agents, of actions taken), and this is precisely from what Lincoln retreats in his so-called restraint. Lincoln's Second Inaugural thus suggests that he should have resigned (he cannot carry out his duties), as I discussed in chapter 1. Burt, *Lincoln's Tragic Pragmatism*, 692, 696.

41. For many leaders, of course, perfectly calibrated justice was identifiable. Lincoln had no problems executing Union deserters when called for. They damaged the war effort and cost lives. Southern traitors such as Davis and Lee did far greater damage to the Union and were responsible for hundreds of thousands of deaths. In Lincoln's political world, they, too, belonged in front of a firing squad or at the end of a rope. Still, there are opportunities for leniency the further down the chain of command one proceeds. Why was the South spared the kind of discrimination Lincoln (allegedly) brought to bear against the Dakota Sioux?

42. Wills, "Lincoln's Greatest Speech."

43. Ibid.

44. Ibid.
45. Ibid.
46. Ibid.
47. When Lincoln's imagery reaches its most violent and retributive, White can only write that Lincoln's language "pointed to two and a half centuries of the unfair and unacceptable burden borne by black American slaves who longed for freedom." What kind of moral sensibility characterizes the evils of slavery as unfair and unacceptable? Lincoln's failure to write about slavery in nitty-gritty terms leads to this kind of rhetorical and moral laxity bordering on cowardice. White, *Lincoln's Greatest Speech*, 158.
48. White discusses the importance of Lincoln's letter to Albert Hodges in April of 1864 as a veritable dress rehearsal of the themes Lincoln would develop about God and slavery in the Second Inaugural. In this letter Lincoln speaks of North and South paying *fairly* for their complicity in slavery, but seems to overlook the inescapable conclusion that the South, the part of the country where this peculiar interest was located, must assume a much greater share of the burden than the North, according to Lincoln's own criterion. Lincoln, moreover, offered the Border States gradual emancipation coupled with compensation, and they rejected it out of hand. This kind of setback affects what it means to assign responsibility fairly for the war, but not somehow in Lincoln's ledger book. White, *Lincoln's Greatest Speech*, 113. See also 145, where White does not distinguish Northern and Southern assumptions of responsibility for slavery, as if they were and ought to be identical.
49. White and Donald do not consider the racial dimensions of this "exact retribution," in Donald's words. Donald, *Lincoln*, 567.
50. The South would be unlikely to affirm Lincoln's providential reflections since they considered themselves the aggrieved party in the conflict, an assessment that would never change. This does not mean the South was right, but insofar as the South balks at Lincoln's divine punishment scheme, how will it receive his words about malice and charity?
51. Burt's account of Lincoln's God strikes me as astute, but he somehow misses the narcissism informing it, that is, the bloody retribution that will not be inflicted just upon each other. "The purpose of Lincoln's rendering of a wrathful, unforgiving God who sees through all of our pretenses and uses our own vanities to cause us to inflict bloody retribution upon each other is to rebuke us for seeing ourselves as the instruments rather than as the objects of God's wrath, for by seeing ourselves as the instruments of God's wrath, we ourselves became the agents of it against ourselves. We can only actually serve God by giving up the illusion that we know his will well enough to serve it in purity." Could Lincoln make whites—to know their place and render their service to God—more important to Him? Narcissism can take active and passive forms. To claim that God is on our side of a political conflict and that we are doing his bidding (because we know his will) is only one of the active forms. Burt, *Lincoln's Tragic Pragmatism*, 699, 700.
52. White notes of Lincoln's opening that "there seems to be nothing in Lincoln's beginning paragraph that would arouse the passions of his audience. . . . In these initial words Lincoln did not seem to build bridges to the aspirations of his Union audience." I would argue that this remains true throughout the entire speech.

53. Lincoln, "Second Inaugural Address," 429.
54. Donald, *Lincoln*, 567.
55. Ibid., 566.
56. White misses this aspect of Lincoln's presidency when he moralizes about Lincoln's critics: "One may criticize Lincoln for his attitudes on race, or the timing of emancipation, but only if there is a prior acknowledgment of the centrality of the Constitution in both his political and moral thinking. The integrity of this fidelity to the Constitution shines through in sentence after sentence." Again, Lincoln's is a limited and flexible fidelity, which White inadvertently reveals when he writes, "Fidelity to the Constitution, when it came to the issue of slavery, worked to restrain the actions of the president." I would alter the formulation and say instead, "when it came to the issue of race." White, *Lincoln's Greatest Speech*, 96, 94.
57. Wills, "Lincoln's Greatest Speech."
58. Ibid.
59. Ibid.
60. White argues that "the true test of the aims of war would be how we now treated those who have been defeated. If enmity continued after hostilities ceased, the war would have been in vain. . . . In this final paragraph, Lincoln offered the ultimate surprise. Instead of rallying his supporters, in the name of God, to support the war, he asked his listeners, quietly, to imitate the ways of God." White is again treating his audience in monolithic fashion, as if it were purely white. Moreover, the true test of the war's aims has to be the new birth of freedom promised at Gettysburg and thus how we now treat those who have been emancipated. Lincoln's rejection of malice toward "Confederate leaders, soldiers, or citizens" needed to be conditional upon Southern response, nowhere mentioned. White makes the fatal mistake—for blacks—of assuming that enmity can come in only one form—the intent to harm others. The Union needed to maintain a spiritualized enmity toward the South to ensure the new birth of freedom would not arrive stillborn or die in early childhood. Such enmity would not humiliate the South, but it could, for example, call for reparations. The South started the war (defending monstrous evil) and brought enormous destruction down on the nation for no good reason. It needed to pay its debts. In short, for the nation as a whole to practice charity to all would first require doing justice to blacks so they are in a position, if and when asked, to "imitate the ways of God." The war would only be in vain if the South lived on after the war with its Confederate identity and ambition intact, if also reconfigured. Ronald White, *Lincoln's Greatest Speech*, 165, 171.
61. George Kateb, *Lincoln's Political Thought* (Cambridge, MA: Harvard University Press, 2015), 201.
62. Ibid.
63. Ibid., 202.
64. Ibid., 203.
65. Ibid., 204.
66. Ibid.
67. Ibid., 205.
68. Ibid.
69. Ibid., 206.

70. Ibid.
71. Ibid.
72. Ibid.
73. Ibid., 206–7.
74. Ibid., 209.
75. Ibid., 210.
76. Ibid.
77. Ibid., 211.
78. Ibid.
79. Ibid.
80. Ibid., 214–15.
81. Ibid., 215.
82. Ibid.
83. Ibid.
84. Steven B. Smith, "Lincoln's Second Inaugural Address," in *The Writings of Abraham Lincoln*, 484.
85. Ibid., 486.
86. Ibid., 487.
87. Smith quoting Lincoln's "Letter to Albert G. Hodges." Ibid., 488.
88. Ibid., 491.

Conclusion

Lincoln's Tragic Revenge

> At what point then is the approach of danger to be expected? I answer, if it ever reach us, it must spring up amongst us. It cannot come from abroad. If destruction be our lot, we must ourselves be its author and finisher. As a nation of freemen, we must live through all time, or die by suicide.
>
> —Abraham Lincoln, "Address to the Young Men's Lyceum"

Given Lincoln's (un)timely assassination forty-one days after the commencement of his second term of office, the Second Inaugural has received perhaps undue attention and praise, as I argued in the last chapter. Therefore, I would like to conclude this short meditation on Lincoln's iconic condition with a brief treatment of one of his first public speeches, the so-called Lyceum Address. It reads like a document for today. In it Lincoln warns the country of the grave dangers it faces—from the lawlessness of mob rule wreaking havoc across much of the nation and from the potential emergence of an American dictator who would make a name for himself by destroying America's experiment in self-government, "whether at the expense of emancipating slaves, or enslaving freemen."

Lincoln's early speech is noteworthy not so much because the analysis is prescient, especially insofar as he eventually becomes the dictatorial danger he identifies, as some have maintained. Rather, it is noteworthy because Lincoln, thanks to the conduct of his presidency coupled with the American people's response to it, becomes, both alive and dead, an all-too-predictable danger to the republic, a kind of danger that he did not identify. Remember, Lincoln could not do it alone. He said: "*we* must *ourselves* be its author and finisher."

As a young lawyer Lincoln was invited to speak to the Young Men's Lyceum of Springfield, Illinois, on the theme of "the perpetuation of our political institutions." Since the subject was perpetuation rather than creation, Lincoln, somewhat predictably, began with a tribute to America's founding fathers for their extraordinary achievement and fabulous bequest to future generations. "We find ourselves in the peaceful possession, of the fairest portion of the earth, as regards extent of territory, fertility of soil, and salubrity of climate."[1] More than invaluable land, the American people also enjoy "a system of political institutions, conducing more essentially to the ends of civil and religious liberty, than any of which the history of former times tells us."[2] The self-assigned "task" of the founders was to "possess themselves, and through themselves, us, of this goodly land."[3] They performed it nobly.[4] It is the duty of the current generation to protect the land from conquerors and preserve "the political edifice of liberty and equal rights" for its posterity.[5] This duty, Lincoln adds, entails "love for our species in general."[6]

What, if anything, might prevent the American people from fulfilling its patriotic duty to protect and transmit its inheritance? What existential threat does Lincoln fear? While the oceans afford the nation considerable security, should America nonetheless worry that some singular military power might cross these vast waters and conquer it? In a word, no. "All the armies of Europe, Asia, and Africa combined, with all the resources of the earth (our own excepted) in their military chest; with a Buonaparte for a commander, could not by force, take a drink, from the Ohio, or make a track on the Blue Ridge, in a trial of a thousand years."[7] Rather, Lincoln insists that only America can endanger America, that if it finds itself threatened with destruction, the danger necessarily lies within.[8]

More specifically, Lincoln names two threats to the republic, one already manifesting itself in the streets from North to South, the other an ever-present possibility well-known in the history of politics. His discussion of the lawless spirit of the mob, resulting in the "alienation of [the people's] affections from the Government" and eventually in the dissolution of government itself, and his theorization of the rise of someone of "ambition and talents" who would not be content with tending to the prior accomplishments, however brilliant, of predecessors but rather must do something grand on his own, including destroy whatever came before him, are chilling and still resonate.

Some sixty years after the Declaration of Independence and fifty-five years after the Revolutionary War, Lincoln feared that American citizens can no longer recall the heroism, especially the sacrifices, required to introduce and secure republican government in North America. The last generation—prominent thanks to its scars, broken bodies, and riveting stories—with direct ties to founding events has all but disappeared from the political scene. While they will never be "entirely forgotten," Lincoln assumes that "they must fade upon the memory of the world, and grow more and more dim by the lapse of time." They knew how to deal with threats. Still, Lincoln thinks their loss can be addressed by renewed commitment to the rule of law in the name of those who died so that we might enjoy it.

Lincoln's ardent patriotic reflections, despite or even because of their perspicuity, deflect attention from the emergence of another, perhaps more likely danger, namely, the political actor of undeniably good faith and intention who seeks to defend republican institutions in the spirit of the founding generation and succeeds in doing so at the price of their subversion—all of which unfolds unnoticed in front of a grateful nation that, over time, comes to idealize and worship him and his office.

How could American institutions disintegrate before a watchful citizenry? Ironically, the founders started something of an American tradition in which the country violates its basic norms at decisive moments, one dimension of the glorious revolution that Lincoln does not address. If it is the fate of the great men and deeds that inaugurated the American republic to be forgotten, what is the fate of the crimes they committed that played an equally decisive role, crimes that never became an official part of American civic discourse? Public memory tends to single out what it admires and forget the remainder. This habit comes as no surprise, but what are its political implications? Selective memory reflects and reinforces a collective judgment about the acceptability of problematic political actions, as well as their cost, that sets a standard and then establishes a pattern of conduct enabling each and every generation to enjoy a certain kind of license when fulfilling their duties and exercising their powers to protect or enhance the founding legacy.

And Lincoln's memory is nothing if not selective. The Lyceum Address makes its own contribution to national forgetting: America, believed to be a land governed by the rule of law, was born in utter lawlessness. Lincoln's iteration of American exceptionalism assumes such grandiose proportions that it blinds him to the violence lodged in his narration of America's origins. What's more, by Lincoln's own standards, not only has the American polity already committed suicide, as we have seen repeatedly in previous chapters. It was born suicidal. Death coincided with its birth—a result reenacted by post-founding generations. Eschewing a "love for our species in general," Lincoln's beloved founders first occupied and then conquered a land that was not theirs. What's more, slavery made their freedom possible. Yet the institutions they designed to control and regulate the new nation were meant for their exclusive use. There was nothing noble about the task the founders took upon themselves, nor in the way in which they executed it. Instead, it dishonored them and what they created. Lincoln is thus a rightful and legitimate heir to America's founding insofar as the adolescent United States followed in its forefathers' bloody footsteps. The peace of which Lincoln spoke in 1838 at the Lyceum was purely fictional. Westward expansion—and thus mass killing—had not stopped. Slavery was still legal, too. Subsequent generations of Americans, including Lincoln's, were their faithfully violent followers. Insofar as death, dispossession, and displacement were the conditions of possibility of founding and its perpetuation, they had to be disavowed or, better, ignored altogether. Lincoln's claim of a peaceful inheritance is a life-denying and thus a life-giving fiction. This does not alter its horrific consequences, of course. If anything, Lincoln's fabulous narration enables the perpetual reproduction of such violent repercussions. War is peace. Domination is equality. Killing is love. Death is freedom. Lincoln may speak reverentially about the rule of law and abhor the destructive fury of the mob, but the American people have always constituted themselves as—and acted like—a frenzied mob when it comes to their sense of entitlement to the land on this continent. Lincoln will continue and come to embody this all-American (lawless) tradition.

Rather than warn the public about the possible rise of an ambitious political actor who might not be satisfied with maintaining the founding legacy and, seeking to establish his own reputation, carves out a new path that would undo the founders' Cinderella story, Lincoln needed to reckon with the damage the American experiment in self-government had already incurred.[9] He also needed to reckon with the possible damage the American experiment in self-government would continue to inflict as it defended itself against its many domestic enemies. Lincoln, the ambitious and talented actor who *did* find gratification "in supporting and maintaining an edifice that had been erected by others," would not be the first president to abuse his power, but he would be the first who did so on a grand, systematic scale and was posthumously revered for his efforts, as would the office itself, not despite the terrible things he was willing to do to defend America but precisely because of them. The result: Lincoln's ambiguous iconicity perpetually threatens American democracy with the lawlessness, violence, and terror it makes possible. If Lincoln's 1838 intuition was (more or less) right; if the danger Lincoln did identify in 1838 has finally manifested itself in the twenty-first century; and if a man of enormous ambition and some minor talent is poised to help bring down the country at long last by destroying what came before him; then "our Lincoln" bears much of the burden. He just didn't know how responsible he, with the assistance of an adulatory nation, would be one day for vindicating his own worst fear.

NOTES

1. Abraham Lincoln, "'The Perpetuation of Our Political Institutions': Address to the Springfield Young Men's Lyceum," in *Lincoln: Political Writings and Speeches* (Cambridge: Cambridge University Press, 2013), 11.

2. Ibid.
3. Ibid.
4. Ibid.
5. Ibid., 12.
6. Ibid.
7. Ibid.
8. Ibid.
9. Ibid., 16–17.

Index

Abe Lincoln in Illinois (film), 53, 55–56, 63–67, 68, 71
Abraham Lincoln: Vampire Hunter (film), 54–55, 74–78
Agamben, Giorgio, bare life, 20, 27, 32, 33, 37–38, 92–93
Alexander, Archer, 89, 92–93, 100
Allen, Danielle, 174n13
Ambiguity, xviii, 2–12, 25–29, 47n25, 74, 78, 93, 102–4, 138–39, 141, 199
Ambrister, Robert, 23
American Colonization Society, 109, 112
Anker, Elisabeth, 20
Apess, William, 174n14
Arbuthnot, Alexander, 23

Bacon, Henry, 40, 83
Baker, Jean, 165–66
Ball, Thomas, 85–86, 90–91, 92–95, 104
Barnard, George Grey, 105–6n8
Bates, Edward, 136
Battle of Jenkins' Ferry, 57
Battle of Poison Springs, 57
Bekmambetov, Timur, 54–55, 74. *See also Abraham Lincoln: Vampire Hunter* (film)
Belz, Herman, 45n1, 48n58
Berg, Scott W.
Berns, Walter, 82n32

Blumenthal, Sidney, 13n11
Boime, Albert, 84, 87, 106n16, 106n19
Booth, John Wilkes, 1, 73–74, 81n24, 103, 184, 196
Boritt, Gabor, 171–73
Bromwich, David, 19
Brown, John, 65, 81n20,
Buchanan, James, 126
Burnside, Ambrose, 18–20, 24–26, 46n10, 48n45
Burt, John, 25, 142n3, 142n4, 142–43n11, 143n14, 143n17, 144n18, 146n100, 197n2, 197–98n5, 198n6, 200n40, 201n51

Cahiers du Cinema, Editors, 58, 79n1, 79n7, 80n10, 106n17, 106n20
Calhoun, John, 167
Clay, Henry, 109, 111–13, 142–43n11
Colaiaco, James, 106n17, 106n18, 107n38
Collins, John, 43
Connolly, William E., 14n11
Cooper Union Address, 129–30
Croly, Herbert, 8–9
Cromwell, John, 53. *See also Abe Lincoln in Illinois* (film)
Crosby, Elisha W., 134
Curtin, Andrew, 174

Dakota Sioux, 11–12, 15–16, 35–40, 44, 50n91, 50n94, 51n96, 80n13, 151–52, 160, 164, 200n41
Dargis, Manohla, 74
Davis, David Brion, 141–142n.1, 200n41
Davis, Jefferson, 50n91, 76, 77, 197n4, 189, 200n41
De Beauvoir, Simone, 3
Decisionism, 15–45, 47n36, 70, 114
Declaration of Independence, 66, 112, 122–23, 145, 153–54, 156–57, 161, 162, 163, 166, 169–73, 174n13, 174n15, 182, 191, 206
Delaware People, 119–20
Donald, David Herbert, xvii, 2, 9–10, 189
Douglas, Stephen, 19, 65, 75, 83, 87, 107n36, 107n41, 107–8n44, 108n45, 114, 116–17, 122–24, 125–26, 145n51, 169
Douglass, Frederick, 83, 87, 94, 96–104, 105n8, 106n16, 106n17, 106n19, 106n20, 107n26, 107n36, 107n38, 107n41, 107n44, 107n45, 128, 133, 179, 181, 184, 188, 194, 199n31
Doyle, Don, 168
Dred Scott decision, 65, 122–24, 126–27, 133, 136, 139, 182
Dumm, Thomas L., 34–35

exile, antipolitics of, 18–22
Eyman, Scott, 80–81n15

Ferguson, Kennan, 50n91
Fisher, Louis, 46–47n22
Fonda, Henry, 55–56, 62, 66
Foner, Eric, 46n.15, 109–10, 131, 136, 138–41, 147n114, 164–65
Ford, John, 53, 58, 79n3. *See also Young Mr. Lincoln; The Searchers*
Freedmen's Memorial Monument to Abraham Lincoln, 84, 85–86, 87–96, 99–100, 102, 104, 105n2, 105n8
Frémont, John, 30, 101
French, Daniel Chester, 40, 42, 83

Garrison, William Lloyd, 155
Gettysburg Address, 72, 78, 87, 149–78, 179
Gourevitch, Philip, 13n11
Grant, Ulysses S., 71, 96, 97, 103, 106n19, 108n45, 144n18, 160, 172, 183, 186, 189
Guelzo, 149, 177n50

Harding, Warren, 105n5
Hayne, Robert, 167
Holzer, Harold, 16, 149
Honig, Bonnie, 79n4
Hosmer, Harriet, 94

Indians, 118–22, 153–54, 157–58, 160, 162, 163, 167–72, 175n24

Jackson, Andrew, 22–24, 34, 55, 47n36
Jaffa, Harry, 173n2, 174n10, 176n42, 176n43–77n43
Jefferson, Thomas, xvii, 35, 94, 98, 109, 111, 116, 118, 120, 129–30, 131, 143n14, 150, 161, 172, 174n10, 182, 189

Kalyvas, Andreas, 45n6
Kaplan, Fred, 9
Kateb, George, 31–34, 45n2, 49n58, 72, 136–38, 146n97, 192–95
Kleinerman, Benjamin, 29–31
Kutz, Christopher, 45n9, 49n78

Lee, Robert E., 33, 50n91, 76, 81n20, 108n45, 150, 151, 172, 183, 189, 198n21, 200n41
Lin, Maya, 99
Lincoln (film), 53, 55, 56–57, 67–74, 160–61
Lincoln, Abraham: and American exceptionalism, xviii, 6–7, 12, 38–39, 110, 113, 154, 168, 181,

196, 199n32, 207; and American founding, 5–8, 39–40, 44, 58, 63, 67, 68, 111–12, 122, 125, 129, 139, 141, 150, 153–58, 160, 170–71, 175n17, 175n24, 176n40, 177n50, 184, 206–8; assassination, 1, 2, 35, 64, 67, 70, 73–74, 78, 81n24, 84, 85, 96, 103, 108, 184, 205; babe magnet, 76–77; and colonization, 109–41; and constitutional crimes, 15–40, 63, 67, 74; Emancipation Proclamation, 11, 78, 85, 89, 93, 101–2, 128, 135–36, 138, 166, 171, 190; First Annual Message to Congress, 130–32; First Inaugural, 100, 198n6; Fugitive Slave Act, 98, 100, 133, 136, 139, 167, 182; habeas corpus, xviii, 16–18, 21–25, 28, 31, 45n9, 47n25, 73; House Divided speech, 124–29; Icon, xvii–xix, 1–3, 5–12, 14n11, 15–16, 53–55, 77, 78, 83–84, 94, 106n16, 109–12, 141, 149–50, 156, 179–81, 205–8; Kansas-Nebraska Act, 11, 65, 113–23, 125–26, 133, 136, 139, 182; Lamar, Eric, 105; Letter to Albert Hodges, 30, 74, 184; letter to Erastus Corning, 22, 24–29; Letter to Matthew Birchard, 27–28; mass execution of Dakota Sioux, 11–12, 80n13; and military necessity, 21, 31, 33, 70, 92, 129, 136, 138; and narcissism, 179–97; and Oedipus, 54, 63, 70; and patriotism, 31–32, 71, 76, 78, 83–84, 96–97, 103, 109, 118, 159–60, 161; Peoria speech, 113–18, 143n17, 144n18, 158; and resignation, 33–35; 200n40; Second Annual Message to Congress, 35, 72, 135–38; and slavery, xviii, 6–7, 9, 11–12, 33, 50n91, 58, 64–70, 72, 74–78, 81n20, 93–99, 101–3, 109–29, 132, 135–39, 141–42n2, 142n11, 143n14, 144n18, 145n75, 147n104, 149, 153, 155, 162, 167, 169, 171, 173, 177n50, 179–90, 192–95, 198n5, 199n36, 200n40, 201n47, 201n48, 202n56, 207; Thirteenth Amendment, 68–72, 92–93; Young Men's Lyceum Address, 61, 205–8
Lincoln, Mary (Todd), 70, 76–78
Lincoln Memorial, 1, 40, 43–45, 57, 58, 83–85, 87, 106n8, 196
Lincoln's God, 12, 72, 109–41, 182, 184, 185, 187–89
Little Bighorn National Monument, 43

Magness, Phillip, 128, 147n104
The Man Who Shot Liberty Valence (film), 60
Manning, Chandra, 162–64
Massey, Raymond, 71
Masur, Kate, 133–34
Masur, Louis, 166–67
McBride, Joseph, 79n3
McPherson, James, 47n37, 47–48n38
Missouri Compromise, 113, 116, 117
Moton, Robert, 84–85, 87

Native Americans. *See* Dakota Sioux; Indians
Neely, Mark Jr., 21
Nichols, David A., 36, 40
Nietzsche, Friedrich, 45, 150

Page, Sebastian, 147n104
Peace through Unity Memorial, 43
Pericles, 157, 176n39
Peterson, Merrill D., 46n12, 79n6, 107n26
Pierce, Franklin, 126
politics of elimination, 15–51, 114, 130, 147n104, 181–82, 199–200n40
Pope, John, 164

Ramsey, Alexander, 164
Richardson, William, 123
Rogin, Michael, 37, 50n89
rural cemetery movement, 157
Rutledge, Ann, 63–64

sacrifice, 159–60
Sandburg, Carl, 1
Savage, Kirk, 40, 88, 93–96
Schaar, John, 149, 175n18
Schantz, Mark, 157, 161–62, 176n40
Schlesinger, Jr., Arthur 13n.3
Schmitt, Carl, 15, 16–17, 45n7
Schneider, Bethany, 40
Scott, A. O., 81n31
Scott, Charlotte, 88
Scott, Winfield, 100
The Searchers (film), 62
Second Inaugural, xviii–xix, 50n91, 72, 78, 99, 150, 161, 168, 179–203, 205
Seneca Falls, 165–66
Sherman, William T., 103, 186, 189
Shields, James, 123
Smith, Steven B., 175n24, 195–96
Snee, Brian J., 79n5, 81n16, 81n18
Socrates, 64
Spielberg, Steven, 53, 57, 67–71, 73–74, 109–10, 160, 188. *See also Lincoln* (film)
Stanton, Edwin, 128–29
Stephens, Alexander, 71–72
Stone, Geoffrey, 27, 45n5
Symonds, Craig, 167

Taney, Roger, 122
Thomas, Christopher, 104–5n1
Thomas, Edward, 133
Towers, Alison, 43
tragedy, 33–35, 55–56, 57, 66–67, 74, 80n8, 80n15, 205–8
Trump, Donald, 13–14, 208

Underwood, James, 49n77

Vallandigham, Clement, 15, 16, 18, 19–23, 24–33, 35, 38, 46n10, 46n15, 47n37, 47n38, 94, 128, 141, 191

War of Southern Aggression, 17, 57, 71, 102, 150–51, 167, 180–81, 198n21
Washington, George, xvii, 6; and genocide, 12, 158
Washington Monument, 40, 44, 83
Weber, Jennifer, 21–22, 46n12, 46n18
Weber, Max, 33, 48n43, 49n77
Webster, Daniel, 167
Western Sanitary Commission, 88, 94, 95
White, Ronald, 181–82, 188, 189, 197n4, 198n14, 199n32, 199n34, 199n35, 199n36, 199n38, 201n47, 201n48, 201n49, 201n52, 202n56, 202n60
Whitman, Walt, 53
Wilentz, Sean, 155, 175 n23
Wills, David, 173n8
Wills, Garry, 151–52, 155–56, 158, 161, 156–58, 173n4, 176n40, 181, 183–86, 187–88, 189, 190–91, 196, 199n33, 199n36
Wilmington, John, 79n3
Wilson, Douglas L., 47n25
Wilson, Edmund, 1
Wood, Fernando, 69–70, 73

Young Mr. Lincoln (film), 53, 55–56, 58–63, 68, 69, 81n25

Zarefsky, David, 127–28, 145n75

About the Author

Steven Johnston is professor and Neal A. Maxwell Chair in Political Theory, Public Policy, and Public Service in the Department of Political Science at the University of Utah. He is the author of *American Dionysia: Violence, Tragedy, and Democratic Politics* (2015), *The Truth about Patriotism* (2007), and *Encountering Tragedy: Rousseau and the Project of Democratic Order* (1999). He has published articles in *Political Theory, Theory & Event, Contemporary Political Theory, Strategies, Political Research Quarterly*, and *Polity*. He is currently finishing a volume on *It's a Wonderful Life*. In 2013 he founded the Neal A. Maxwell Lecture Series in Political Theory and Contemporary Politics.

CPSIA information can be obtained
at www.ICGtesting.com
Printed in the USA
LVHW052025060519
616799LV00009B/136/P

9 781442 261303